SECRETS OF
SOCIAL
MEDIA
MARKETING

SECRETS OF SOCIAL MEDIA MARKETING

How to Use Online Conversations
and Customer Communities to
Turbo-Charge Your Business!

Paul Gillin

Quill
Driver
Books

Fresno, California

Printed in the United States of America.

Published by
Quill Driver Books
an imprint of Linden Publishing
2006 South Mary, Fresno, CA 93721
559-233-6633 / 800-345-4447
QuillDriverBooks.com

Quill Driver Books may be purchased for educational, fund-raising, business or promotional use. Please contact Special Markets, Quill Driver Books at the above address or phone numbers.

Quill Driver Books Project Cadre:
Doris Hall, Christine Hernandez, Dave Marion,
Stephen Blake Mettee, Kent Sorsky

35798642

ISBN 978-1884956-85-0 • 1-884956-85-8

To order a copy of this book, please call
1-800-345-4447.

Library of Congress Cataloging-in-Publication Data

Gillin, Paul.
  Secrets of social media marketing : how to use online conversations and customer
communities to turbo-charge your business! / by Paul Gillin.
     p. cm.
  Includes index.
  ISBN-13: 978-1-884956-85-0 (trade pbk.)
  ISBN-10: 1-884956-85-8 (trade pbk.)
  1. Internet marketing. 2. Social media--Economic aspects. 3. Customer relations.
4. Interactive marketing. I. Title.
  HF5415.1265.G55 2009
  658.8'72--dc22
                                                              2008029764

*For Ryan and Alice,
who are the future*

Links indicated in the text of this book may be found at SSMMBook.com. Also visit SSMMBook.com for online footnotes, updates, special interviews, and a constantly updated list of social media resources.

Contents

Foreword

When Paul Gillin asked me to write the foreword for his new book, I was honored but a little reticent, as I was starting to get social media and marketing burnout. I had been eager to move on to my next "future of marketing" musing, but then I read *Secrets of Social Media Marketing* and, like after staying locked up in a Starbucks for four hours, I was ready to be rocketed right back into the fight. "A fight?" you might ask. Yes, that is what is still going on. The old media tycoons are nervously still holding on to what the broadcast era of intrusion marketing wrought, not knowing they are the Berlin Wall of communications.

Everywhere I travel—in the world or on the Web—the beautiful sound and depth of social media is undeniable. We are all media now, and it is not a fad but a complete change of platform. Marketing as dialogue and content creation will be the prevailing elixir for a planet overloaded with one-way attacks on our intellect.

The Web, in this fourth phase of emotion and broadband, will only deepen in experience, conversation, and commerce. As Sir Tim Berners-Lee reminded me last year, the semantic Web will finally begin to change all human interaction for the better. The micro-segmented topics wrapped in advanced social networks will be so numerous that cable television will pale in comparison. Soon we will all look back at the 75-or so-odd years of the broadcast era with confusion and relief as the screen fades and a new powerful digital landscape becomes the closest thing to real life we have. For marketers, the new social Web innovation will become the nucleus of customer celebration, conversation, and commerce.

Marketing really is everything. *Secrets of Social Media Marketing* is a strong hammer that will help close the lid on the past and create a new environment where the words "Web" and "marketing" will eventually disappear.

The first maps of a previously undiscovered area are often the hardest to make. Paul was one of the first master mapmakers of social media with his first book, *The New Influencers*, and now—with this new book—offers well-learned lessons, the discoveries of more social Web innovations, and a very practical "how to" approach. Paul has written a master map for enterprises to succeed in the era of customer conversation and customer control.

Seldom does a book come along (excuse the liberal borrowing from E.B. White's *Charlotte's Web*) that is both a good friend and so well written. Read this book and celebrate! Paul Gillin gives us a clear and commonsense instruction set on how to work in this compelling new environment, an environment soon to be the most dominant communications platform of our lifetime.

Larry Weber
Cape Cod
Late summer, 2008

Acknowledgments

The research for this book began in November 2005, when I attended a meeting of the Massachusetts Technology Leadership Council. Dan Bricklin, who organized the meeting (and whom I profiled in *The New Influencers*), asked for volunteers who were willing to blog about the proceedings. I obliged, and the 800 visitors I received from a single link on Dan's blog changed my life. I was captivated by the idea that the rules of influence had changed and that a single blogger could duplicate the results of a massive marketing campaign.

I've learned so much in the three years since then that it's impossible to thank everyone. I'm particularly grateful to Steve Mettee at Quill Driver Books for giving an unknown author a contract to write *The New Influencers* in 2006. He didn't hesitate a moment to commit to publishing this sequel. Andrea Wright and Christine Hernandez lent publicity support. I hired Catherine Marenghi to promote *The New Influencers*, and her skill and tireless work ethic were no small part of that book's success. My agent, Neil Salkind, has been both a valuable business adviser and a steady fan.

I'd particularly like to thank the experts who contributed sidebars to this book: Maggie Fox, B.L. Ochman, and Tamar Weinberg. Maggie has been particularly helpful in sharing her experiences from the field and promoting my earlier work. B.L. was one of the first marketers to describe the mechanics of a successful campaign to me with her "Up Your Budget" promotion for Budget Car Rental three years ago. She has a gift for this stuff.

I met David Meerman Scott when I was researching *The New Influencers*, having come across his profile on Marketing Sherpa and deciding he would make a good interview. Little did I know that he would publish a much more successful book—*The New Rules of Mar-*

Links indicated in the text above may be found at SSMMBook.com

keting and PR—only about a month after *The New Influencers*. We have collaborated on several projects since, and his wisdom and experience as a successful author has been of immeasurable help.

Larry Weber was an early influence on my thinking about the changing role of media and its effects on marketing. We have stayed in close touch for the last two years and his creativity and insight have never ceased to fascinate me.

Many people gave generously of their time for profiles in this book, including Michelle Alter, G. Kofi Annan, Richard Binhammer, Bobbie Carlton, Geno Church, Olivia Cutitta, Todd Defren, Merrill Dubrow, Jason Falls, George Faulkner, Maurene Grey, Fritz Grobe, Reba Haas, Chuck Hester, Christine Hight, Howard Kaushansky, Jim Nail, Dan Neely, Robert Pearson, Ben Popken, Greg Peverill-Conti, Mike Prosceno, Julie Wittes Schlack, Toni Sikes, Stephen Voltz, Debbie Weil, and George Wright.

Laura Fitton revealed to me the wonders of Twitter. Jody DeVere taught me about the value of syndication. I was lucky to meet her when she was just launching AskPatty two years ago and am delighted to see how well her vision has turned out. Diane Hessan and Jill Miller from Communispace Corporation and Karen Orton of Lithium Technologies helped track down customers for interviews. Don Fry had no formal role in this book, but what he taught me about writing and reporting infuses several of its chapters.

BtoB magazine editor Ellis Booker offered me a chance to write a regular column about social media more than two years ago, when I had no track record in this area. He has fed me a steady stream of assignments that have kept my name in front of some influential people and helped me earn income writing about something I love. John Gallant also gave me a regular column in front of his marketing clients at Network World. Peggy Rouse of Whatis.com has been a constant source of insight about the Internet in general. Her perspective is always unique. David Strom has co-hosted the MediaBlather podcast with me for over a year, helping me to meet interesting people and shape my perspective on this topic.

Links indicated in the text above may be found at SSMMBook.com

Jennifer McClure runs the nonprofit Society for New Communications Research (SNCR) with tireless devotion and incredible energy. It has been a privilege to contribute in a small way to the excellent work she is doing. Several of the case studies in this book came from research projects that originated in her group. Other SNCR Fellows who have helped guide me are Nora Barnes, Joseph Carrabis, John Cass, Sally Falkow, Susan Getgood, Francois Gossieaux, Shel Israel, and Katie Paine.

I'd also like to thank two non-humans for their support. <u>Diigo</u> is a social bookmarking site that permitted me to save and annotate more than 1,000 articles that were invaluable in primary research. Much as this book pays homage to del.icio.us, the reality is that Diigo rocks. I'm also a big fan of Dragon Naturally Speaking, a voice recognition program published by Nuance Communications. Much of this book was originally spoken into a microphone, enabling me to save dramatic amounts of time and wrist pain.

Most importantly, I want to thank my wife, Dana, for her unyielding support and for her extraordinarily detailed edit of the original manuscript. She not only read the entire manuscript under deadline pressure in a week but contributed observations and corrections that I never would have noticed. I would not have written these last two books without her love, support, and unqualified devotion.

Introduction

Two pals from Maine videotape themselves dropping candies into bottles of diet soda, triggering spectacular geysers. Four weeks later, they're performing the stunt on the Letterman show.

A Seattle real estate agent books $3 million in new business by promoting her knowledge of the local market through online channels without spending a dime on advertising.

The CEO of a major airline averts a potential customer relations fiasco by floating an idea for policy change on the company blog before taking action and received hundreds of helpful comments.

A pet products company analyzes online conversations to identify a previously untouched market opportunity.

A small company that makes kitchen blenders videotapes its CEO pulverizing everyday objects with its product and quintuples sales in one year.

A government agency selects five low-level employees to explain its controversial practices to a global audience.

These are just some of the stories you'll read about in this book. They are part of the growing body of evidence that the revolution in online conversations is delivering tangible and often dramatic results.

While some business people continue to fret about ROI and measurement standards, many individuals and organizations are diving in and experimenting with blogs, online video, corporate communities, and public networks. They are learning how to live in a world in which mail and phone messages are increasingly ineffective, but direct engagement is yielding returns that were once unimaginable. These individuals and organizations are embracing the changes going on around them and preparing themselves to lead the next wave of marketing innovation.

Embracing change is the only sure success strategy in a business world that is evolving faster than we have ever known. Students of the information technology industry know that failure to adapt to change can obliterate even large and successful companies with blinding speed. In this book, I'll make the case that the changes now roiling the marketing world are the best thing that's ever happened to the profession. Start embracing these changes now, and you'll propel your company and your career to new heights. Deny them, and you'll watch as the skills that have served you well for many years move rapidly toward irrelevance.

A Story About Change

I remember clearly the first time I ever experienced the World Wide Web. I was at PC Forum, a tony industry conference for well-heeled technology executives and venture capitalists, in March of 1994. People were just waking up to the Internet, and at that conference the talk was all about interactive publishing. Online upstarts like CompuServe and America Online were there showing off their flashy new graphical interfaces, along with media giants like *The Washington Post* and Ziff-Davis.

These companies had spent the past year, and many millions of dollars, creating destination websites that delivered the news and community features. All were built on proprietary platforms, using software and programming languages that the companies had invented at great expense. But the payoff was clear: Consumers and businesses were beginning to go online and the brands that captured their loyalty would dominate the digital age.

On Tuesday morning, John Gage, the chief scientist at Sun Microsystems, got up to address the crowd. Using a monochrome Apple laptop computer and a slow dial-up connection, he logged onto the Internet and pulled up a simple Web page created by a high school student in Los Angeles. It was the most basic of web pages, with a photo and text in the Times Roman font.

As Gage talked matter-of-factly about the technologies underlying the Web, I looked around at the ashen faces of the executives in the audience. They knew they were witnessing the virtual destruction of all that they had accomplished during the past year. Here a high school student was using freely available tools to publish to the world. The technologies were rudimentary for sure, but they were open and available to anyone who wanted to use them. These businessmen knew that the quality of the tools would only get better.

Platform Shift

Within a year, every publisher exhibiting at that conference had scrapped its proprietary products and remade its services around Web standards. Those that succeeded in the long term were the ones that recognized that power had passed into the hands of ordinary people and that their survival strategy hinged on not only adapting to but applauding that transferral.

It would be a decade before the promise of what I witnessed on that day was fulfilled.

The first few years of commercial Internet use saw the rise of three basic kinds of websites:

- The static "brochure ware" model, in which businesses posted their marketing literature and a few pages of basic company information;
- Online catalogs that permitted visitors to read about and order products; and
- News sites such as CNN.com that delivered articles prepared by professional journalists.

That was the first stage of the Internet revolution, and it quickly got boring. The second began early this decade with the arrival of blogging and what Stanford University law professor Lawrence Lessig has called the "writable Web." Blogs were the first "hit" social media tool because they were easy to create and update, required little formatting, and could be maintained by individuals.

At the same time, the first rumblings of social network activity were happening. Classmates.com was launched in 1995, followed by Six-Degrees.com in 1997. These sites introduced the concept of "friends," which were really circles of people who either knew each other or shared some common interests. People had been able to create online profiles since the early dating sites, but friends extended that metaphor. Now people could organize themselves and form ad hoc discussion groups without oversight. More importantly, people's online activities were tied to a distinct profile, which gave them status and personal influence.

It would be six years before blogs would go mainstream. In early 2004, the search engine Technorati counted about one million blogs on the Internet. By early 2008, the figure had swelled to 112 million. While that number is impressive, it's also somewhat misleading. Technorati has estimated that less than 30 percent of blogs are updated at least once every 90 days. The landscape is littered with blogs that exist principally to display advertising, to attract search traffic, as well as the abandoned blogs.

Nevertheless, what occurred beginning in 2004 was revolutionary. For the first time, large numbers of people across the globe were publishing online and finding audiences through the magic of links and search engines.

The Web began to become a platform for multimedia. Groups formed and networks sprang up, connecting people to each other along a broad range of shared interests. The genie was out of the bottle and the world of media would never be the same.

A Game-Changer

Social media will alter our lives and institutions in ways that we are only beginning to comprehend. Researcher eMarketer estimates that more than 75 percent of the U.S. adult population is now online. By some estimates, more than one billion people will be posting information online by 2012, whether through blogs, social networks, or photo/video-sharing services. They will be sharing their experiences, observations, and opinions with a global audience as freely as we pick up the telephone today.

These developments will pressure businesses to engage with their constituents in unprecedented ways. The age of one-way messaging is over. At best, a message is only the starting point for a conversation in which a community of voices seizes control and adapts and fine-tunes the message to its own liking. As PR visionary Larry Weber says in his book, *Marketing to the Social Web*, "The marketer's primary job is to be the aggregator of customers and potential customers. The marketer's secondary job now and in the future is to create compelling environments that attract people."

Some people still believe that social media is a fad, a bubble that will burst as suddenly and dramatically as the first Internet bubble did. They are very wrong.

Social media isn't about money or institutions. It isn't about stock-holders making billions of dollars. It isn't about corporate ownership. Social media is about ordinary people taking control of the world around them and finding creative new ways to bring their collective voices together to get what they want. Whether you like it or not, it is the world to which institutions must adapt. And we have only the barest inkling of what will happen when a new generation of digitally empowered kids joins the workforce.

Sure, there will be fluctuations in the market and new media ventures will come and go. That's a natural cycle of any growth industry. But it's clear that we will never go back to the day when marketers funnelled messages through a few media monoliths.

The stunning speed with which these changes are occurring has blindsided business marketers. Having spent decades refining tactics built around messages, they are now being told that the messages don't matter. They need to become "Chief Conversation Officers." This book is for them.

A How-To Manual

In my 2007 book, *The New Influencers*, I documented the impact that citizen publishers are having on markets and institutions. That book was written less than three years after the blogging explosion began. Much has changed in the short time since then. Social networks were only beginning to gain traction in the spring of 2007. Today, their memberships number in the hundreds of millions. Viral video campaigns have, in some cases, achieved more impact than network television buys at less than 1 percent of TV's cost. Small businesses have rocketed to success on the backs of online customer buzz, while some corporate titans have fallen with a thud. Facebook, which was almost unknown to the general public in early 2007, achieved a $15 billion valuation by the end of that year.

Writing a book about a market that's changing so fast is like trying to catch lightning in a bottle. Any book about this topic is out of date the moment it is published, so I've attempted to distill the lessons learned from the early successes of social media pioneers. This book isn't intended for the 10 percent of marketers who are on the leading edge of this phenomenon. It's for the 90 percent who are still trying to figure out how to start.

Some social media experts are quick to dismiss reluctant marketers as being clueless Luddites who can never understand this new world. I beg to differ. There is nothing mysterious about social media. The practices that we all use to maintain meaningful relationships in our personal lives apply just as well online. It's just that the media is different. Marketers aren't stupid or reactionary. They recognize that the world is quickly changing around them. They're trying to change as well, but a variety of internal and external factors make it difficult to do that very quickly. They're scared and nervous, but that's okay. No one is an expert on all these new trends and no one knows where it's all going. Marketers need to start learning and experimenting, because the only sin in social media right now is inaction.

The critical success of *The New Influencers* was gratifying, but nothing was more rewarding than to read reviews praising the book's readability and constructive tone. In *Secrets of Social Media Marketing*, I have attempted to dispel some of the jargon and mystique that characterize these new marketing disciplines and to do it with respect and encouragement for readers who are making an earnest attempt to understand and adapt. If this book does nothing more than give you confidence about the future, it will have been successful.

And the conversation doesn't end here. Visit the book's website at SSMMBook.com, where you'll find continuously updated online resources, footnotes, audio interviews, and other bonus features. Like social media marketing, this book is just the starting point for a conversation that should grow richer and more useful over time.

Paul Gillin
Framingham, MA
April, 2008

How to Use This Book

Secrets of Social Media Marketing is intended to cover all aspects of social media campaigns, from inception through measurement. Each of the sixteen chapters in this book examines a different stage in the process. In addition, a series of short profiles, called vignettes, look at notable examples of social media success. There is a glossary at the back of the book to help you with terms used. Links indicated in the text of this book may be found at SSMMBook.com. Also visit SSMMBook.com for online footnotes, updates, special interviews, and a constantly updated list of social media resources.

Chapter 1 (Making the Case) is about making the argument for social media investment. Fears of negativity, uncertain ROI, and doubts about the staying power of the social media phenomenon frequently frustrate advancement. This chapter offers some arguments and tools of persuasion.

Chapter 2 (Making Choices) is about matching tools to objectives. Many people still make the mistake of leading with technology. This chapter is about how to put the business objective first and then select the most appropriate tools.

Chapter 3 (Ear to the Ground) is a tactical lesson in listening. Lots of great tools exist to monitor conversations, and Google is only one of them. In "Ear to the Ground," we take a hypothetical company and demonstrate how it can tap into what people are saying about it and its market in various online forums.

Chapter 4 (Courting Online Influencers) offers advice on engaging with online influencers, measuring their importance and understanding how patterns of influence develop in highly distributed communities.

Chapter 5 (Corporate Soapboxes) examines business blogging and podcasting. Blogs are the simplest technology to use, but there are many ways to apply them. This chapter includes the seven most common applications of blogs and principles for making them work.

Chapter 6 (Customer Conversations) is about the social network phenomenon. This chapter delves into the sudden popularity of these services, their common features, and the distinct segments of the market.

Chapter 7 (The Social Network Gorillas) looks at the biggest brands in social networking and the opportunities they present for marketers.

Chapter 8 (Niche Innovators) profiles 14 smaller social networks that represent special interest or vertical categories. These can be appealing venues for targeted marketing.

Chapter 9 (Learning from Conversations) tells how companies can work with groups of customers and constituents in private and public communities to build trust and improve products and services.

Chapter 10 (Basics of Social Media Content) is the first of four chapters about creating content that customers and prospects find useful and engaging. This demands some skills that may be new to many marketers. This chapter covers the fundamentals of setting objectives, choosing media, and understanding online behavioral standards.

Chapter 11 (Picking Your Spots) is about packaging information. Here we get tactical about choosing topic, voice, approach, and medium, which are the first steps in developing a distinctive online presence.

Chapter 12 (Telling Stories with Words and Images) is about the finer points of communicating with words, photos, and video. The chapter includes lots of tips derived from my 20+ years of editing experience and advice from other successful practitioners.

Chapter 13 (Engagement through Interaction) looks at interactive marketing devices like games, contests, and reviews.

Chapter 14 (Promote Thyself) covers the fine points of content promotion. Creating good content is pointless if no one knows about it. Fortunately, there are lots of tricks for getting the message out.

Chapter 15 (Measuring Results) presents a commonsense approach to social media metrics. It cuts through the numbers debate to focus on the numbers that are meaningful to you.

Chapter 16 (Celebrating Change) speculates on the next five years, which is about as far ahead as anyone dares to look in this constantly changing field. I suggest that the only two sins of the new media world are fear and inaction, while offering encouragement for marketers who are trying to sort it all out.

1

Making the Case

"The more in control we are, the more out of touch we become. But the more willing we are to let go a little, the more we're finding we get in touch with consumers."

—A. G. Lafley, CEO, Procter & Gamble, in a speech to the Association of National Advertisers

Fiskars, a maker of high-quality scissors and crafting tools, was frustrated by the low emotional connection its customers had with the brand in the United States. The nearly 400-year-old Finnish company made some of the world's finest cutting tools. Its orange-handled scissors (a pair of which is on exhibit in the Museum of Modern Art) were a favorite of crafters and the emerging cult of scrapbooking enthusiasts. Yet research showed that while people were aware of the Fiskars brand, there was no passion surrounding the products. The timing was bad: Big box retailers were beginning to draw down their selection of crafting supplies. Shelf space would become harder to find.

Fiskars had to shift its distribution toward specialty retailers. The company knew the old adage that people don't buy drill bits; they buy holes. Fiskars knew that marketing scissors would be less effective than marketing what people do with scissors. It seized on scrapbooking, a popular hobby of preserving family history through decorated albums, as its target.

Conventional wisdom held that Baby Boomer moms were the most enthusiastic scrapbooking segment, but Fiskars wanted to test this assumption by analyzing online conversations. It hired the identity strategy company Brains on Fire, which enlisted the conversation mining company Umbria to validate the strategy.

Umbria monitored scrapbooking discussions and used text and language analysis to discover who was talking. The results surprised everyone. The analysis determined that younger women—the so-called Generation Y—were actually more passionate scrapbookers than Baby Boomers. The Fiskars strategy was revamped to engage that group. Brains on Fire conceived of an exclusive community of scrapbookers to be led by four part-time, paid enthusiasts who exemplified the members' passion for the craft. Members—called Fiskateers—knew they were involved in a two-way relationship which encouraged them to share their passion with one another. The four lead Fiskateers were taught how to keep up the conversational momentum.

Exclusivity was important. Members had to apply to become a Fiskateer. The leads were equipped with samples and literature and encouraged to visit local craft shops to help merchants sell scrapbooking supplies—but as enthusiasts rather than as sales reps. An online community was set up for the Fiskateers to exchange ideas and designs.

Response to the promotion exceeded Fiskars' expectations by orders of magnitude. About 200 women were expected to apply; more than 4,200 had become members as of mid-2008. The Fiskateers proved to be so passionate about their hobby that Fiskars staged events solely for group members. The four lead Fiskateers maintained a blog devoted to family, crafts, and everyday life. Some of their entries sparked hundreds of comments.

The bottom line: Within a year, sales of Fiskars supplies in stores that had been visited by a Fiskateer more than tripled. Online mentions of Fiskars products increased six-fold. Engineers in the U.S. headquarters began calling themselves "Fiskaneers." The influence of the scrapbooking enthusiasts convinced the conservative company to take its product line in directions it never before conceived, including the introduction of designer scissors with skull and crossbones on the blades. In short, the Fiskateers transformed Fiskars.

The Fiskars story embodies the best of what social media can accomplish on several levels. It started with listening to online conversations to develop a segmentation strategy. It continued with communities built around shared enthusiasm and conversation. It turned a team of a few thousand unpaid customers into a national field marketing force. And, it transformed the culture of one of the oldest companies in the Western world.

If a company founded in 1649 can do this, so can you.

If you're reading this book, you've probably already bought into the idea that social media has some marketing value for your organization. Maybe you monitored some blogs or customer review sites and have witnessed people discussing your company and its products. You know that these people can be powerful advocates for you and that word-of-mouth marketing can spread a message more quickly and convincingly than conventional advertising.

Most marketers already understand this, at least at some level, but most also harbor some skepticism. The newness and unpredictability of the medium is scary, and measuring results is still more art than science. They also face resistance from higher-ups who think that conversation marketing is a flash in the pan or who simply can't adapt themselves to the atmosphere of trust, transparency, and two-way communications that this new world requires. The older higher-up people are, the more cynical they're likely to be. There's also a good chance that you report to them.

That's why this chapter will be devoted to making the case for social media in your organization. We'll start by looking at the most common objections and then present just some of the wealth of new statistical evidence that indicates the marketing profession is changing forever.

I'll state my biases up front. I spent more than 25 years in the publishing business, two-thirds of that time putting printed words on paper. So I understand conventional media pretty well. My specialty was technology, so I've also seen more than my share of fads. I've watched momentous change in which new markets emerged and venerable companies collapsed with blinding speed. Disruptive change can have cataclysmic results.

The growth and acceptance of the Web as a means to disseminate information has been nothing short of astounding. Many experts now predict that the Internet will become the world's largest advertising medium within the next three to five years. That means that the Internet will have gone from infancy to market dominance in just 17 years. In contrast, television took nearly 40 years to reach two-thirds of American homes.

Social media has given voice to millions of ordinary citizens who can now relate their experiences and opinions to a global audience at little or no cost. This is not a fad. People don't abandon technologies that make it easier for them to communicate. The sooner marketers dive in and begin experimenting with these new channels, the more success they'll have. In the chapters that follow, I'll try to offer you advice and examples from the early adopters that will help you focus your efforts and avoid mistakes.

I'm not one of those zealots who wants to convince you to abandon traditional marketing. Broadcast and print advertising, direct marketing, events, and other tried-and-true channels will have value long into the future. However, all the evidence points to these traditional media becoming less important over time, as the power to publish is distributed to you and me. The age of broadcast is nearly over and we must prepare ourselves for the new reality of small, highly focused communities.

Embrace Change

Social media challenges nearly every assumption about how businesses should communicate with their constituencies. The most important change to understand and to accept is that those constituencies now have the capacity to talk—to each other and to the businesses they patronize. In the past, those conversations have been limited to groups of at most a few hundred people. Today, they are global and may include millions of voices. Once a shift like this occurs, a lot of change happens, both predictable and unforeseen.

Most marketers have their own definitions of social media, but let's just quickly define terms. According to Wikipedia's surprisingly brief definition: "Social media use the 'wisdom of crowds' to connect information in a collaborative manner...[they] depend on interactions between people as the discussion and integration of words builds shared-meaning, using technology as a conduit." Stanford University law professor Lawrence Lessig has called social media "the writable Web," a description I like for its brevity. I think of it as "personal publishing."

Social media is all about people sharing opinions. These opinions can be expressed as written entries in the form of blog posts or comments, spoken words via podcasts, video presentations, and votes on social news sites. These opinions are often direct and unfiltered. In contrast to mainstream media, which scrubs content for appropriateness and civility, the social media world is full of people talking about topics they care about, often in blunt terms.

This frankness is often startling to veteran marketers, those who have been accustomed to delivering messages via one-way media and receiving feedback only in heavily filtered and homogenized form. The first time they are the victim of a blog attack, their instincts are either to get mad or to walk away in disgust.

Take it easy. This is simply a new form of expression and it's nothing personal. To work productively with social media, you need to embrace the idea that feedback of any kind is useful, not only to your messaging, but also to the way you develop products and run your company. Executives who deny or trivialize the value of customer feedback are not good candidates for social media marketing. However, it's becoming harder and harder for anyone to do business the old way.

Let's start by looking at three of the most common objections to social media adoption and how to overcome them.

"People Will Go Negative"

Secret: Don't fear negativity.

In my conversations with marketers, I frequently hear this fear voiced as the number one impediment to embracing social media. Marketers fret that if they acknowledge these new media channels as legitimate, they automatically endorse the whining and complaining that sometimes takes place in them. Control is their central issue. They believe that no one can control what customers say, but if you ignore them, you are not validating their comments.

This observation was supported by research conducted by TWI Surveys for the Society for New Communications Research. It found that "fear of loss of control" was cited by nearly 47 percent of the 260 marketers surveyed as an impediment to social media adoption, second only to manpower constraints, at 51 percent.

Let's examine a few famous examples of negativity at work:

• Jonah Peretti of the online news site Huffington Post tried to use Nike's sneaker customization site to request a pair of sneakers with "sweatshop" written on the side, a reference to the sporting goods maker's allegedly exploitative labor practices. The request was denied, but Nike never admitted that the sweatshop issue was at the root of the denial. Instead, it said the order was refused because of the use of "inappropriate slang." Peretti forwarded the ludicrous e-mail exchanges to a few friends, who in turn sent them to their friends. Eventually, e-mail spread the story to millions of people.

"The only force propelling the message was the collective action of those who thought it was worth forwarding," Peretti wrote in *The Nation*. "Unions, church groups, activists, teachers, mothers, schoolchildren and members of the U.S. armed forces sent me letters of support." Peretti ended up being interviewed on "The Today Show," where he was portrayed as an expert on offshore labor, despite the fact that all he had done was try to order a pair of shoes.

• In June 2006, New York blogger Vincent Ferrari tried to cancel his America Online account. The AOL customer service representative refused to let him do so. During a five-minute phone call, Ferrari asked no less than 15 times to "cancel the account." The customer service rep's refusal went from comical to absurd. Ferrari recorded the phone call, and a week later he posted the recording on his blog. Word-of-mouth took things from there, and within a few weeks the story had been picked up in more than 40 newspapers and Ferrari had landed on "The Today Show" and "Nightline." AOL characterized the incident as isolated and remained mostly silent as the story spread to tens of millions of people. But two months later is excited the consumer Internet service provider business, a decision prompted, in part, by customer service complaints. I provide an expanded account of this incident in the first chapter of *The New Influencers*.

• The 21st most popular story on Digg (a prominent so-cial news site) in 2007 was about a man who was arrested for using $2 bills in a Baltimore Best Buy store. The story was covered in more than 600 online journals. Best Buy is a favorite target of consumer advocacy sites. Its tacit policy is not to lower itself to commenting upon such incidents. Two-dollar bills, by the way, are legal U.S. tender, but local police were suspicious because the brand-new currency was in sequential order.

• In June 2006, a UK-based blog called The Inquirer post-ed a photo of a Dell laptop exploding into flames at a Japanese conference. It was three weeks before Dell responded, and its comments amounted to a weak dismissal of the event as an iso-lated incident. However, online chatter quickly established that the problem was anything but isolated, and five weeks later Dell was forced to issue the largest battery recall in history.

Secret: Be willing to admit fallibility and promise to improve. Nothing will stop a negative discussion more quickly.

All of these problems could have been mitigated if the companies in ques-tion had responded more quickly and constructively. A few years ago, there would have been time to craft carefully worded responses and get them blessed by the company's legal department. But no one has that luxury any more. News spreads so quickly today that a story can jump from an individual blogger to the national news media in a few hours. "Disney has a situation where an incident happens in a theme park and there's video of the incident online before the PR team even knows about it," says Josh Hallett, a prominent public relations blogger.

This puts pressure on corporate communications organizations to marshal their forces quickly. This is challenging but not impos-sible. The good news is that a negative story can die as quickly as it can spread.

A few examples:

- In October 2007, an AT&T customer service representative foolishly refused to waive a $300 equipment return fee for a California couple who had called to cancel their service after their home was destroyed in the California wildfires. The story racked up over 44,000 visits on The Consumerist consumer advocacy blog and 2,100 votes on Digg in just six hours. Fortunately, AT&T acted quickly. Within an hour of issuing an apology, the story had died out almost completely.

- Dell was at the center of another controversy in June 2007, when The Consumerist posted "22 Confessions Of A Former Dell Sales Manager," a list of tips for getting better deals from the computer maker (this format is a Consumerist favorite). Dell made the initial mistake of sending its corporate lawyer in to solve the problem, and her cease-and-desist letter was gleefully published by the site. The Digg factor also kicked in as The Consumerist readers began recommending the story on the popular social bookmarking service. Two days after the firestorm began, Dell's chief blogger stepped in and issued an apology for the company's belligerent reaction. The story died in a matter of hours.[1]

- Comcast has been a favorite target of hate blogs because of its reputation for spotty customer service. When The Consumerist posted a list of more than 75 e-mail addresses of Comcast executives and employees, one frustrated customer used it to carpetbomb service managers in his area with e-mails. After the customer dug up phone numbers from out-of-office messages and called one manager at home, a fleet of eight Comcast trucks were dispatched to fix his problem. "Once you get ahold of [executives], they bend over backward for you," he told *BusinessWeek*.[22]

---

[1] Lest you think The Consumerist exists solely to bash businesses, the site does also recognize acts of corporate kindness, such as Tiffany's decision to forgive a customer's $255 charge for a bracelet that was held up in shipping.

[2] Comcast got the message. It has recently mounted an aggressive campaign to respond quickly to complaints. Type "comcast customer service" into Google and you'll see why.

You can see that rapid response is key to stopping stories in their tracks. While this isn't true in every situation, crisis management experts agree that what most people want to see is an admission of guilt and a promise to address the problem. However, few large firms are organized to do this. Corporate statements typically require multiple levels of approval and are dumbed down into a bland mush. The irony is striking: Businesses empower their frontline personnel—who are often under-trained because of heavy turnover—to represent them to the public with little or no approval, but then stand in the way of empowering communications professionals to speak quickly when a crisis arises.

Conversation marketing can proactively prevent firestorms from occurring. When customers believe that companies earnestly care about their concerns, they are more likely to give them the benefit of the doubt before taking to public forums. It's no surprise, for example, that cable television and utilities companies, which historically demonstrate the worst customer relations practices, are among the favorite targets of hate and consumer advocacy blogs.

Here's why negativity concerns are overblown:

For most companies, it's not an issue. If your products suck and your customers hate you, you probably have good reason to fear negativity. However, most successful businesses have good products and fairly happy customers, so it's unlikely they'll have much of a problem. However, even the best companies have some dissatisfied customers. As long as the number of these dissatisfied customers is small, they're unlikely to do much damage.

Most dissatisfied customers can be mollified with a receptive ear and a constructive approach to problem-solving. In fact, your harshest critics can quickly become your biggest fans if they believe you are really listening. My favorite example of this is Microsoft, which launched a blog called Port25 in early 2006 and invited its most vocal opponents to give it feedback on the company's fledgling open source software initiatives. My earlier book, *The New Influencers*, has a detailed account of this story.

Microsoft's critics initially had a field day, posting all kinds of angry and even obscene comments on the website. Microsoft was ready for this, and its people responded with courtesy rather than defensiveness. Within two weeks, the entire tone of the conversation turned constructive. Microsoft will probably never be popular with this group, but at least it demonstrated that it was listening.

In January 2008, the Transportation Security Administration (TSA) launched a blog. Written by four mid-level employees from around the U.S. and monitored by a TSA press relations officer, the blog is an earnest attempt to draw the traveling public into a discussion of airline security. Initial reaction was predictable: Visitors piled on with more than 700 comments to the blog's "welcome" post; many of them were negative, some profane. True to the spirit of transparency, the TSA deleted only the most offensive remarks, but let most of the comments stand. It was a gutsy move by an organization that has the luxury of ignoring its customers if it desires. While it's too early to assess the value of the blog to the TSA, its boldness should serve as an example of new attitudes toward open discussion.

Unhappy customers are a fact of life; the only difference today is that these customers have a way to organize themselves. They're going to do so whether or not you participate. In the same way that a "no comment" is seen as the quintessential PR dodge, refusing to acknowledge and respond to customer concerns is simply an invitation to more criticism.

Negative feedback isn't necessarily bad. We know that criticism is often more useful than praise. It helps us to understand our shortcomings and make our products and business better. If customers are willing to offer you free advice, why would you not want to listen? If negativity exists, wouldn't you rather find out now than wait until it turns up in *The Wall Street Journal*?

Negativity can actually boost awareness. Consider General Motors' 2006 Chevy Apprentice campaign, in which people were offered the opportunity to construct their own video ads for the Chevy Tahoe SUV from clips posted on a website. About 15 percent of the ads criticized the Tahoe and SUVs in general for their poor fuel economy.

Today, people often cite the campaign as an example of a failed social media effort. But the fact is that people are still talking about that campaign nearly two years after it ended. If GM's goal was to raise brand awareness in a crowded market, then the Chevy Apprentice campaign was massively successful. The daring move also contributed to General Motors' image as an innovator, a perception it very much wants to encourage. Tahoe sales were up 35 percent in the month following the campaign's launch, so the campaign can't have been that bad an idea.

When Bank of America and MBNA merged, a couple of executives wrote a song about the merger to the tune of U2's "One" and performed it before a group of employees. I don't think anyone outside of the room was supposed to see the act, but someone videotaped it and posted it on YouTube. The performance was a little weird: two middle-aged bankers trying to sound like new-age rockers. A lot of YouTubers trashed it. But you have to give these guys credit; it was different and they actually sang pretty well. There was no harm done and hundreds of thousands of people who didn't know about the merger before the video was leaked out knew later. Was that really all that bad?

I don't mean to minimize the difficulty of selling this idea inside an organization. Engineering-driven companies, in particular, tend to resist customer feedback, believing that engineers know better than customers. Even the proudest companies, however, usually understand the value of user group meetings, town hall forums and other types of customer engagement. While those gatherings are more controlled than the freewheeling public conversations on the Internet, the brass tacks honesty of unfiltered commentary can be a quick and compelling route to understanding customer needs. All you need to do is listen.

Most feedback is positive. Research has shown that active bloggers are six times more likely to write positively about brands and products than they are to write negatively. *Word of Mouth Marketing* author Andy Sernovitz notes that "one of the quickest and easiest ways to express our personality and individuality is to talk about the products and brands that we like."

Nearly 90 percent of respondents to a survey of online commenters conducted by customer-feedback software vendor Bazaarvoice and

Tone of Online Feedback for Products and Services Written in the Past Month by US Internet Users*, August-October 2007 (% of respondents)

Equally split 11%
Negative everytime 1%
Negative most times 1%
Positive everytime 36%
Positive most times 51%

Note: *who posted one or more reviews to Bazaarvoice client Web sites
Source: Bazaarvoice conducted by Keller Fay Group as cited by Marketing Charts, November 27, 2007

090066   www.eMarketer.com

Keller Fay Group said they usually left positive reviews, with ratings averaging 4.3 on a five-point scale. Nine out of 10 respondents said they wrote reviews in order to help other people make better buying decisions and four out of five said their intention was to reward a company.

When you think about it, this isn't surprising. While it's human nature to complain, people get most excited when they're telling their friends about an experience that they love. You can see this trend for yourself on a user review site like Yelp. For example, in ratings of 40 steakhouses in the Denver area encompassing more than 450 user-contributed reviews, not a single restaurant was rated at less than 3.5 stars. Is the beef really all that good in Denver or is it more likely that happy customers were quicker to share their experiences with others?

Think of your own experience. How often do you get angry enough to actively complain about a service or product? Chances are it's not very often. Most people tolerate annoyances with resignation and only complain when they're hopping mad. I've seen cases in which people tried to start blog swarms by posting accounts of mildly irritating experiences. These stories go nowhere.

"The ROI Is Unclear"

This is a difficult argument to overcome, in part because it's true. Social media is such a new marketing channel that the metrics for measuring returns are still relatively undeveloped, although they are evolving rapidly (see Chapter 15).

Nevertheless, what's wrong with experimenting? You can look at ROI as meaning "return on investment," but it can also refer to "risk of inaction." There are two factors in the ROI equation, and the investment denominator is often overlooked. The cost of starting a business blog or creating a special interest group on Flickr is zero dollars. If you don't get much in return, you haven't lost much, either. You will at least gain some valuable experience.

One of the appeals of social media campaigns, in fact, is that they're not very expensive. Marketing strategist B. L. Ochman estimates that costs begin at $50,000 for a two-month campaign, but they can be lower. She reported the following on her blog:

> As a rule, a $50K budget can cover the creation of a simple multi-media micro-site which becomes the center of an online community; perhaps some widgets to help distribute the content, and the formation of a Facebook and/or Flickr, Jaiku, Twitter, or other networking group to enhance the community aspect of the campaign. Complex functions add to programming and design costs.

Secret: Social media campaigns are cheap.

Forrester Research analyst Josh Bernoff concurs: "Facebook pages and blogs are two examples of social programs that you can start for next to nothing. Even more sophisticated programs like a full-blown customer community typically don't cost more than $50,000 to $300,000 to get going."

While these costs aren't trivial, they are small compared to those of prime-time network television, which may cost $200,000 to $600,000 for one 30-second ad, according to *Advertising Age*.

One way to counter the ROI objection is to point to the many established corporate activities that have indefinite ROI. These include public relations, employee relations, and, to some extent, research and development. Businesses invest in these functions because executives have faith that they work and their confidence is rooted in decades of experience. The returns on social media are still being tabulated, but the initial results are positive.

Another response is to cite the numerous case studies that are emerging from successful social media campaigns. You'll find many examples in this book and many more online. You can keep your ear to the ground by subscribing to newsletters and reports from some of the many services that document these trends. Some of my favorites are MediaPost, Min, eMarketer, iMediaConnection, the Word of Mouth Marketing Association, MarketingSherpa, and MarketingProfs.

As David Churbuck, vice president of global Web marketing at PC maker Lenovo, recently wrote on his blog: "The number of success stories are now so pervasive that no one can reasonably express doubts that a social media marketing practice is an option. Today it's a must-have operation."

"It's a Fad"

Some executives still maintain that social media is a fad. The boom has even been compared to the Internet bubble of the late 1990s. There's some validity to this comparison, but people have forgotten the extremes of the early Internet investment frenzy, when companies like Webvan were able to raise $1 billion for a service that was never actually launched. In comparison to Web 1.0, the Web 2.0 financial bubble has been tiny.

There is also a lot more evidence this time around that people's information consumption habits have changed significantly and permanently. The next time you hear the "fad" charge, cite statistics about the growth of new media and the decline of the old. The evidence is overwhelming that traditional channels are producing poorer and poorer returns for marketers as mainstream media fades in importance. Consider the following:

> • Newspaper advertising revenues totaled about $43 billion in 2007, which is about 20 percent lower on an inflation-adjusted basis than 1997 levels. Declines accelerated sharply in 2008. U.S. newspaper circulation is at the same level it was in 1946, when the population was half as large. My NewspaperDeathWatch.com blog has plenty more details on these trends.
> • Television advertising is being zapped by a combination of the Internet and digital video recorders. Jupiter Research estimated that $12 billion worth of television advertising was blown away by TiVo and similar devices in 2007. Accenture has estimated that the cost to advertisers is actually twice that high.

• The Ketchum public relations firm and the University of Southern California Annenberg Strategic Public Relations Center found in 2007 that <u>consumer confidence in nearly all media fell from the year before</u>.

• The overall trend was summed up by Paul Woidke, vice president of Comcast Spotlight: "Ad dollars are leaving the cable, broadcast TV, and newspaper business at a rate of roughly $5 million per day."

Meanwhile, the gold rush is on for online advertising:

• <u>Internet ad spending will surpass newspaper advertising</u> to become the nation's leading ad medium in 2011, according to private equity firm Veronis Suhler Stevenson. Online ad spending will total nearly $62 billion that year.

• Publicis Groupe's ZenithOptimedia expects Internet advertising spending in the U.S. to eclipse radio in 2008 and magazines by 2010.

• A survey of 260 senior marketing PR and marketing communications professionals by the Society for New Communications Research found that <u>two-thirds planned to increase spending on social media during 2008</u> and 81 percent expect to spend at least as much on social media marketing as on traditional marketing within the next five years.

• <u>General Motors will shift half its $3 billion annual advertising budget to digital and one-to-one channels between 2008 and 2011</u>. That's a huge jump from the $197 million it spent online in 2007.

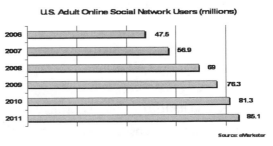

U.S. Adult Online Social Network Users (millions)

Year	Users
2006	47.5
2007	56.9
2008	69
2009	76.3
2010	81.3
2011	85.1

Source: eMarketer

• Spending on word-of-mouth advertising was $981 million in 2006 and will grow at a compounded annual rate of 30 percent through 2010, <u>according to PQ Media</u>.

• A Deloitte survey found that 62 percent of the U.S. consumers read consumer-generated online reviews; 98 percent of them believe those reviews are reliable and 80 percent of them say customer reviews have affected their buying intentions.

So the ad spending trends are pretty clear. But what happens when the current generation of teenagers moves into the workforce? That's when change really kicks in. Consider the following:

• On average, teens spend 60 percent less time watching TV and 600 percent more time online than their parents, according to a report by the Arthur W. Page Society.
• A total of 141 million U.S. Internet users collectively watched more than 10 billion videos in December 2007, according to comScore. The average YouTube visitor watched 41.6 videos in a month.
• Emory University surveyed its freshman class and found that 97 percent of the students had Facebook accounts and 24 percent logged on to Facebook 18 or more times a day.
• The Pew Internet & American Life project says that 64 percent of online teenagers engage in at least one type of content creation, up from 57 percent in 2004.

The numbers cited above are just a fraction of the statistical evidence that online marketing is overwhelming traditional media in effectiveness and business spending intentions. For a large and constantly updated list of the latest market research in this area, please visit this book's website at ssmmbook.com/Research.

With all this evidence, you'd think that marketers would be rushing to invest in social media campaigns. You would be wrong: Despite Google's findings that Americans now spend as much time online as they do watching TV, marketers still spend more than three times as many advertising dollars on traditional broadcast.

- The Ketchum/USC Annenberg survey found that less than a quarter of business communicators report having a word-of-mouth program in place.
- While 78 percent of respondents to a Coremetrics survey said social media marketing is a way to gain competitive edge, it commands less than 8 percent of their online marketing spending.
- Despite the finding that six in 10 Internet users research health and beauty products online, TNS Market Intelligence reported that U.S. health and beauty advertisers' spending on online display advertising remained almost flat between 2004 and 2006.
- Only 12 percent of respondents to a survey of 444 business marketers conducted by online marketer com.motion said they plan to increase social media spending in 2008. Nearly a third said they spent nothing in 2007 and won't start in 2008.

Why the disconnect between business leaders' positive perception of social media and their tepid spending plans? The economy is one factor, but I believe there are several explanations:

Social media is still new and the sheer pace of change has paralyzed investment. When I completed *The New Influencers* in October 2006, Facebook was almost unknown and YouTube was so new that it merited only a sidebar mention in the book. Over the next 12 months, Facebook exploded to include more than 50 million members and a $15 billion market value. YouTube has become a cultural icon. Social networks sprang up by the hundreds. This dizzying pace of change has prompted many marketers to sit on the sidelines until some winners emerge.

Social media is cheap. With full campaigns costing far less than a single 30-second TV spot, even an aggressive pilot program may amount to a rounding error on a large firm's marketing budget.

Metrics are immature. The online marketing industry hasn't settled on standards to measure social media campaign results. As I'll explain in Chapter 15, this is a straw man issue, but it's an excuse for cautious marketers to hold back on their investments.

Politics. Even the best-considered social media marketing strategy may be derailed by a CEO who likes seeing his ads on TV during a golf tournament. Demographically, the people who are mostly likely to lead corporations are also the least likely to be active Internet users. Skepticism and lack of knowledge are powerful impediments to change.

Many marketers measure their importance and influence by the size of their budgets. Social media campaigns are so cost-efficient that marketers may actually see their budgets—and their status—fall over time. While resistance to this dynamic this doesn't make much sense, it is a fact of corporate life.

This is just a sampling of the abundant evidence that online marketing is displacing traditional marketing with stunning speed. Social media will continue to capture a growing share of the online dollars. For more evidence of these trends, subscribe to some of the newsletters listed on page 14.

What About B-to-B?

There is a widespread perception that social media is mainly a business-to-consumer play. Businesspeople are too busy to squander their time on goofy videos and trivia games, or so the thinking goes.

Certainly, the scope of b-to-b social media applications is smaller than in consumer markets. Some industries have also been slower to adopt the tools because the audience is technology-averse or because buying decisions are individualized.

Nevertheless, social media is taking hold in many sectors and there is evidence that once b-to-b marketers find value in it, they move more quickly than their consumer counterparts. In a survey of b-to-b, b-to-c and "hybrid" marketers, *BtoB* magazine found that 31 percent of b-to-b marketers were allocating at least a fifth of their media

Links indicated in the text above may be found at SSMMBook.com

budgets to new media, compared with only 5 percent of b-to-c marketers. What's more, the magazine reported that "21.2 percent of b-to-b marketers have been using blogs for between one and three years, compared with only 10.3 percent of b-to-c marketers, and 12.3 percent of b-to-b marketers have been using wikis for between one and three years, compared with only 5.6 percent of b-to-c marketers."

In some b-to-b industries, blogging is already mainstream. Nearly every major information technology firm now has blogs in place and most are at least dabbling in podcasts. The financial services, travel, and transportation industries have also used blogs to reach business customers. The CEO of Beth Israel Hospital in Boston writes about the complexities of his job. Accenture shows off the expertise of its consultants. McDonald's uses a blog to tell readers what it's doing to be a more responsible corporate citizen[3].

Corporations find YouTube to be a convenient place to post informational videos, executive Q&As, and other content aimed at professional audiences. Such content, which once would have been relegated to forgotten archives, can live for months or years online. HP and IBM are just two of the tech firms that post customer testimonials and marketing materials as Web videos. Microsoft's Channel 9 has expanded far beyond its short-video roots to include several regular programs and even a collection of wikis where customers can post product recommendations. It also has nearly 1,500 archived interviews with Microsoft employees.

There have even been some fledgling b-to-b experiments with the video contests that are so popular in the consumer market. Software developer VMware staged a competition called Become Virtually Famous in which

[2] I maintain a fairly complete list of corporate blogs on my website.

customers were invited to upload videos showing "what rocked your world" during the company's user conference. The promotion generated only 55 videos—a drop in the bucket compared to consumer contests—but the traffic was impressive, with the winning entry polling over 20,000 downloads.

Many social networks serve b-to-b users. LinkedIn is the most notable, but Plaxo and Visible Path also help business professionals manage professional networks. NotchUp pays people to interview for jobs. Jigsaw and Salesconx are contact directories aimed at sales, marketing, and recruitment professionals. We look at some of these niche innovators in Chapter 8.

The consumer market will likely lead the way in social media innovation for the foreseeable future, but b-to-b marketers may actually be quicker to mine the business value of new ideas.

2

Making Choices

"Social media is just another evolution of consumer-to-consumer communication that marketers are getting to listen in on. Only the people in social media are not playing the role of consumers with purchase intent; rather, they are just being social with each other."
—Joe Marchese, writing on <u>MediaPost</u>

Let's say you've run the in-house approval gauntlet and are ready to launch a campaign. It's now time to stop and figure out just what you're trying to accomplish.

If this seems like an obvious step, then the number of abandoned blogs, discontinued podcasts, and deserted islands on Second Life would indicate otherwise. A surprisingly large number of companies launch social media campaigns without any clear strategic goal. Perhaps they're just experimenting with the technology or maybe they're drawn by the low cost of entry. Experimentation is better than inaction, but it's better to have a plan.

Because there are so many social media options today, strategy is vital to sorting through them. A couple of years ago, blogs and podcasts were about all that marketers had to work with. Today, social networks have proliferated into all kinds of vertical and special-interest areas, each with its own nuances and peculiarities. Layer on top of that the social bookmarking sites like <u>Digg</u>, <u>StumbleUpon</u>, and <u>Sphinn,</u> as well as burgeoning categories like social shopping and microblogs, and choices quickly become unmanageable. Marketers frequently tell me they're overwhelmed by this. I tell them not to worry: People who follow this stuff for a living feel the same way!

Author Malcolm Gladwell has said that when people are faced with an abundance of choice, their inclination is to not make any choice at all. That's an understandable impulse given the quantity of social media options available, but choosing to wait out the market is a bad idea. This sector will remain chaotic for years, and the early movers are learning the ropes and making the mistakes that will lead to future success. The fundamentals of social media marketing are falling into place, even if the tools aren't. The cost of experimentation is low and the market is forgiving. In fact, stubbing your toe on an ambitious project at this point can actually enhance your image as a risk taker and innovator.

Tools Are Secondary

When marketers talk about applications of social media, they typically start with the tool and work backwards. Management has issued an order to start blogging, perhaps, and the marketing team has to make the initiative work.

Secret: Start with the business goal, not the tools.
But this method is all wrong. The choice of social media tools is no more relevant to the success of a campaign than the choice of paint is to the structural integrity of a house. Many tools are flexible enough to be used for multiple purposes and some strategic goals require leveraging many tools in concert.

In fact, social media tools work best when integrated with traditional marketing. For example, a television ad for a bank may send visitors to a website where they can interact with a specialist about financing a college education. Or, a television ad may find new life as the basis for a video contest. Evidence is growing that the most successful campaigns use conventional marketing to jump-start conversations when activity slows.

Leading with tool selection can create a lot of unnecessary work. When I was a young technology reporter covering the software market in the mid-80s, I was amazed to witness the applications that people found for their Lotus 1-2-3 spreadsheets. Some people used the software for word processing or presentation graphics, tasks for which 1-2-3 was never intended. They used 1-2-3 because it was familiar;

however, they wasted time and got inferior results because they didn't make the effort to figure out first what they were trying to accomplish and then apply the tools.

No matter which technology you choose, at any given time there is likely to be something coming down the road with more bells and whistles. Technol-

Secret: The best technology is usually not the best choice.

ogy vendors love to freeze buying decisions by promising that they are weeks away from delivering something better. Don't fall for this. The history of the information technology industry is littered with failed products that were functionally superior to the market winners. Cool features are meaningless if all the customers are already using something else. Factors like market share, vertical industry focus, adoption rate, and market momentum are more important than features and functions.

If you need to come up to speed with tools, play it safe and use them behind the corporate firewall first. Your mistakes won't have much impact that way, and by the time you implement your public campaign, you'll know what you're doing. The most exciting social media experimentation is taking place right now behind closed doors. Companies are learning to apply technology to well-understood internal problems, and they only go public when they've worked out the bugs.

The chart on the next page is one way to look at the tool selection issue. Start with the business objective in the left column and then read across to find out which tools may help you. Keep in mind the importance of balancing between ease of use, simplicity of deployment, and functionality. Many social media tools can be used for multiple purposes. You may be better off using a tool that you understand really well rather than deploying a more elegant solution that carries a steep learning curve.

Not Right for Every Job

There are also some functions to which social media is poorly suited. Among them are the following:

Business Goal	Appropriate social media tools						
	Blog	Podcast	Video	Social Network	Private Community	Customer Review Engine	Virtual World
Build customer community	•		•	•	•	•	•
Counter negative publicity	•	•	•			•	
Crisis management	•	•	•	•		•	•
Customer conversation	•			•	•		•
Expose employee talent	•	•	•		•		•
Generate website traffic	•		•			•	
Humanize the company	•	•	•		•		•
Market research/focus group testing	•			•	•	•	•
Media relations	•	•	•			•	•
Generate new product ideas	•		•	•	•		•
Product promotion	•	•	•	•		•	•
Product support/customer service	•	•	•		•		
Product/service feedback	•			•	•		
Recruit brand advocates	•		•	•	•		•
Sales leads	•	•	•	•		•	•

Branding—While there are many examples of video and blog campaigns being used effectively for branding, you still can't beat conventional marketing for speed and reach. This is particularly true for consumer products with large target customer bases. Consider social media as a targeted add-on that engages customers and provides feedback. The 30-second ad spot still has its value.

Channel relations—While some companies have used private blogs and gated communities to communicate with channel partners, face-to-face and phone contact still rule the roost here.

Direct marketing—When the goal is to generate rapid response to a coupon or incentive, traditional direct marketing channels still do pretty well. Coupons work well online, but conventional media scales up better. You can, however, use social media to add value to the customer interaction by driving target customers to an interactive website or other informational area.

Business-to-business—Consumer markets are leading the charge right now with b-to-b lagging by at least a couple of years. There are exceptions, such as the information technology market, but any business that sells specialized, high-cost items to a business audience probably does a lot of direct sales work. Media in general may be less interesting to them.

Demographic targeting—You'll be more successful reaching an over-50 audience with conventional marketing than an under-20 audience. Low-income groups are also less likely to be active social media users.

High-ticket items—One reason many high-end lifestyle magazines and television networks haven't felt the sting of Internet competition is that their products don't present well on computer screens. Magazines and cable TV travelogues are still effective here. However, be aware that luxury items are a favorite topic of bloggers and social network groups. These can be effective channels for creating peer recommendations that customers find so important.

No matter what social media you choose, it's important to remember your basic guidelines and to prepare yourself and your colleagues for a different approach to marketing.

Secret: Embrace niche markets.

Small Is Still Beautiful

Social media markets are by definition small. This is a difficult concept for many business executives to internalize, because marketing has historically worked on the principle of messaging large groups of prospective customers in hopes that a small percent would respond. Executives may believe that campaigns targeted at a few hundred or even a few thousand prospects aren't worth their time.

Niche markets, however, are the future of marketing. As customers become increasingly numb to mass-market advertising and pay less attention to mainstream media, specialty channels have flourished. Cable television and specialty magazines have been sucking market share away from big brands for the last 30 years. Social media continues that trend by enabling individuals to interact with very specific groups of like-minded people. Marketers must learn to engage with people according to their narrow interests because there may be no other way to reach them.

Howard Dean's 2004 presidential campaign dramatized this idea. The campaign understood that thousands of highly motivated and empowered enthusiasts could generate more awareness and excitement for their candidate than expensive ads in mass-market media. The tools that were available to the Dean campaign were rudimentary compared to the vast new online venues of today. In 2008, Barack Obama broke from the Democratic presidential pack in part because he understood that candidates can now choose to be in the media spotlight every hour of every day. Obama decreased reliance on the 30-second ad in order to narrowcast his messages through every conceivable electronic media every waking hour. That's a big reason his campaign resonated with young people.

The power of small markets was dramatized to me during the year following the release of *The New Influencers*. The book benefited from a number of initial positive reviews from mainstream media organizations, including *The Wall Street Journal* and the BBC. That gave early sales a boost, but the book's Amazon rankings soon fell.

What got the book into the ranks of the top 5,000 titles on Amazon and kept it there for many months were the dozens of positive reviews on blogs and in small publications. I would like to say that this success was the result of some great marketing strategy, but it was really a matter of necessity. My publisher didn't have the means to mount an expensive marketing campaign, so I simply made it a point never to refuse a request for a conversation with a blogger or podcaster. The stream of coverage provided consumer awareness long after the media reviews had faded. A year after the book was published, it delivered more than 500 daily search results on Google.

Have a Conversation

Secret: Customer service is your weakest link.

It's also important to understand that markets are conversations. This concept, which headlined the landmark 1999 book *The Cluetrain Manifesto*, marks a major evolution in marketing practice. Customers now have the capacity to respond to messages and to discuss their opinions among themselves. They do this whether companies invite them to do so or not, so it is incumbent upon businesses to become involved in these conversations.

Obtaining feedback takes time and attention. In the past, many businesses have had the luxury of ignoring their customers. Feedback was relegated to call centers and satisfaction surveys. Even if there was an undercurrent of customer dissatisfaction, it could take months or years for that trend to impact the bottom line, if it ever did. Customers had limited means to speak to each other, and companies had little incentive to listen if they didn't care to.

Today, almost nobody calls customer complaint lines. Customers take their problems directly to the Web, whether through consumer advocacy sites like Consumerist.com, RipOffReport.com, My3Cents.com, ConsumerAffairs.com, and PlanetFeedback.com or through their own blogs and social networks. *BusinessWeek* highlighted this phenomenon in a March 2008 cover feature entitled "Customer Vigilantes." It said: "Customer angst sites are no longer just shouting 'YourCompanySucks' into the cyberdarkness, but acting as gathering spots for sharing call-center secrets and trouble-shooting tips. And as the audience for more blogs and social-media sites such as Digg reach critical mass, it's easier than ever for consumers to wallpaper the Web with their customer-service nightmares."

The Consumerist editor Ben Popken sees his site's role as being "to empower consumers by informing and entertaining them about the top consumer issues of the day. We give them a voice by directly publishing their tips and e-mails and then following up on them as warranted." At 26, Popken has never worked for a mainstream media organization and he doesn't abide by the standard rules of journalism. The Consumerist editors do little fact-checking. They don't have time given the volume of material they process. If something is wrong, they expect readers to quickly correct it.

The Consumerist gets the occasional legal threat, but these have never amounted to much. And its laser focus on reader interests has won it a fanatical following. Have you ever sent a letter to a newspaper about a story you read and failed to get a response? At The Consumerist, you are the story.

The payoff: The Consumerist was getting 15 million unique visitors per month in early 2008 and had passed the venerable *Consumer Reports* in audience reach, according to the Web metric service Alexa.com. While the comparison is somewhat misleading (*Consumer Reports* charges for enhanced services), the performance is remarkable for a site that's less than three years old. Perhaps more importantly, The Consumerist is closely watched by mainstream media outlets. For example, *The New York Times* has referenced the site 381 times, *The Wall Street Journal* 114 times, and *BusinessWeek* 37 times. Consumerist gets picked up on the popular social bookmarking site Digg.com constantly—34,000 citations and counting. Popken was featured in a cover story in *BusinessWeek* in early 2008 and invited to write a 2,300-word article for *Reader's Digest*. Popken accomplished all of this without a day of formal journalism training.

This phenomenon dramatizes an important new factor in customer relations: Your frontline employees are increasingly the most important link between you and your customers. Advocacy blogs like The Consumerist specialize in promoting stories told by individual customers, making them the new power brokers in cyberspace. All the branding and positioning in the world won't do much good if street-level employees aren't treating customers well. The story outlined in Chapter 1, in which an AT&T employee nearly caused a customer-service crisis by refusing to forgive a couple's equipment deposit fees after their house was destroyed, is a classic example of this.

The consequences of poor customer service is dramatic. As Andy Sernovitz sums up in *Word of Mouth Marketing*: "Let's look at a certain major cable company…that infuriates its customers…with absurdly poor service. When you look up the company online, what do you see? Expensive ads, official news stories—and tens of thousands of posts from angry people…The company can never buy another online ad without having it placed next to the words of a customer they've messed with."

Today, you need to communicate your positioning and customer-service policies to your company's front lines more effectively than you communicate them to customers. You also need to be willing to acknowledge mistakes when they happen. Unfortunately, many companies marginalized and outsourced their customer service operations during the 1990s. This disconnect has become a liability.

Empower Your People

In the age of mass media, most messages were delivered by large, vertically integrated print and broadcast entities,

Secret: Empower your people to speak for the company.

which had elaborate fact-checking and approval cycles and well-documented procedures for dealing with exceptions. Not surprisingly, corporate communications organizations developed in the same way. Any message coming out of the company was vetted and approved through an approval structure that ensured that everything was "on message." When problems emerged in the media, there were established procedures for addressing them. Negotiations with media entities were conducted behind closed doors and corrections and make-goods efforts were carefully crafted. It was all very civil.

Today, it is all very irrelevant.

Social media entities don't operate by formally established policies and procedures. In fact, complaints and demands for corrections are likely to be posted on the Web. Some sites knowingly publish speculation and then wait for the community of readers to fill in the facts. Like it or not, the rules have changed and it's incumbent upon businesses to react to that.

This doesn't mean unleashing every employee to speak freely, but it does mean loosening some of the reins of power. A few companies, like Microsoft and Sun Microsystems, have gone to the extreme of providing company-branded blogging platforms and giving individuals the power to speak more or less freely.[1] One of their goals is to identify and resolve issues before they require corporate attention. However, this approach may be too radical for most corporations.

A common approach is to deputize a few select employees to speak on behalf of the company in designated forums or on the company blog. People are given special training and sign documents that govern their behavior. If you go this route, choose well-rounded individuals with demonstrated experience and loyalty and an ability to communicate the company position with vigor. Don't just hand this task to the corporate communications group. The audiences you need to address are often interested in highly specific topics, and the standard "We'll get back to you on that" response doesn't hold water.

Managers sometimes try to jump-start a blogging initiative by making it a job requirement. This is a terrible idea. Blogging requires enthusiasm, dedication, and time commitment. If people are forced to do it, they'll do it badly and then quit at the first opportunity. There's nothing to be gained from this approach.

A better approach is to identify a few people who are genuinely enthusiastic about the opportunity to blog and let them lead the charge. Celebrate their accomplishments and give them promotions. Others will quickly get the message. Look for the following characteristics in potential bloggers:

- Passionate about their work/product
- Enjoy sharing with others
- Risk takers
- Goal oriented
- Have a sense of humor
- Ambitious
- Receptive to feedback

---

[1] Within limits. While many corporations post their blog policies publicly, there are surprisingly few recent collections. A good place to start is the Fortune 500 Business Blogging Wiki. *The San Francisco Chronicle* carried a long story on this topic, but that was three years ago.

Note one item this list does not include: good writing skills. Some of your most popular bloggers will be people who have a lot of domain experience, like developers and engineers. These people often don't write very well. That shouldn't be an impediment. Chapters 10 through 13 offer tactics that even weak writers can use to express themselves clearly.

In late 2006, Intel launched "Four Days of Dialogue," an online pow-wow between customers and the engineers who were building products. "Just a year before, Intel would have rented hotel rooms and asked partners and customers to fly in," to see a new product, *BtoB* magazine reported. "Instead it put the chip architects online for one hour each day for four days." The event got 22,000 visitors in four hours, most of them highly engaged in the topic of chip design. The engineers loved the experience.

One temptation is to pile this task on top of the existing corporate communications group. This is usually a ticket to disaster. Those people already have their hands full dealing with a flood of new influencers and they are unlikely to be equipped to deal with the product or customer service challenges that dominate online discussions. They should be involved in setting policies and procedures, but it's the people with specialized knowledge who should communicate directly with knowledgeable influencers. Yes, it's hard to find technical people with the time or inclination to do this. You need to point out to them the career benefits of being seen as problem-solvers and visible company representatives. Once they start taking direct feedback from customers, they tend to get addicted. Direct customer relations is like a drug.

Incidentally, small businesses usually have much less of an issue with this kind of free interaction. They have fewer corporate policies that limit employees from dealing directly with customers. This is one reason some of the most innovative social media use has come from the smallest companies.

Relax

Most big corporations take themselves very seriously. The traditional pressure from Wall Street, the press, and customers has forced them to think that way. Any admission of imperfection was a potential

Nine Common-Sense Secrets of Social Media Marketing

By B. L. Ochman

1. The purpose of social media marketing is to engage with enthusiasts and existing customers in interactive communities in order to drive more traffic and sales. This type of engagement—when it is genuine—facilitates a highly involved audience that wants to interact with the brand. The more people a company can interact with who already have strong social networks, the more likely it is that a message can be spread through those networks—but only *if* the company is already a trusted member of the community.

2. Incorporating social media into your marketing isn't a quick fix, magic elixir, or sure thing. It's about creating community, and that doesn't happen overnight. Consistent participation in social media delivers its best results months, or even a couple of years, down the road. You need to be in it for the long haul.

3. Establish credibility. One aspect of social media is a set of tools that people can use to recommend products and services to others. Absolutely anyone—including big corporations—can use these tools to establish credibility and trust. Social media levels the playing field. Participants in social media have a zero crap quotient and will not stand for thinly veiled corporate messages. Be ready to be credibly involved or don't get in.

4. Embrace *all* feedback. CMOs, CEOs and CFOs fear they'll lose their jobs if people say bad things about their company online. Well guess what? If there's something bad to be said, people are going to say it. Get used to that. Everyone's playing by new rules.

Customers who complain are an opportunity. Engage them in conversation. Find out what would make them happy. Then make changes that knock their socks off. Zappos, with more than 250 employees on Twitter, and several other smart companies, pay attention to conversation and respond immediately when complaints crop up, earning the respect of the community. That respect often leads to favorable blog posts—endorsements money couldn't buy.

5. The value is the network. By the way, if you *do* lose your job, you can use social networks to find a better one. Consider IT Toolbox. It's a social network that helps people connect with and be evaluated by their peers. On Twitter, valued members of the community often recommend their friends for jobs, or even post jobs they are trying to fill. CEO Jason Calacanis used Twitter to seek a president for Mahalo. Zappos CEO Tony Hsieh has also posted jobs listings.

6. Social media can change the world. A message that resonates can make an enormous difference. The Frozen Pea Fund began as a series of Twitter posts and became a global campaign for breast cancer awareness. Al Gore's multi-year, multi-million dollar campaign to solve global warming is anchored by a community organized to spur massive action for change.

7. Build a genuine connection with your audience so you can experiment with prototypes and new ideas. People love to be heard, and the ideas you get from people outside the company are often more objective and original than those you get from insiders.

8. Resisting the voice of the customer is futile. Your customers are already talking about you. They'll keep doing that whether or not you respond. But if you do respond, you have the opportunity to surprise and even delight people who might otherwise never have bought from you again.

9. Think globally and speak in tongues. Global marketing is no longer just for giants like P&G and Microsoft. The Internet brings globalization to firms of all sizes. Speak in many tongues. Hire a human translator rather than relying on machine translations (which make you sound like the village idiot). Communicate in simple words. Avoid idioms and complex sentence construction.

B. L. Ochman has been creating Internet marketing campaigns since 1995. She heads the creative team of whatsnextonline.com *and publishes the internationally respected* What's Next Blog. *Her* Clutter Control Freak *campaign is described in Chapter 10.*

blow to the stock price and to the veneer of invincibility that the companies spent years refining. This is one reason most corporations do a terrible job of dealing with crises.

When you look at the most successful companies of the last decade—companies like Southwest Airlines, Dell, Google, Starbucks, and Apple—you'll note that nearly all of them have in common a freewheeling culture, tolerance for risk, and a willingness to laugh at themselves. In today's consumer-driven market, these traits are actually assets.

It's unfortunate that more companies don't see this. In mid-2005, Federal Express served up a cease-and-desist order to a cash-strapped Arizona programmer named Jose Avila III, who had decorated his apartment in furniture made out of FedEx boxes. Avila had posted pictures of his creations online and had won a following for his creativity and resourcefulness.

FedEx didn't think the stunt was funny at all. Its legal swipe was an effort to protect its brand equity, a spokesman said. Unfortunately for FedEx, Avila's case tapped a wellspring of online sympathy. As bloggers rallied to his support, the David vs. Goliath story caught the attention of mainstream media, eventually landing Avila on "The Today Show" and CNN, among other outlets. A Berkeley law professor offered to defend him pro bono. As viral publicity built, FedEx looked more and more like a vicious corporate monster trying to crush an innocent customer who was, after all, endorsing its brand.

In pointing to FedEx's missed opportunity in this case, new-media marketer Joseph Jaffe suggested what the delivery company could have done differently. "FedEx should have called a 'pull-out-all-stops' with its media and creative efforts and figured out how to embrace Jose," Jaffe wrote in *Join the Conversation*. "When you start referring to your customers as violators, you are most certainly not a creator of brand life but rather a prophet of brand death." Equally perplexing was that FedEx's competitors didn't rally to Avila's defense, perhaps by paying him to create more elaborate furniture out of their own branded products. Why weren't these companies able to let their hair down and celebrate a customer's creativity? Why did they take themselves so seriously?

Listen

This last bit of advice seems obvious, but it is painfully difficult for many organizations to implement. When customers take to the Web with problems or suggestions, they usually just want to be heard. Responding with a curt, "We'll take that under advisement," will only leave them frustrated. Responses need to show that the company hears the message, even if it can't act at the time. Don't say, "We'll get back to you on that" unless you earnestly intend to do so. Your failure to follow up will simply become fodder for negativity. Think of social media as an evolution of the company suggestion box, only the suggestions are now contributed in public. Failure to listen will only be taken as evidence that the company doesn't care. On the other hand, repeating the message back to the source and delivering a well-reasoned response can go miles toward demonstrating concern.

In the chapters that follow, you'll find many examples of businesses that leveraged active listening and a feedback loop to achieve remarkable results. Now that you've prepared yourself for a social media foray, let's look at the options that are available, the pros and cons of each, and the best practices for taking advantage of them. Start by listening.

Dell's Social Media Transformation

Perhaps no company has historically had better reason to steer clear of social media marketing than Dell Computer. Yet few companies have embraced these new media with more enthusiasm.

In 2005, Dell was the victim of a legendary blog swarm kicked off by prominent blogger Jeff Jarvis, who posted a rant entitled "Dell lies. Dell sucks." on his BuzzMachine blog. His complaints about Dell service resonated with thousands of other customers, who piled on with their own tales of woe.

A year later, a British blog called The Inquirer posted photos of a Dell laptop erupting into flames at an Osaka, Japan conference. The incident brought Dell critics out of the woodwork. Photos of smoking and burning Dell laptops began to show up on sites like Consumerist, which has long delighted in tweaking the nose of the Texas computer maker.

Unbowed, Dell introduced its first corporate blog, Direct2Dell, in July 2006. Response from the blogosphere was swift and merciless. Critics trashed the site as being overly promotional and devoid of useful content. Dell listened, made changes, and began to use the blog to address customer complaints and preview new products.

Then, in what was showing signs of becoming an annual event, Dell was taken to the woodshed again in June 2007. Consumerist posted "22 Confessions Of A Former Dell Sales Manager," a long list of tricks that consumers could use to get better deals out of the company.

Dell fumbled the crisis by sending a corporate lawyer after Consumerist with a cease-and-desist notice. Not surprisingly, Consumerist posted the lawyer's letter on its site, along with its response and the year-old photo of the flaming laptop. The confrontation logged more than 3,600 votes on Digg and threatened to become a major headache for Dell until its chief blogger, Lionel Menchaca, stepped in and quickly put out the fire with a mea culpa statement on Direct2Dell.

Given these experiences, it would be understandable if Dell developed a skeptical attitude toward social media. However, the company actually did the opposite. It launched a site called IdeaStorm and encouraged customers to contribute product suggestions. In the spring of 2007, Dell began offering the Linux operating system on its desktop computers as a result of feedback posted on IdeaStorm.

When *BusinessWeek* magazine sent Jarvis to visit Dell in late 2007, the onetime critic found a company that was embracing customer conversations at the highest level.

"Michael Dell starts to sound like a Cluetrain convert himself," Jarvis wrote, referring to the seminal 1999 treatise, *The Cluetrain Manifesto*, which launched the social media craze. "'There are lots of lessons here for companies,' [Dell] says. 'These conversations are going to occur whether you like it or not. Ok? Well, do you want to be part of that or not? My argument is you absolutely do… I'm sure there's a lot of things that I can't even imagine but our customers can imagine,' Dell says, sounding darned near like a blogger himself."

In early 2008, Dell claimed that 27 product and process innovations had come about as a direct result of ideas submitted on IdeaStorm. The same month that Jarvis' article appeared, Forrester Research gave Dell a Groundswell Award, recognizing its use of social technology. The category: company transformation.

	Blog	Podcast	Photo	Video	Social Network	Virtual World
Distinctive Voice	■	■	◢	■		■
Visual appeal			■	■		■
Easily Updatable	■				■	■
Translatable	■		■		■	■
Time-Efficient	■		■			
Technically Simple	■	◢	■			■
Taggable	■	■	■	■	■	
Syndicatable	■	■			■	
Searchable	■				■	
Navigable	■				■	■
Personal	■	■	■	■		
Mobie	■	■	■			
Interactive	■				■	■
Flexible	■				■	■
Entertaining		■	■	■		■
Distinctive		■	■	■	■	■
Easily Deployable	■		◢			
Cross-cultural			■	■		■
Cost	■	◢				
Categorizable	■	■	■		■	
Adaptable	■	■			■	■

■ = Strength
◢ = Situational

3

Ear to the Ground

"How much control do you give up? That's like asking the person holding you up at gunpoint how much money to give them."
—Ted McConnell, Interactive Innovation Director, Procter & Gamble, speaking at ad:tech 2006

"We've been talking to people as if they were morons and now they're punching our lights out."
—Joseph Jaffe, author, *Join the Conversation*, speaking at NewCommunications Forum, April, 2008

Each morning, before his first Coke of the day, Greg Peverill-Conti logs on to his Twitter account. His circle of followers and people he's following have been chatting away overnight, and if there's any important news about topics that interest him, he'll find it there first.

When he arrives at work at the Cambridge, Massachusetts offices of PR firm Weber Shandwick, the 41-year-old executive fires up Radian 6, a conversation monitoring service. He's got searches stored there for client names and products, as well as topics like "consumer confidence" that clue him into issues that matter to clients. Within 15 minutes, he knows if any influential bloggers are going to cause him trouble that day, or if there's a rave review to pass along.

On his RSS reader, he's saved search results from IceRocket, Technorati, and a few other search engines. There's even Summize, an engine that searches only Twitter comments.

You never know where news is going to pop up. Recently, Peverill-Conti was working on a project for the National September 11 Memorial & Museum. A blogger comment led him to an area in the Second Life virtual world where a member had set up a virtual 9/11 memorial.

Links indicated in the text above may be found at SSMMBook.com

The destination had attracted several thousand visitors, yet it was invisible on traditional search engines.

And then there are the international communities. For another client, Peverill-Conti was seeking to promote a speaking program featuring Nobel laureates. The largest Facebook group on the topic had 3,000 members, but it turned out that Orkut, a social network site that's popular internationally, had 54,000 members in a similar group. Bingo.

Welcome to the new world of influencer marketing. Not that long ago, public relations professionals typically scanned three or four newspapers every morning. Today, that routine has been replaced by a complex network of search engines, RSS feeds, and paid monitoring services.

Tap into the Conversation

The first step to social media engagement is social media awareness. That means learning what's being said about your company, people, and products. More importantly, it means knowing where to focus your energies. Finding those pockets of influence has almost become a science in itself. In this chapter, we'll get our hands a little dirty looking at the tools—all of them free—that can help you identify and classify influencers.

Nearly every social medium has a hierarchy. In the blogosphere, this can be measured by inbound traffic, inbound links, comments, mainstream media attention, search performance, and other metrics. Some factors are easily measurable and others aren't. In social networks, it's the number of "friends" or followers that a person has. On social news sites, it can be the number of recommendations a person has made. Even social bookmarking sites have hierarchies because some users are more active than others.

Hierarchy creates levels of influence. Though there is no direct correlation between inbound links or friends and influence, it's a safe bet that people who get a lot of attention have disproportionate influence. One of the trickiest aspects of measuring influence is getting a handle on the scope of a person's online activities. Not long ago, a person might contribute to one or two blogs. Today, she may also be active in a half-dozen social networks and also contribute to news or topical sites clustered around areas of interest. The fact that many social networks and discussion groups are invisible to search engines makes finding and ranking these influencers all the more difficult.

Secret: Google indexes less than 20 percent of the Web.

It's no longer enough just to set up a <u>Google Alert</u> for your company or product name and trust the search engine to do the rest. For all its awesome scope, Google indexes less than 20 percent of the Web, according to several estimates. To really find people, you need to dig into members-only networks where they might be active. Social bookmarking sites like Digg, <u>Netscape</u>, <u>Newsvine</u>, <u>Sphinn</u>, and <u>Shoutwire</u> add to the complexity. Influence in these communities is driven by member consensus, and there is no reliable way to measure or predict their impact. It's not so much the content that's important, but the votes the content receives.

Nevertheless, search is a great place to start. In the following section, I'll offer some highly tactical advice on identifying influencers through search. Next, I'll offer some guidelines on the ins and outs of sorting through podcasts, video sites, social networks, and social news sites. Finally, I'll briefly cover the emerging class of paid services that can do a lot of the drudge work for you.

There is also a vast amount of free advice available on the Internet from people who specialize in understanding each of these areas. At the end of this chapter I'll provide a list of some of the best resources.

How to Deal With New-Media Overload
By Tamar Weinberg

So much new information comes online every day that trying to keep up with it all seems futile. And it is. You can't read, watch, and listen to everything that could possibly interest you, but by using the tools of the trade, you can keep up with major trends and satisfy most of your specific needs. Here are some tactics I use. I'm a big fan of social media sites and aggregation tools that make it easier to consume massive amounts of information. My primary one-stop-shop is Bloglines, a Web-based news aggregator that makes it easy to read information published using RSS (really simple syndication), which is a format that "pushes" information from Web publishers to subscribers. There are lots of free RSS readers available. Use them to simplify. They can combine information from hundreds or thousands of websites into one display.

I have over 150 feed subscriptions to a wide variety of sites. I categorize them in order of priority, from breaking news to fun reads that are entertaining but not urgent. I often check Bloglines more than once a day, because new information always flows in, even during the wee hours of the night. If I fall behind, I'll ignore the entertaining feeds and focus on the more important news.

Social bookmarking sites are another great way I find interesting information I wasn't aware of. My favorite choices in this category are social news services like Digg and Mixx, and social bookmarking sites like del.icio.us and StumbleUpon.

With social news sites, I navigate first to the section that interests me, such as technology or education. If the title and description of an article catch my eye, I read it and maybe even add the RSS feed for that site to Bloglines. Social bookmarking sites are different. You can search based on tags, which are labels that people add to text to improve searchability. This is a great way to find out what other people have already bookmarked as interesting in a given category.

If these options sound intimidating by themselves, there are many tools that aggregate popular content. For technology news, <u>Techmeme</u> identifies and discusses the most popular topics based on algorithms and blog links. Political aficionados may be interested in <u>memeorandum</u> which does the same thing in the political sphere.

The blog search engine <u>Technorati</u> highlights news stories and blog posts that are gaining attention. The most popular stories of the hour are right on the home page. Finally, entrepreneur Guy Kawasaki's <u>alltop</u> aggregates the best blogs in a variety of topics, from culture to living to geekery and more.

As you find new sources, you'll often see old sources become stale. Constantly reevaluate your RSS subscriptions to avoid becoming overwhelmed. Eventually, you'll find a comfort zone where you can freely add new and interesting content and discard that which no longer fits your needs.

Tamar Weinberg is a freelance writer and Internet marketing consultant specializing in blogger outreach, viral marketing, and social media. She maintains a personal blog at <u>techipedia.com</u> *about social media and marketing and also writes for* <u>Lifehacker</u>, <u>Search Engine Roundtable</u>, *and* <u>Mashable</u>, *three major blogs in the technology sector.*

Getting Started

For the purposes of demonstration, let's assume that you're marketing a resort destination in Quebec, Canada. You need to identify people who are interested in Canadian travel and who have an audience of regular readers or viewers. These people may turn up in several different venues, including blogs, video- or photo-sharing sites, and social networks like Facebook. Let's start with the bloggers, and specifically with blog search.

Secret: Learn to use advanced search—it'll save you boatloads of time.

Most people go to Google when they want to find something on the Internet, but there are plenty of other options to consider. In addition, there are capabilities buried within Google and other search engines that most people don't know about. These can save you lots of time. For example, you can cut down the time you spend waiting for results pages to load simply by registering with a search engine and specifying in your preferences that you want to display 50 or 100 results per page instead of 10.

There is a vast universe of search engines that aren't Google. Wikipedia has a pretty good list of these. One of my favorites is Mahalo, which is a meta search engine. Meta search aggregates result from multiple search engines. Mahalo also has human guides who aggregate information about a topic, similar to About.com. Most search engines use Google, Ask, MSN or Yahoo! as their core technology and add value on top. The results you get from these engines won't differ appreciably from those of the core technology providers, but the added features can be useful.

You should also know about the power of advanced search. Most search engines have an option to specify all kinds of search conditions and results options. Google's advanced search page, for example, lets you specify sites that originate in a particular region or pages that were first found within the past day, week, month, and so on.

This latter capability is particularly useful because you often want to strike while the iron is hot. If you can identify someone who is writing frequently about a topic, chances are that person or organization will be interested in hearing from you.

There are gems buried in other search engines, too. Excite advanced search, for example, lets you specify a date range for when a Web page first appeared. Yahoo! has Search Assist, which suggests alternative search terms that might get you closer to what you're looking for. Ask.com has a similar feature and can also give you thumbnail previews right in the search results.

For mining the blogosphere, the options expand. There are dozens of blog-specific search engines (you can find a good list at aripaparo. com/archive/00632.html), but the most popular ones are Technorati, Google Blog Search, IceRocket, Blogdigger, Blogpulse, and Bloglines. Zuula is a new meta search engine that just does blog search. There's even Twittersearch, Terraminds, and Twittermeter, which search only Twitter messages.

Blog search engines work fundamentally differently from conventional ones. Google, Yahoo!, and MSN all use "spiders." They visit a website periodically—anywhere from once every few hours to once every couple of weeks—and index the newest information they find. Spider-based search is comprehensive but slow.

Blog search engines work by listening for RSS "pings." Whenever a ping is received, the content is immediately indexed. As a result, blog search engines are very fast; new entries may be posted in as little as a few minutes. However, sites that don't use RSS may not be indexed at all. Blog search engines thus sacrifice comprehensiveness for speed.

These alternative engines each have unique features. Blogdigger, for example, can organize results by date and has an option to find only multimedia results like video and podcasts. IceRocket has dedicated searches for MySpace.com. Bloglines lets you make a personal home page composed of RSS feeds. AideRSS incorporates ranking criteria from other services to filter feeds based upon the popularity of the source.

Most of these search engines have the option of allowing you to subscribe to search results either by e-mail or RSS feed. As noted earlier, Google's Alerts service is a valuable way to get new Web mentions dropped into your e-mail box. Every marketer should have Google Alerts set up for the products, brands, executive names, and competitors that matter to them.

Subscribing to search results via RSS feed is a little clunkier than e-mail but can be rewarding, especially since most search engines don't offer e-mail alerts but do support RSS. Just copy and paste the RSS address into your reader and check it every so often to see what new results have turned up. Aggregation sites like Bloglines and iGoogle also make it possible to gather many RSS feeds on a single page.

Secret: When searching, think like the customer.

Don't ignore the universe of vertical search engines, either. For example, ChemIndustry. com searches for products, suppliers, and articles about the chemical industry. Ebuild is for the construction industry. GlobalSpec is an engineering search engine. SearchMedica indexes medical journals and sites. ThomasNet searches supplier information for industrial parts. Lawyers.com and Findlaw.com mine legal content. Biocompare searches products and articles of interest to life scientists. AgWeb.com is a search engine about agriculture.

Get Creative with Terms

Your choice of search engines doesn't matter much if you don't ask the right questions, and here's where it pays to know the advanced options that are available to you and how to be creative with search terms.

Of course, you'll want to start by searching for your own brand in the various engines. Then you'll probably want to find people who are talking about your industry but who aren't familiar with your business. They can help build awareness.

Think like a customer. Experiment with combinations of words that describe not only the destination but also what people expect to do there. For example, *Québec resorts fishing, Québec resorts skiing, Québec lodging winter, Québec luxury hotel, Québec resorts recommended,* and *Québec hotel best* all deliver different result sets. Substituting "Canada" for "Québec" will give you different results that may also be useful.

One powerful timesaver is to narrow your results using quotation marks. This will deliver pages that have words in the exact sequence that you specify between the quotation marks. This can make a huge difference in the size of the results domain. For example, *"best Québec hotels"* returns only seven results on Google while *best Québec hotels* returns nearly 2.3 million![1] You can also combine quoted and unquoted search terms in interesting ways: *Québec luxury hotel* and *Québec "luxury hotel"* actually return somewhat different results, with the latter query identifying specific hotels on the first results page that don't show up from the first query.

Most search engines allow you to narrow your search either using quotes or by specifying your exact terms on the advanced search page.

---

[1] The numbers cited throughout this book were current at the time of my research, but these results change all of the time.

For example, you can specify that search results may not contain the word "Montreal." Advanced search is also where you can specify whether words appear in the title, text, page name, or other locations. This is another way of winnowing down your result set to a more manageable number. For example, a page that mentions "Québec luxury hotels" in the headline is likely to be more specific to that topic than one that doesn't.

Secret: Use 'site' and 'link' to drill down on search.

You can even use advanced search to specify results for a single site. This is useful in assessing influence because it quickly shows you the level of activity about a particular topic on any site. For example, the Google query *"québec luxury" site:tripadvisor.com* delivers a small number of articles from the TripAdvisor.com site that specifically mention the keywords. This filtering is useful if you've discovered a site that seems relevant to your area of interest and you want to find out how active it's been.

Another useful Google filter is the "link:" command. This quickly shows you a list of all other pages linking to a site or page you specify. It's a quick way of assessing influence. For example, if you want to

That Damned Spam!

Unfortunately, the spam problem isn't limited solely to e-mail. Spam blogs and comment spam are a growing problem on the Internet and they can make the process of finding legitimate influencers a real chore.

Spam blogs are created by computer robots that take advantage of the open nature of sites like Google's blogger.com to set up online outposts that push cheap pharmaceuticals and get-rich-quick schemes. The spammer's goals are to get these sites into search engines and fool users into landing on their ad-laden pages. Many of them steal content randomly from legitimate sites to do this, and they're remarkably good at their odious work. Blog hosting services and search engine providers work hard to keep up with the bad guys, but they're no match for the robots. Spam blogs can usually be identified by the random words that turn up in their descriptions on search result pages. You can often also identify them by the name of the site, which may be full of garbage characters or closely resemble the name of other sites.

Comment spam is another automated scheme to harvest search engine traffic. Many bloggers don't moderate comments submitted by visitors, and spammers take advantage of this to stuff their comments sections with advertising. One blog I administer receives over 30 such comments per day, even though there is software in place to deflect them. This is frustrating for blog owners because it requires them to manually filter their comments and to delay posting legitimate feedback just to weed out the junk.

Sadly, there is no total solution to the spam problem on the horizon.

determine the popularity of The Informed Traveler blog, you'd type *link:traveler.fivestaralliance.com* and immediately learn that 1,240 pages link to this site. You could visit a sampling of those pages to see if they come from influential sources.

Blog Search

Search engines do an excellent job of mining the Web as a whole, but if you want to focus on social media, you need to tap into a specialized search engine.

Google's "link" comand shows the number of sites that link to a specified URL.

For blogs, the two most popular engines are Technorati and Blogpulse. You can perform searches on these sites the same way you would on Google or Yahoo!, but the results look very different. For one thing, both sites make an effort to index only social media sources, which they do with reasonable success. Both also take a stab at assessing the authority level of the blogs that they index. Technorati does this with an authority ranking based upon the number of blogs linking to a website in the last six months. There's also a ranking metric that assesses the authority of a blog relative to all of the two million-plus blogs in Technorati's database.

BlogPulse links to a profile page that lists a blogger's recent activity, links from other blogs, posting activity, and other bloggers that have

What's a Blog?

Most veteran Web surfers know a blog when they see it, but a blog is merely a way of displaying information. Most blogs use a highly templated format incorporating a fixed outer shell and a variable interior that displays new entries in reverse chronological order. Blogs are often personal, but they don't have to be. Also, the blog format may be used in business websites to display various kinds of information.

Blog search engines generally work by indexing RSS feeds. That's a good start, but many kinds of websites other than blogs use RSS. Google Blog Search, for example, frequently turns up articles from mainstream media that aren't blogs in any sense. Unfortunately, there are no programmatic standards that blogs use to identify themselves. The only way to really tell a blog from some other kind of website is by looking at it. That's time-consuming, and no one—not even the costly conversation marketing services—does it perfectly.

People also display their opinions in forums that can't be called blogs. Advisory sites such as ThisNext, Yelp, and TripAdvisor are loaded with information that marketers might want to see, yet they can't be classified as blogs.

This means that you should take blog search services with a grain of salt. Personally, I don't think the distinction is very meaningful. Most marketers simply want good information, regardless of where it comes from. In-

Links indicated in the text above may be found at SSMMBook.com

fluence is the most important factor, and tools like the Technorati ranking metric, Google's "link:" command, and social network "favorites" ratings are more important indicators of authority. Not to mention old favorites like circulation and traffic.

similar interests. You can also track conversation threads for posts that generate a lot of activity. BlogPulse's "Neighborhood" feature is one of its most interesting services. It attempts to identify authors who have similar interests based upon the words they use and where they link. Click the "Tools Overview" link to learn about these distinctive features.

Technorati indexes many more blogs than BlogPulse and includes photo and video results. Many bloggers also register themselves on Technorati and provide profiles and photos (BlogPulse doesn't have this capability). This makes it easier to put a name with a face, which is useful information to have at hand when making contact with an influencer.

Technorati also offers the option of viewing search results by authority level. Use this option to screen out spam and occasionally updated blogs. This can save you time. Going back to our example of the Québec resort, if we look for travel-related influencers, searching *Québec travel* on Technorati, we find over 10,000 mentions on sites that are classified as having "any authority." However, there are less than 4,000 results on sites that are classified as having "a lot of authority." Both services also offer the option of tracking mentions over time, which is useful in identifying topics that generate swirls of activity.

Many blog search engines also track tags, which are keywords that authors associate with their content. Tags are useful to marketers because they are a sort of human-powered description engine. This can greatly narrow the list of results. For example, searching *Québec travel* in Technorati delivers nearly 4,000 results. However, searching on *Québec travel* in blogs and posts that are tagged as being about travel turns up just 111 results. We'll take a closer look at tags in a moment.

Mining Search Results

So, let's assemble all our search tools and try to identify some influencers. We start at Technorati, where we go to advanced search and type *Canada resort* into the search bar. We then specify that we only want self-described travel blogs. We get a list of 44 results for "canada AND resort in blogs tagged travel."

We see that the top results are all from a site called TravelPod, which describes itself as "The Web's Original Travel Blog." We go to the home page of this rich site and type *Québec* into the search box. Our top result is a traveler named "Cobi," who has posted more than 100 entries and whom the site identifies as a "Top Pick." We also see that 39 of those entries are about a Canadian trip. Even though Cobi lives in Great Britain, she could be a good candidate for a repeat visit. We bookmark her profile page, where we can send her a message.

Our search yields another top pick named "kevandsian" who has traveled 21 percent of the world and logged over 190,000 views from visitors. We also bookmark this traveler's profile.

Returning to Technorati, we see that the second page of search results lists Jaunted, The Pop Culture Travel Guide. Technorati assigns it an authority of 670, which is very high. There are quite a few articles about Québec here, so we hunt around for contributors who have written a lot about the topic. One of them is Alex Robertson, who describes himself as "Senior Features Editor at EuroCheapo.com, as well as a freelance travel writer." There's a link to EuroCheapo.com. A Google search on *alex robertson site:eurocheapo.com* takes us directly to a staff listing and an e-mail address for Alex.

Not all of our searches are as successful. Ask.com points us to AndrewLog, a blog written by a Canadian that has several posts about travel. But how influential is Andrew? If we enter the blog's URL into Technorati, we find no links and the "link:" command in Google turns up just five. While it's possible that this blogger hasn't gone through the Technorati registration process, the low link count indicates he's probably not a good target for us.

Back at Ask, though, we stumble across SmartCanucks.ca, a Canadian site that features deals and discounts for Canadian consumers, including travelers. The site includes a page of editor profiles. A Google "link:" search turns up 113 citations. That isn't bad. It might be worth offering some kind of coupon or other incentive to visitors.

As you can see, there is nothing fast or easy about identifying influencers. Even though a clutch of services has emerged to handle some of the dirty work, it's still up to human beings to assess whether an influencer deserves attention.

Our task doesn't begin and end with search, though. There are elements on each site that may lead us to other influencers. Blogrolls, for example, are links to other sites that bloggers find useful. This can be a quick way to discover new resources. You should also look at the profiles that authors provide of themselves. Frequently they list other sites to which they contribute, and you can often find other enthusiasts there.

Seeing Is Believing

Our task also doesn't end with blogs. A variety of other social media outlets can point us to people whose preferred medium is photos, video, and the spoken word. Head over to Yahoo!'s Flickr, which is one of the largest photo-sharing sites. Type *Québec resort* into the search box and select "Tags only." This returns 272 results of photos that have been specifically tagged with these terms, either by the photographer or someone else. Scroll to the list of photos and look for the photographers whose names come up most often.

One of them is "ash2276," who's submitted more than 1,100 photos and who belongs to more than 100 groups. Look at a sample of ash2276's photos and note the large number of comments from visitors. This is someone with a following. Look at the photos tagged "Quebec" (there are 98 of them) and click on some of them. Note the enthusiastic comments. Ash2276 is an accomplished photographer, the kind of person you might want to invite to your resort for a photo weekend.

Flickr has over a half million groups, and while some are small or inactive, others are very large. Search for groups about Québec and you get about 1,800 results. Most aren't about Québec specifically, but if you sort by group size and scroll down, you come across a group called "Canadian Beauty" with nearly 1,800 members, another called "Photo Quebec" with 144 members and a group titled simply "Quebec" with 591 members. Wade into the discussion forums and photo galleries for these groups and look for user names that appear frequently. These are also potential influencers.

There are plenty of other photo sharing sites on the Web, including Snapfish, Shutterfly, Photobucket, and Kodak Gallery. They each have different features and nuances, but they all enable people to categorize and share their photos.

Video and Audio Connections

We're not done yet. Go to YouTube, the most popular video-sharing site, and type *Québec resort* into the search box. You get 29 results. Looking at the user names, you note that "zenwaiter" has posted several videos. Click through to his profile and you read, "In the winter I travel all over Québec…and I shoot video clips." He even has a link to his website, zenwaiter.com.

Remembering our earlier search techniques, we look up that URL on Technorati and find 131 posts linking to it. Some of these bloggers might be good targets for you. The activity certainly indicates that zenwaiter is a promising influencer.

While we're looking at multimedia, let's check out whether there are any good podcasts in this area. Podcasts are Internet audio and video programs that you download and play on computers or portable media players.

The Who's Who of podcasting is Apple's iTunes. Searching on *Canada travel podcast* we come up with 150 results, which iTunes lets you sort by popularity. The service will also tell you which programs are explicit or clean, which is something you want to know. The trick with podcasts is to identify programs that are still active. Many series go dormant after just a few episodes but they aren't removed from the iTunes directory. You can tell by clicking through to the description or the website and looking for when the program was last updated.

Podcast Alley lists 200 results for the same query, but they're in no particular order. You need to look for promising titles and click through to the details page, where Podcast Alley provides a nice summary of popularity and recent episodes. Beware: Many podcasts are produced by businesses—even your competitors—and probably aren't good targets for you. We do quickly find a couple of good candidates, though, including Travelrific and Travel Advice Show. Most podcasts have accompanying websites, so it's pretty easy to find contact information.

Tag, You're It

Secret: Learn the value of tags—the social search engine.

We're in the home stretch. The search isn't complete until we've visited the sites where people share opinions about and vote on the best Web content. These are called social bookmarking and social news sites, and they can give you a glimpse into crowd psychology that no other online service can.

Del.icio.us isn't the most functional social bookmarking site, but it's the most popular. Here's where people save links to websites that they want to remember and also apply tags to describe them. Tags are a little-understood but very powerful method of describing information. A tag can be any combination of letters and numbers; the choice is up to the user. Many search engines give tags special treatment, meaning that content that has been labeled with certain tags rank higher in the results. Tags are very popular with photo-sharing sites, but they can be applied to any kind of information.

Social bookmarking sites are kind of like search engines, only the results are selected by the members. The more people who've applied a certain tag to a bookmarked page, the more likely that page is relevant to that term. There are dozens of these sites on the Web. Some of the more popular are Ma.gnolia, StumbleUpon, Backflip, Chipmark, and Linkroll.[2] If you search on *tag:quebec tag:travel* on del.icio.us, for example, you get more than 450 results. Some are obvious, like the official government tourism site. But others may be new, like Montrealfood.com, a blog about Québec restaurants, or 1000 Islands, a beautiful photo blog. Del.icio.us makes it possible for you to see that

---

[2] Mashable has a list of more than 50 social bookmarking sites.

1000 Islands has been bookmarked by more than 350 people, which is a good indicator of influence. The person who runs this site is another candidate for a photo weekend.

Your trip wouldn't be complete without a stop at Facebook, the hottest social network of 2007. Facebook's adult, professional membership has made it a favorite of marketers, and it boasts thousands of groups of all sizes. One group called "Coups de Coeur pour découvrir le Québec" appears to focus on Québec exclusively. Its membership is small, but it may be worth joining just to keep an eye on discussion topics. You might also want to submit a friend request to the group's organizer and ask how you can become involved. Don't jump right in. Lurk for a while and see what the members are talking about. When you do enter the conversation, be sure to fully disclose your affiliation. Social network users don't mind engaging in discussions with marketers, but they don't like to be deceived.

What's Next

At this point, you may have spent an afternoon or even an entire day navigating social media sites and accumulated a list of maybe 30 to 40 potential influencers. And you've barely scratched the surface. Travel sites like BootsnAll, Gusto, RealTraveler, TripAdvisor, VirtualTourist, Where Are You Now?, and LonelyPlanet.com all provide gathering places for travelers to share ideas and experiences.

You also haven't tapped the emerging class of people search engines such as Zoominfo and Spock. These tools can build remarkably rich profiles of people based solely on publicly available information. Professional networks like LinkedIn, Visible Path, and Plaxo also make it possible to learn people's professional affiliations and even personal contacts.

If you feel like your head is about to explode, don't despair. The social media landscape is seemingly endless, and new sites launch all the time. No one can keep up with it, and no one should try. If you make it a goal to explore one new network or search engine for a few minutes every day and to identify a couple of new influencers that way, you will make steady progress. You can also give much of this work to junior staff, if you have any, once you learn the ropes.

However, I recommend against outsourcing this task entirely. Marketers need to learn the ways and means of social networks if they are going to interact with them. Younger staff members actually may be more adept at using the tools, but they are less able to think strategically about them.

You also can't necessarily computerize the process, although tools are emerging that can apply sophisticated algorithms to conversation analysis to determine sentiment. At some point, human-to-human communications defies automation. PR blogger Phil Gomes tells of looking at a post about Starbucks that said, "This is the greatest f***ing cup of coffee I ever had." The machine, in its infinite wisdom, had categorized the comment as negative.

Tool Talk

Identifying influencers requires a lot of Web surfing, and productivity tools that cut down on repetitive tasks can go a long way toward eliminating boredom and making you more productive. Here are three that I use:

Firefox—the big attraction of this popular free web browser is that it supports tabbed browsing. That means that you can open new Web pages in tabs within the browser and easily navigate between them with the Control-Page Up and Control-Page Down keys. Opening a new tab is as simple as holding down the control key while clicking on a link. Most browsers now support tabbed browsing, including Microsoft's Internet Explorer, but Firefox is faster and easier to use than any other I've tried.

Roboform—This shareware program costs $30, but is well worth it. Roboform can quickly remember log-on information for hundreds of websites, but its greatest value to me is that it stores much of the information you typically need to provide when registering for new sites. So instead of going through the slow and error-prone process of typing in a name and address every time, you click a couple of mouse buttons and all the forms are filled in for you.

Social bookmark sites—Services like del.icio.us enable you to save web pages to a central location, tag them, and provide some descriptive information. This makes them far superior to the local bookmarks that come in Web browsers, especially as your bookmarks run into the hundreds and you lose track of why you saved things in the first place. I personally use Diigo, but there are many options (Here are just a few). and any of them will do the job.

4

Courting Online Influencers

At this point, you might want to start contacting some of the influencers you've identified to engage with them and find out if they're open to learning more about your business. Perhaps you've done this in the past with journalists. It's important to understand that social media influencers are not reporters. They don't cover a beat and they don't feel obligated to write or comment about anything that doesn't interest them. That makes it critical that you understand the issues that get their attention. In the case of Canadian travel, it may be skiing, snowmobiling, outdoor photography, fishing, hunting, boating, business meetings or other interests. You'll be much more successful if you can frame your interactions in the context of these topics.

Influential bloggers have always told me that the most important step a marketer must take before contacting them is to read their work. This doesn't need to be time-consuming. In the case of a blogger, scanning a few recent posts, reading a biography, and noting the categories or tags that the person uses can give you a pretty quick idea of what motivates him. This is literally a five- to 10-minute process. In the case of a person who contributes to a group blog or to recommendation sites such as TripAdvisor, start

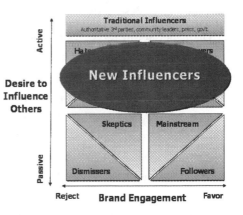

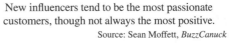

New influencers tend to be the most passionate customers, though not always the most positive.
Source: Sean Moffett, *BuzzCanuck*

as you would with a blogger: Consult the person's profile and list of recent posts to learn this information. Then take a measured approach to initiating contact. Consider the following guidelines:

Secret: Flattery will get you everywhere, but be sincere.

Make your initial contact meaningful and positive—Never start a relationship on the wrong foot. Even if you don't like what the writer has said, find something you do like and post a comment on her blog or Flickr portfolio telling her what you like and why. Don't limit your comment to something simple like, "Great post!" Tell her why you thought it was great, and perhaps add a bit of context or new information. If you have a blog, contact the influencer and ask if you can add her to your blog roll. You don't have to do this, but it's a nice gesture and will establish in the person's mind that you're paying attention. Bloggers love comments and links. Show that you respect them by offering this small acknowledgement of their value.

Ask the person's advice—In *Word of Mouth Marketing*, Andy Sernovitz talks about the emotions that compel people to share their thoughts and opinions. One is that we like to look smart. Another is that we want to feel important. "Being a frequent flyer used to be as much about the gold luggage tag as the miles and rewards," he says. The same rules apply online. Asking someone for his opinion and showing that you take that opinion seriously is the fastest way to make a friend. That doesn't mean always doing what the person says, but it does mean showing that you understood him.

Take the conversation off-line—If you're serious about building a relationship, offer influencers something special. This doesn't have to be expensive; it can be a discount, free sample, trial offer, or just a link on your website. Keep these interactions private, using e-mail or the telephone. Also use this opportunity to ask permission to add someone to your press list or to invite him to attend an insider event. If the e-mail address isn't on the site, use resources like Zoominfo or LinkedIn to find an alternate means of contact.

Follow through—One of the most common mistakes public relations professionals make is to contact the media only when they have something to promote. That's not a relationship; it's a transaction. It's easy to keep track of what influencers are saying. Subscribe to their RSS feed and keep an eye on new activity. Send e-mails or leave comments on their site every so often to show them that you are engaged. You won't believe how rarely this is done and it will pay huge dividends for your relationship.

One temptation is to try to co-opt influencers by offering to advertise on their sites or to pay them. I recommended against this approach if you want to secure future editorial coverage. Social media influencers are like journalists in their resistance to mixing advertising and editorial interests. They may take your ad, but they are actually less likely to write about you once they do.

Give them the same privileges and access that you would give the media—Online influencers are, after all, just another kind of media voice. They should be part of your everyday press communications and should be granted the same access to events, interviews, and news stories as mainstream media.

Some companies worry that this is a slippery slope. If they legitimize bloggers by treating them like journalists, then there is no going back. They're right. Once you start inviting new media influencers to your press conferences and giving them access to your executives and employees, this will have to become part of your standard operating procedure. This can add cost and complexity to your press relations program and you have to think carefully about whether the value is there. Keep in mind, though, that excluding influencers from your communications channels won't stop them from talking about you. If you believe in the power of word-of-mouth influence, then you're better off engaging these people in a conversation than pretending not to listen. It's better to be part of the conversation than to stand mute on the sidelines.

The question often comes up of whether all social media influencers should be treated the same. I say no. A blogger who writes only occasionally about a topic that's relevant to you, or who has a small following, does not have to be treated the same way as a true influencer. In reality, most of them don't expect that. You're no more obliged to invite every blogger to a press conference than you are to accept anyone who has journalism credentials. In the rare event that someone challenges your inclusion criteria, be ready to explain honestly what those criteria are. The person may not be happy with your decision, but if you've articulated a rational argument, you've done your part.

Craft a Program

Influencers appreciate being recognized and taken seriously, so think of how you can entice them to get involved with you. This doesn't have to be expensive, but it does have to be special. Here are some ideas for our fictional Canadian resort:

Photo weekend—Your research has shown that photo and video enthusiasts are an important constituency, so consider hosting a weekend gathering of top photo bloggers. Invite 10 key people to bring their cameras, with accommodations on the house. Don't require them to publish their photos online, but ask them to tag any images they publish with your resort name. Then feature the best work on your site.

Contest—Raise the stakes a little and sponsor a photo contest. Winners will have their work featured on your home page and win a weekend trip for two. Or offer to feature the winning photo on your brochure. You can even have the community vote on entries.

License content—Sponsor a ski weekend and invite some ski bloggers and videographers to record the event. Offer to review their best work from the weekend and incorporate it into your collateral for a small licensing fee. Offer to introduce them to some of your travel industry colleagues in the area, too.

Free trials—Even easier is to contact a few influencers and offer 50 percent off the price of a weekend stay. Make it clear that they were chosen for the quality of their work. Flatter them. It'll get you everywhere.

Search Engine Magic

One appeal of blogs—and one of the reasons they can be so frightening to marketers—is that they perform very well on search engines. Why is this? The main reason is that the basic unit of blog content, called a permalink, typically uses a page title that is derived from the headline of that entry. Most search engines assign great importance to page titles when indexing content. Writers who use descriptive headlines can thus become magnets for search engine attention. Bloggers also tend to write frequently about a few topics, which further improves their search performance. Search engines are attracted to frequent updates and revisit sites more often if the content changes frequently.

In contrast, many large companies have two strikes against them when it comes to search. Some use content management systems that assign arcane content ID numbers to their file names. Search engines don't know what to do with a file named "index.php?option=com_content&task=blogsection&id=3&Itemid=86" and so they ignore that critical file information. That's strike one. Many search engines also use keyword and pattern analysis to suppress content that appears to be a promotion or catalog listing. That's strike two. Bloggers enjoy a double advantage: Both their content and their page titles are search-friendly.

Blogs' remarkable search performance is one reason that marketers are often shocked to find fan or hate sites on the first page of Google results right below their own homepage. This is because a blogger may talk about a company online almost as much as the company talks about itself, only the blogger has the advantage in search performance. This is a good reason to consider launching one or more company blogs. They can help level the playing field.

Many bloggers also do a better job of optimizing their sites for search engine performance than the businesses they cover. Free online resources like Business Blog Consulting, Conversion Rater, Search Engine Journal, B2B SEO, Dosh Dosh, Mashable, and BlogStorm are loaded with tips and tools. HubSpot has a free service that evaluates your search engine performance. In contrast, it may cost a corporation months of time and millions of dollars to optimize a sprawling website for search. They can't match bloggers for speed.

Finally, most search engines consider inbound links to be the gold standard for content quality. Because many top bloggers have active and enthusiastic readers, their inbound link counts can actually exceed those of even large corporate entities. By human nature, people are more likely to link to content written by individuals than by corporations. The personal nature of blogs is a strength.

How Important Is Influence?

For more than half a century, marketers have accepted as conventional wisdom the thesis that a few people exert disproportionate influence over many other people. The idea was first outlined by Elihu Katz and Paul Lazarsfeld in their 1955 book, *Personal Influence: The Part Played by People in the Flow of Mass Communications*, and epitomized in the title of a 2003 book by Jon Berry and Ed Keller: *The Influentials: One American in Ten Tells the Other Nine How to Vote, Where to Eat, and What to Buy*. The idea is that if you can get the ear of that 10 percent of the market, word-of-mouth will do the rest of the work for you. The concept makes intuitive sense, and has been the thesis behind the best-selling book, Malcolm Gladwell's *The Tipping Point*. However, the influentials theory is facing some new challenges.

Among the challengers is Duncan Watts, a former professor of sociology at Columbia University and now a lead researcher at Yahoo! Using simulations and detailed mathematical models, Watts has built a controversial case that influencer marketing underestimates the complexity by which messages are spread and that marketing campaigns that rely solely on reaching influencers are at a high risk of failure.

"Reliably designing messages to exhibit viral properties is extremely difficult, it turns out, as is predicting which particular individuals will be responsible for spreading them," Watts wrote in a May 2007 _Harvard Business Review_ article. He went on to characterize viral marketing as being successful only when each person who receives a message passes it on to more than one other person. When that pass-along rate falls below 1:1, the campaign can quickly fizzle out. A detailed description of Watts' theory appeared in _Fast Company_ magazine in early 2008.

A more reliable approach to marketing, Watts argues, is to supplement viral campaigns with conventional media marketing. By continually re-seeding the market with the original message in this way, campaigns have a greater likelihood of long-term success.

In their excellent 2008 book _Influencer Marketing_, authors Duncan Brown and Nick Hayes argue that most companies don't even know who their most important influencers are and that bloggers are greatly overrated as sources of influence. Most bloggers, they argue, focus on very small niches and audiences. While bloggers can exercise great influence in their niches, their overall importance isn't that great, at least not yet. Further, they state that based on their work mining thousands of influence sources for clients over the years, "Our best estimate is that, for any one market there is a maximum of seven blogs that have measurable influence. That's it—seven."

These relatively minor influencers attract a great deal of attention, the authors state, because marketers are hyper-focused on the media, and bloggers are seen as a new media channel. The authors propose that there are actually more than 20 sources of influence on purchase decisions, including government regulators, financial analysts, channel partners, and systems integrators. Most marketers can identify, at best, 20 percent of the influencers in their markets.

Brown and Hayes' holistic approach to influence merits attention, although I differ with some of their conclusions about the blogosphere. As mainstream media outlets relentlessly cut back on reporting staff, bloggers are arguably acquiring more influence as sources for these channels. I related several stories in *The New Influencers* in which discussions started by bloggers made the jump to mainstream media. The emergence of aggregation sites like Consumerist and My3Cents can powerfully amplify the voice of even the most little-known individuals.

Even the most prominent influencers can't create a viral storm if the conditions aren't right. Anecdotal evidence suggests that even great ideas fall flat if people aren't yet ready to embrace them. In a May 2007 article in *InformationWeek* magazine, Janet Edan-Harris, CEO of Umbria, was quoted as saying, "It's much more important to identify those themes that are gaining momentum than try to find opinion leaders." "You want to ride the wave rather than trying to start one on your own."

In that article, author Alice LaPlante concluded, "[A] growing school of thought is that influentials aren't so much leading trends as acting as mouthpieces for underlying social movements that are either already in progress or lying fallow waiting to be triggered. Thus successful marketing doesn't depend so much on finding influential people and seeding them with ideas as doing the kind of research that exposes embryo trends, and then helping influentials discover them."

If the influentials theory continues to lose favor, it could cause marketers to re-examine the fundamentals of viral campaigns. That could threaten viral marketing's rapid growth. MarketingVOX estimates that more than $1 billion was spent on word-of-mouth marketing in 2007 and that the category is growing at 36 percent annually.

Conversation-Mining Services

A handful of companies have emerged in recent years that listen in on online conversations, report on activity, and even assess influence—for a price. These services range from a few hundred to a few thousand dollars per month and vary widely in the features they offer. Here are capsule summaries of a few of the leaders. Keep in mind that new competitors are emerging all the time. Pricing of their services vary widely.

Andiamo—Launched in early 2007, Andiamo provides an attractive dashboard and many reports to measure conversations on blogs and in some social networks. The service ranks authority of the authors, relevance of conversations to a brand, the sentiment expressed by their postings, and competitor analysis, among other things. Pricing is on a per-mention basis.

Biz360—Biz360's Market360 line of services ropes in print and broadcast outlets as well as online conversations. Like others, it can be customized to specific topics and it features real-time analytics and drill-down capabilities.

Brandimensions—This company's BrandIntel services identifies appropriate online communities, profiles discussion leaders, tracks content, and synthesizes all the information with a staff of human analysts.

BrandsEye—Developed by Quirk eMarketing as an adjunct to its marketing consulting services, BrandsEye scours the Internet for every mention of a brand and rolls that information up into a weighted "Reputation Score" that companies can use to compare their online image to their competitors.

CyberAlert—A small media monitoring company founded in 1999, CyberAlert has added daily monitoring of more than 25 million blogs and 100,000 message boards.

Factiva—This Dow Jones subsidiary has a suite of products that monitor various media sources with a focus on mainstream media. It is less capable in the consumer-generated media area.

Magpie—Magpie's BrandWatch service continuously scours blogs and websites identified as influential for mentions of clients' brands. It uses a database of articles classified by humans as positive, negative, or neutral and compares new information to that content as a way to estimate sentiment.

MotiveQuest—This is a marketing consultancy with a technology twist. The company's tools for monitoring buzz and online trends are used to support a suite of brand development and positioning services. The linguistic model is customized for each domain and project. The service also claims to be able to determine emotions using linguistic modeling.

Nielson BuzzMetrics—This company's BrandPulse and BlogPulse services have been around as long as anyone's. The service excels at tracking overall trends in blogger conversations and reporting on the most influential sources.

Onalytica—This UK-based company's InfluenceMonitor service measures the topical influence of blogs and media and uses statistical mining to flag content that has the greatest impact on sentiment.

Radian6—A 2007 newcomer that generated quite a bit of buzz, Radian6 is an online service that provides customized monitoring of blogs, video-sharing, image-sharing, microblogging, discussion group, and mainstream media sources. The company uses algorithms to determine influence based upon a variety of factors and its dashboard interface has been praised for being functional and easy to use.

RelevantNoise—This online service monitors more than 80 million blogs and applies algorithms that evaluate the importance of the bloggers and the tenor of conversations. It provides useful charts showing total activity, positive/negative tone, and activity by influence level.

Seer—This service performs all the standard conversation monitoring tasks but adds a visualization layer that depicts nodes of influence and the paths that topics take as they travel through online communities.

TNS Media Intelligence/Cymfony—Cymfony's Orchestra platform monitors online chatter to understand how companies are perceived and how trends develop. The service monitors not only blogs, but also mainstream media outlets, and it provides a real-time dashboard, campaign measurement, and influencer rankings.

Umbria—A relatively recent entrant to the market, Umbria uses conversation analysis to help clients with brand positioning and audience segmentation. Its specialty is in identifying new classes of customers and audience segments that aren't readily apparent without this analysis.

Visible Technologies—Self-described as the only solution that completes the conversation, Visible's TruCast service monitors social media comments and context, allows for tracking over time, identifies trends, and enables users to publish real-time responses. Users can "teach" the engine how to analyze and group conversations and they can respond to comments from within the engine.

5

Corporate Soapboxes

"A company's true character is expressed by its people. The strongest opinions—good or bad—about a company are shaped by the words and deeds of its employees...It is the responsibility of corporate communications to support each employee's capability and desire to be an honest, knowledgeable ambassador to customers, friends, shareowners and public officials."

—From <u>The Authentic Enterprise: Relationships, Values and the Evolution of Corporate Communications</u>, Arthur W. Page Society, December 2007

On June 21, 2006, the chief executive officer of Southwest Airlines wrote an entry on the company's <u>Nuts about Southwest</u> blog, which was just two months old at the time. "I'm new to this whole blogosphere thing," Gary Kelly admitted at the outset, adding that he was "humbled that so many people are as enthusiastic and nuts about Southwest as we are."

Kelly then went on to address an issue that had the rumor mills buzzing for more than a month: reports that Southwest was considering modifying or discontinuing its distinctive open-seating policy. Open seating had long been a topic of controversy in the airline industry. It's a far faster and more efficient way to board an aircraft than assigned seating, and many die-hard Southwest customers love it. However, the practice baffled and annoyed customers who were accustomed to other airlines' procedures.

Kelly explained that new technology could make it feasible to adopt assigned seating without too big a hit to efficiency. A month earlier he had alluded during a shareholders' meeting to the possibility of moving to assigned seating in the future. He wanted to get some honest feedback.

He got it.

Over the next few weeks, hundreds of Southwest customers weighed in with their comments on the blog. Some wrote epics of several hundred words, describing their own interpretation of the pros and cons of open seating. Between 80 percent and 90 percent of the contributors didn't want Southwest to do away with the policy. More than 650 comments accumulated over the next few months.

Kelly evidently got the message, for on October 13 he returned to thank customers for all their input and to issue a vague "no decision." However, the outpouring of customer sentiment had clearly made an impact. More than a year later, Kelly returned to announce that after extensive testing, Southwest had decided to keep open seating with modifications. His post included a link to a video demonstrating the new system. That drew another 500 comments, most of them favorable.

Gary Kelly has been an infrequent contributor to Nuts about Southwest, but the blog in which he occasionally participates has become a staple of the company's communication strategy. With new entries posted almost daily by an assortment of Southwest employees, the site is a showcase for the company's friendly, customer-focused style. Equally important: It has evolved into a critical tool for announcing new services and for floating ideas without the intercession of media gatekeepers. The blog has won awards and frequently been cited as a shining example of how businesses can use new media to create meaningful dialogue with their customers.

Southwest was a perfect candidate for blogging success. Over 75 percent of its reservations come through its website, and its freewheeling culture is a natural fit for the open discourse of the blogosphere. Few companies have it so easy. Perhaps that's why, nearly five years after blogs exploded onto the online scene, less than 15 percent of the Fortune 500 companies use them, according to Forrester Research. There are many reasons for this; corporate politics, unease about openness, regulatory concerns, and time constraints are just a few. But as blogging matures and finds new niches in the business communications hierarchy, resistance is beginning to melt.

In this chapter, we'll talk mainly about blogs and podcasts, which are the safest and most demonstrably successful steps busi-

Secret: Blogs are your best bet for controlling the conversation.

nesses can take in moving into social media. Both vehicles have been around for several years and have demonstrated success. They also offer companies the greatest control over conversations, which is a critical factor. While having control doesn't mean manipulating the conversation, the flexibility to dictate the terms of engagement is reassuring for many businesses.

Business Blogs: An Online Podium

Blogs have been compared to business presentations. The speaker has the microphone and most of the control over the conversation, including the option to shut it down if necessary. Cutting off a conversation is rarely a good move, but having the power to seize back the microphone when a response is needed can be useful.

Blogs are taking on new roles as businesses learn to leverage their flexibility and ease of use. I classify business blogs into seven categories, but it's first worth reviewing some terms.

When many people think of blogs, they think of the personal, often intensely opinionated diaries that seem to pop up randomly in search results. While this is the most popular use of the medium, it's by no means the only one. A blog is simply a container for information, a crunchy outside with a soft middle, if you will.

The templated shell that runs around the outside of the blog contains information about the topic and the

Secret: Blogs are flexible. Use them with photos, audio, and video.

author, as well as a few rudimentary navigation aids. The soft middle is a continually changing collection of articles called permalinks that are usually displayed in reverse chronological order. Articles almost always contain text but may also include graphics, video, and audio content. The most recent permalink appears at the top of the page with older entries following below it. Almost all blogs support RSS (Really Simple Syndication) capability, which means that new entries are automatically shuttled out to a variety of aggregation engines across the Internet (as mentioned in the previous chapter, this is how blog search works). This feature ensures that new blog entries are quickly spread about the Internet and is one of the most powerful features of the medium.

Blogs are fast and easy to update and require little technical skill to use. That's one of the characteristics that make them such valuable communication tools. They are a way to respond rapidly to developing stories or to disseminate news. However, their rudimentary navigation scheme and design inflexibility makes them ill-suited to a lot of purposes. Few organizations would want to build their company website on a blog platform, for example.

Many new companies, particularly in the technology industries, now make a blog an essential part of the company website. The value is the ability to update constituents quickly on rapidly changing business and product conditions, troubleshoot questions and add a human element to functional but often bland and impersonal business language. Startups have an advantage, though; relatively few regulators and stakeholders are looking over their shoulder and they have little to lose.

Is Blogging Right for Your Business?

Although some social media consultants will tell you that business blogging is a no-brainer, the reality is that the medium isn't for everybody. Here's a short quiz you can take to determine if your company is a good candidate. Answer appropriately and then compare your score to the key at the end.

Do you want to do it? A blog isn't a short-term project. Once you start, you need to consistently update your site, at least once per week. The novelty will quickly wear off, so ask yourself whether you have the stamina and a wellspring of ideas to keep you going beyond the first few months.
Yes: 5 points; No: 0 points

Do you have a topic in mind? Ideally, your topic should be expressible in less than a dozen words displayed under your blog title. This isn't always easy. Some markets (marketing, entertainment, and sports, for example) have hundreds or thousands of bloggers. In an environment like this, you need to focus your topic very precisely. Other markets (architecture and construction, for example) are nearly wide open. Pick a theme for your blog and be sure it doesn't duplicate what's already being said. The more distinctive your topic, the faster you'll achieve success.
Yes: 3 points; No: 0 points

Are you passionate about the topic? Good blogs have personality and personality is a product of enthusiasm. That doesn't mean you need to be a cheerleader; in fact, some very successful blogs are negative in tone. It does mean that your topic should be something that you can talk about for hours, because that's basically what you'll be doing over time.
Yes: 3 points; No: 1 point

Are you knowledgeable about the topic? A public forum isn't the place to go to school, particularly if you represent a business. It's important to engage in dialogue and learn something from your readers, but you should also have a point of view backed by expertise and experience that makes you credible.
Yes: 2 points; No: 0 points

Do you communicate well? Some people don't, and a blog is probably not the right promotional vehicle for them. You don't necessarily have to be a good writer; many successful bloggers use video and sound to great effect. But you do need to be able to express your thoughts coherently in some form. Most people can actually write at least passably if they use a style that's comfortable for them. Blogging should be natural.

Yes: 2 points; No: 1 point

Do you have a thick skin? If you're opinionated enough to sustain a blog, you need to accept the fact that others may differ with you. Assuming that you accept comments (and I strongly recommended that you do), be prepared to accept pointed responses to what you say without losing your cool.

Yes: 2 points; No: 1 point

Score:
12 or more points: What are you waiting for?
8 to 12 points: You're on track, but you need more focus or enthusiasm. A multi-author blog might bc a good idea.
5 to 8 points: Think hard about whether this is the right vehicle for you.
Less than 5 points: Don't bother.

For established entities with stakeholders and media attention, the issues are more complex. Heavily regulated industries like financial services and health care have legitimate concerns about writing too openly about their businesses. However, even they may find value in offering customers advice through a topical blog (see below). Small businesses have much less reason for concern, and some of the most successful business blogs have been created by them.

There has been a lot written on the subject of blogging and many websites cover it on an ongoing basis. A few are noted in the resource list at the end of this chapter. Below I summarize the options and best practices that I've gathered through three years of hands-on client work. Let's start with the most common types of business blog.

Bill Marriott's CEO blog.

Choose Your Weapon

There are seven basic blog formats that have had demonstrated success:

1. CEO blog—If your chief executive has the desire and discipline to maintain a personal blog, count yourself lucky. Very few CEOs use this tool, but those who do find it an excellent mechanism to connect with all kinds of constituents. For one thing, the media who cover the company become immediate subscribers.

Popular CEO bloggers include Sun Microsystems CEO Jonathan Schwartz, GoDaddy's Bob Parsons, RedBalloonDays' Naomi Simpson, and Marriott International's Bill Marriott. Many CEOs of small companies also have blogs.

A CEO usually doesn't need much guidance when it comes to knowing what to say, but he or she may need writing and editing help. It's important that a CEO blog has a voice and style that is appropriate to the executive's objectives. For example, a brusque or "strictly business" style may not work if the company is trying to soften its image. On the other hand, a style that's too chatty or informal may confuse readers about whether the boss is serious about his work. A certain amount of detachedness may also be needed to satisfy regulators.

Marketers should play a role in creating stylistic guidelines and supporting the CEO in writing and copyediting. They should also make sure that images and videos are available to illustrate the topics the CEO chooses to cover. But don't try to be too heavy-handed. If the CEO is willing to talk, there are bound to be people who'll listen.

As a rule of thumb, blogs are most effective when updated regularly, at least once a week. A CEO blog is the one exception I'd make to this rule. CEOs will get good readership regardless of when they write, so if they want to go a month between posts, so be it. Constituents understand that CEOs have severe time constraints and they're forgiving if the entries are somewhat sporadic.

When David Neeleman was CEO of JetBlue Airways, he contributed only infrequently to the company blog. However, it was a critical tool in JetBlue's handling of a February 2007 crisis that left thousands of travelers stranded. In the two months that followed, Neeleman used the blog to apologize, announce a new customer Bill of Rights, and post a video explaining how JetBlue would avoid future outages[1].

2. Executive blog—A company that wants to showcase the talent of its management team can handpick a select number of senior managers and set up their own personal spaces on a company website. Good examples of this are PriceWaterhouseCoopers UK, Hewlett-Packard (which has greatly expanded its blog presence beyond executives), Oracle Corp. and the public relations firm Edelman.

> Secret: Focus corporate blogs on topics rather than people to insulate against turnover and re-assignments.

The trick here is to make sure that the executives have the will and time to write regularly. With busy people, it's easy for early enthusiasm to give way to scheduling reality. It's usually a good idea to build blog content around topics rather than people. This gives you some protection against the inevitable turnover and executive reassignments. It's also a good idea to have backups in reserve to pick up the ball in case an executive leaves the company or is reassigned.

Executives need support in this effort. Many have come up through the ranks in disciplines where writing skills were not important. They need coaching and editing assistance to make sure they get their points across. Don't be heavy-handed; remember that this is a medium of personal expression. Let their personalities come through and encourage them to go off the business topic occasionally and write about personal experiences, even those outside of the office.

Do encourage them to think of their audience's perspective over the company's message. The biggest problem

> Secret: A safe approach to blogging is to answer frequently asked customer questions.

---

[1] The strategy didn't save Neeleman from taking the fall for the fiasco, though. He was removed in favor of a new CEO just three months later. Neeleman retains a seat on JetBlue's board.

I encounter with executive blogs is that the authors, who are often under intense P&L pressure, start using the blog to deliver a sales pitch. This invariably backfires with customers. A better approach is to have executives answer the most common questions they hear from customers and the field sales force. They are in a better position than anyone to do this.

3. Group blog—This is an increasingly popular form of business blog because it's the easiest to maintain and offers the greatest variety. In a group blog, a select team of employees contributes to the site on a rotating basis. The schedule may be fixed or flexible. Some companies find group blogs to be so popular that employees actually bid for a turn at the keyboard.

Popular group blogs include Nuts about Southwest, the Google blog, the Chrysler blog, and Benetton Talk. Eastman Kodak's A Thousand Words blog takes the innovative step of actually including customer entries in the rotation.

Secret: Give company bloggers a list of preferred keywords and ask them to use those words often to improve organic search results.

Group blogs require a lot of internal communication, but they can pay off handsomely when well coordinated. Vontoo, a seller of permission-based voice market messaging services, failed in its first attempt at blogging because the person assigned to the task had neither the time nor the proclivity to do it well. It happened that that person was Dustin Sapp, the company's president. Sapp told BtoB magazine that he decided instead to distribute the task among five blogs maintained by employees. Each blogger was given a list of keywords that Vontoo wanted to emphasize in its search engine optimization campaign. The company also enlisted a service called Compendium to monitor blogger activity and to aggregate articles into a company blog. The result: Vontoo was able to cut its paid search spending by 40 percent, and about a quarter of that improvement was attributable to search engine performance. About 75 percent of Vontoo's targeted search terms now appear on the first page of Google organic search results.

Marketing should take an active and visible role in a group blog. It's important that everyone involved understand the objective, editorial profile, and desired voice. It's a good idea to launch the blog behind a firewall for a few weeks to get people comfortable with the process. It's also appropriate for marketing to approve entries until bloggers get their sea legs. Contributors need to know that they are speaking as authorized representatives of the company and that responsibility accompanies that role. Otherwise, give people as much latitude as possible to tell stories in their own words and to convey enthusiasm for what they do. Marketing shouldn't dictate content, but marketers should watch for potential problems.

4. Company blog platform—A few companies encourage employees to maintain their own blogs on a company-branded site. These may be just a few high-profile individuals (the PriceWaterhouseCoopers approach) or the platform may be thrown open to everyone (Microsoft and Sun both have over 5,000 bloggers at last count).

You don't have to commit to a particular model at the outset. You can start with a select few bloggers at first and open the floodgates over time. For example, HP launched its blogs with a small number of executive journals but is now rapidly expanding its roster of writers and topics. IBM has over 1,000 employee bloggers, but doesn't provide a corporate platform for their work, preferring instead to issue a set of common-sense guidelines and let employees find their own outlets.

A company blog platform is a useful way to put the people who make and sell the products directly in touch with the people who buy them. It's also a way to show the world the talent that exists in your organization (but beware: Recruiters will be lurking).

You can't possibly control or even monitor what everyone is saying in a companywide blog initiative, so don't try. Use a good set of policies built on your existing

Secret: Make your blogging policy simply an extension of your standards of business conduct.

employee conduct guidelines.[2] Make sure employee bloggers sign a statement that outlines what's expected of them. It's also perfectly all right to define topics that are considered off-limits. General Motors, for example, informed readers of its Fastlane Blog that it would not discuss its contract negotiations with the United Auto Workers in that forum. Stating upfront what topics you won't discuss looks decisive. Saying nothing and avoiding those topics looks evasive.

Although the prospect of allowing employees to speak to a global audience without oversight may seem frightening at first, the reality is that there have been no publicized cases of legal or regulatory action that resulted from an employee blog. In fact, most employees welcome the opportunity to speak directly to the market and are only too happy to stay within company guidelines in order to preserve the privilege. Choose bloggers wisely, though. One major manufacturer I worked with got stuck on this issue. Nearly 90 percent of its workforce in one division was unionized and the confrontational atmosphere made it nearly impossible to find good bloggers.

5. Topical blog—This is one of my favorite approaches to business blogging, and it's a wonder more companies don't do it. A topical blog connects with customers about topics that are mutually interesting. Its purpose is to offer practical information that helps readers be more successful and productive, thereby associating the sponsor with that expertise. A great example of this is Extended Stay Hotels' Road Warrior Tips, which is full of useful advice for frequent business travelers. Clutter Control Freak is from Stacks and Stacks, a retailer of storage and organization accessories. Launched in August 2007, it was getting 1,500 visitors per day by the end of the year. GlaxoSmithKline has a blog called AlliConnect that's all about weight loss and is intended to promote its Alli weight-loss treatment.

Advice blogs are relatively easy to maintain because they can be written by multiple contributors and they do well on search engines

---

[2] *The San Francisco Chronicle* summed up some high tech companies' approach to blogger policies in this 2005 article. Forrester's Charlene Li specializes in this area. Her wiki lists some best practices.

because they pertain to keywords that people frequently use. You can also mix practical advice with references to new company products and services, a subtle but effective marketing tactic. Always be transparent about any commercial affiliation. As long as you don't overdo the marketing, you'll be fine.

Topical blogs don't necessarily have to be advisory. They can also cover the news and cross the line into advocacy (see below). One notable example is Miller Brewing's Brew Blog, a newsy examination of the beer industry written by a former *Advertising Age* reporter who now works for Miller. Brew Blog has sparked some controversy for straddling the line between objective news coverage and advocacy reporting, but it has apparently worked wonders for Miller, logging 12,000 unique visitors in one recent month and attracting the attention of mainstream media for its frequent scoops. Brew Blog is an example of a large corporation using social media to become a legitmate news source, an opportunity that would have been unavailable just a few years ago.

6. Advocacy blog—This relatively little-used format addresses a specific public policy or legislative agenda upon which the company wants to make its position known. It's most effective when the topic is controversial and the company wants to burnish its reputation as a thought leader or activist. Examples include McDonald's Corporate Responsibility Blog and the National Association of Manufacturers' ShopFloor.org. Companies like General Motors, Benetton, and Chrysler also frequently use their corporate blogs for this purpose.

Chrysler used ChrylserLaborTalks07 to talk proactively about pending labor negotiations. Its goal was to quickly infuse its opinions into the media and to track and respond to other posts related to labor issues. The site took advantage of a blog format to provide frequent updates on labor negotiations and to set out the company's perspective. Chrysler also engaged off-line with influential bloggers.

Advocacy blogs can gain significant visibility in the media and with legislators and can become powerful platforms to head off attacks from critics. However, if you decide to launch an advocacy blog, do so with your eyes open. Your readers will include the people who are most critical of you and they may try to turn your words against you. You need a thick skin to do this well, and it pays to take the high road. By acknowledging and responding constructively to criticism, you can keep the conversation civil.

7. Promotional blog—Although a rule of thumb is that blogs should never be used to sell, there are instances in which marketers can find the happy medium between marketing and useful content. These are promotional blogs, and they work because they promote while also informing.

In the technology and marketing industries, event blogs are now common. Most web hosting services can add a blog to a conference or seminar site for a small fee. Speakers are then asked to contribute a few entries about topics they plan to address, answer common questions, or debate a topic with another speaker. Their words live on long after the event has concluded and can be used in future promotions.

The BlogHer conference has applied this tactic so successfully that it's become difficult to tell if the blogs support the conference or vice versa. The conference blogs are a year-round fixture, giving a voice to organizers, speakers, and even attendees. The twice-annual event has been running since 2005 and attendance has increased steadily. Meanwhile, the site has amassed a membership of more than 13,000 people, who list their blogs and contribute to a variety of topic areas.

Search on "*event blog*" to find many other good examples. While most of these are operated by independent producers, the same tactics can be applied to business events.

Blogs are also effective in book promotion, giving the author and collaborators a way to sustain awareness of a work by writing about developments in the field, pointing to reviews, promoting author appearances, and the like. Search engine awareness is a benefit in this field, where sales may continue over a period of years, and the blog is a good place to update and correct information in the published work. David Weinberger's Everything is Miscellaneous blog about his 2007 book of the same title is an excellent example.

Choosing a Platform

Wikipedia.org lists more than 45 blogging software packages, most of which you've never heard of. People sometimes obsess about the choice of platform, but the fact is that it makes little difference. As long as the software is easy to use, supports a variety of media types, and delivers RSS feeds, nearly any package will do. The more important technical questions are how the software integrates with a company website.

In most cases, it's important that a business blog retain the look and feel of the company brand while being flexible enough to allow personalization by the author. Blogs have people behind them, and that human touch is a key factor in their appeal. Your web hosting service probably has favorite blogging platforms they work with. In most cases, they'll do the job just fine.

Should You Sponsor a Blogger?

Over the last couple of years, a new model has emerged that harnesses the popularity of established bloggers to serve marketing purposes. This can be an effective way to meld authenticity with a message, but it does carry some risk.

Blog advertising has been around since the early days of the medium and its price/performance can be attractive. The BlogAds network delivers advertising to over 1,500 bloggers. Customers can buy individual sites or "hives" of topics. A one-week ad on Foobooz.com, for example, costs $50 for almost 18,000 ad impressions. You can get even better rates by negotiating one-off deals with individual bloggers.

A more recent trend is for companies to hire bloggers to contribute content to a branded site. TheLobby, which is operated by Starwood hotels and resorts, combines freelance and staff bloggers to create a travel destination site. Griffin Hollow, a distributor of building products, uses paid bloggers to populate a network of home-improvement blogs. Conventions.net, a referral source for trade show organizers, pays a blogger to maintain its Convention Insider blog.

Weight Watchers enlisted popular video blogger Esther Brady to help publicize its new "Stop Dieting, Start Living" slogan. Brady, who blogs under the name of Starlite, lost 70 pounds on Weight Watchers and was enthusiastic to share her advice. Weight Watchers enlisted her to post inspirational videos about her success on its MySpace page and to invite viewers to contribute their own stories. The company tied the campaign to a contest in which people were asked to describe the strangest diet they had ever tried, with the winner featured on a Times Square billboard.

Secret: Sponsoring bloggers will probably make them *less* likely to write about you.

Nestlé used French blog aggregator Blog-Bang.com, which is owned by French advertising agency Publicis, to promote its new Dolce Gusto coffee makers. The site sent a message to its community of 2,000 bloggers, asking them to link to an interactive game in exchange for a link to their blogs from the home page. Within three weeks, the game had 500 links from member bloggers and had been played 320,000 times.

Bloggers can be incorporated into a marketing campaign in a variety of ways, but you should be realistic about your expectations. Most bloggers are fiercely independent and will actively avoid doing anything that betrays a conflict of interest. In other words, your sponsorship won't get you more coverage and may actually get you less. You should also take pains to fully disclose any financial relationship in order to avoid being charged with deception.

Never, ever create a fake blog or "flog." This is a practice that involves hiring a person to blog positively about a company or cause without disclosing their affiliation. It violates nearly every principle of the blogosphere. The few companies that have tried it—Wal-Mart and Sony are prime examples—have become online whipping posts whose transgressions were still being mocked two years later.

Services like Izea (formerly PayPerPost) and ReviewMe.com have also sprung up with a business model that pays bloggers to write about their clients. The return on this kind of paid placement is unclear, although Izea claims to have more than 80,000 bloggers and 11,000 advertisers under contract. These companies have been a lightning rod for criticism, so investigate them closely. At the very least, full disclosure is always the best policy.

Secrets of Success

No matter what approach you take to blogging, there are a few basic tenets to remember. I'll call these the STRAIGHT rules:

Succinct
Transparent
Responsive
Accepting
Insightful
Genuine
Humorous
Timely

Let's look at each in a bit more detail.

Succinct—As a rule, keep entries to less than 500 words. Make your point quickly at the top, remembering that people increasingly read blog entries through RSS readers, which may only show a few sentences. Keep headlines declarative and clear; you'll not only serve your readers but do better in search engine results.

Transparent—Never try to fool or mislead people. Always reveal your objectives and motivations. Deviousness and manipulation will be exposed, you will be punished, and it will be a long time before you regain your credibility.

Responsive—Blogs invite comments by their nature. When people respond, you should acknowledge and thank them. You don't have to recognize every comment, but stop by every couple of days and respond to the most interesting ones. It'll show people that you're listening. General Motors has logged more than 18,000 reader comments on its Fastlane blog, a dynamic that has made Fastlane an essential part of the company's feedback loop.

I always advise companies to use comment moderation. Some comments may contain obscenities or other inappropriate messages and there's always the risk that you'll be targeted by comment spammers. Most commercial blogging software can filter out comment spam, but there are always a few rogue messages that get past the gates.

Accepting—It's inevitable that you'll hear from critics. Accept their comments in the spirit of constructive criticism and respond calmly. If someone is intent on flaming you after you've tried to address their concerns, it's okay to ignore them.

Mike Prosceno is vice president of marketplace communications at software giant SAP. The company has an active blogger relations program that includes outreach and invitations to bloggers to meet face-to-face with SAP personnel. Prosceno himself monitors more than 150

SAP's Proscano: "Just pick up the phone to learn their motivations."

blogs. He says you have to accept negativity as a by-product of the conversation and know your limits. "The blogosphere is a more confrontational style of communication than traditional media because the conversation can continue," Prosceno says. "If the negativity is malicious, it's probably best not to perpetuate a firestorm and to just pick up the phone and call them to learn their motivations. If it's just a negative comment, sometimes those are very valid."

Insightful—Give people a reason to read your blog. Provide insight about an issue or explain the reasoning behind a business decision. You know more about your business or industry than most people. Demonstrate that.

Genuine—Show readers that there's a human being behind the words on the screen. Use personal anecdotes to illustrate a point. Talk about "I" instead of "we." Show that this is an organization made up of people, not press releases.

Humorous—No one expects you to be a laugh riot, but the occasional funny story will go a long way toward making your blog look more human.

Timely—Make your topics current and relevant. Respond within 48 hours to comments. People who monitor your blog from their RSS readers should see a lot of back-and-forth activity.

Podcasting

> Secret: Podcasts are cheap and easy to produce.

What a difference a year makes! In 2006, podcasting was a media darling, becoming so popular that it got its own definition in the *Oxford English Dictionary* and prompted thousands of articles in newspapers and magazines. Some people said the technology that enabled people to customize their listening experience by downloading programs they liked into their iPods or other portable media players would wipe out terrestrial radio.

In 2007, however, podcasting seemed to all but disappear from view. Some bloggers even declared it a disappointment. Could a technology that seemed so promising really fail that catastrophically in such a short time?

Of course not. Podcasting lost its popular appeal in part because online video muscled it out of the spotlight and in part because technical complexity prevented the market from performing up to lofty early projections. However, podcasting is alive and well, and it's gaining a growing following among business-to-business companies that target busy and mobile customers. For many businesses, it may well be a superior marketing alternative to video.

In-depth research is scarce, but a March 2007 survey by Arbitron and Edison Media Research found that the percentage of consumers who had heard of podcasts nearly doubled from 22 percent to 37 percent between 2006 and 2007, although the percentage who had ever

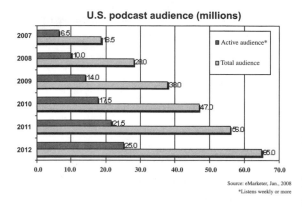

U.S. podcast audience (millions)

	Active audience*	Total audience
2007	6.5	18.5
2008	10.0	28.0
2009	14.0	38.0
2010	17.5	47.0
2011	21.5	55.0
2012	25.0	65.0

Source: eMarketer, Jan., 2008
*Listens weekly or more

listened to a podcast grew only slightly, from 11 percent to 13 percent. The research also indicated that twice as many podcast listeners have advanced degrees as non-listeners and that podcast users are twice as likely to have incomes over $100,000. eMarketer estimates that the U.S. podcast audience grew 285 percent in 2007 to 18.5 million people and will increase to 65 million in 2012. Nearly 40 percent of those people listen weekly, the firm said. The numbers also support the viability of podcasts as b-to-b tools. Arbitron reported that 72 percent of podcast listeners are over 25 and 48 percent are over 35.

Search engine Podnova lists 90,000 podcast programs in its directory and Podcast Alley lists more than 37,000. More important than the numbers, however, is the names of businesses that are using the medium for point purposes, including General Motors, Purina, Hewlett-Packard, IBM, Kodak, Wells Fargo, and many others.

The Lyric Opera of Chicago uses podcasts to take opera-lovers behind the scenes of its productions. The Mayo Clinic has a collection of programs dealing with issues such as cancer and women's health. Wells Fargo Advantage Funds sits a seasoned journalist down with one of its funds managers each week to talk about the state of the market. The city of Louisville, KY posts a monthly program to help attract conventions and tourists. The government of Australia uses podcasts to promote its wine industry. The U.S. Navy has run two successful advertising campaigns with podcasts aimed at recruiting medical professionals.

Secret: Podcasts work well in b-to-b communications.

Disappointment with podcasts developed, I believe, because few programs achieve the kind of subscription momentum that rewarded them with large advertising contracts. However, many companies use podcasts as a companion to their blogs and marketing efforts to highlight interesting people and new initiatives. The medium has also proven powerful for internal applications.

At IBM, for example, podcasts are now second only to wikis in popularity as a social media tool for internal communications, says George Faulkner, who's one of IBM's most visible podcasters. Some 40 percent of IBM's 400,000 employees work primarily outside of an office. IBM's internal podcast program has more than 100,000 unique members and 12,000 files. Its popularity has grown despite some rather onerous regulatory requirements. For example, IBM must transcribe the contents of any executive interview. No matter: Thanks to individual initiative and a corporate hands-off policy, it's the employees who are spreading the word.

One IBM executive used to hold a weekly conference call with 500 people spread across the globe. A live call of that scale is simply impractical, and no-shows were a problem. So the exec switched from a phone conference to a weekly podcast. The move doubled listenership. Now road warriors and people in distant time zones can tune in at their leisure.

IBM now routinely podcasts <u>news for investors</u> and periodically uses the medium to <u>showcase customers and executive perspectives</u> on developing trends. Many of the sessions from <u>the 2007 Lotusphere conference</u> are available as podcasts.

I have produced more than 100 podcasts for major technology companies as part of my content consulting work. In most cases, these programs have been used as part of a suite of communication vehicles to promote new products or marketing programs. They are simply one more way to reach customers, and a relatively inexpensive one at that.

Business-to-business customers love podcasts. When I was involved in the launch of a media property for chief information officers in early 2007, I had the chance to spend some time with a half dozen CIOs who were on the company's advisory board. Every one of them listened to podcasts. They found the audio programs to be an efficient way to take advantage of downtime during their commutes or workouts and learn something in the process.

Podcasts are now routinely accompanied by videocasts, which can be posted and downloaded almost as simply as the audio programs. Videocasts are an effective way to leverage product explainers and customer testimonials, for example, without the cost of mass-producing DVDs or videotapes. We'll look at video content in more detail in Chapter 12.

Podcasts aren't likely to live up to their early billing as a challenge to terrestrial radio anytime soon, but they can be an effective component of your marketing program.

Resources

Blogging Books

Bly, Robert W. *Blog Schmog: The Truth About What Blogs Can (and Can't) Do for Your Business*. Nashville: Thomas Nelson, 2007.

Holtz, Shel and Ted Demopoulos. *Blogging for Business: Everything You Need to Know and Why You Should Care*. New York: Kaplan Business, 2006.

Scoble, Robert and Shel Israel. *Naked Conversations: How Blogs are Changing the Way Businesses Talk with Customers*. New York: Wiley, 2006.

Scott, David Meerman. *The New Rules of Marketing and PR: How to Use News Releases, Blogs, Podcasting, Viral Marketing and Online Media to Reach Buyers Directly*. New York: Wiley, 2007.

Weil, Debbie. *The Corporate Blogging Book: Absolutely Everything You Need to Know to Get It Right*. New York: Penguin Books, 2006

Blogs and Websites About Blogging

A Shel of my Former Self
AndyBeard
AttentionMax
Bloggers Blog
Business Blog Consulting
Dosh Dosh
GigaOm

Joho the Blog
Marketing Profs Daily Fix
Mashable
Micro Persuasion
MsDanielle
Online Marketing Blog
Robin Good
Scobleizer

Podcasting Books

Demopoulos, Ted. *What No One Ever Tells You About Blogging and Podcasting*. New York: Kaplan Business, 2006.

Geoghegan, Michael. *Podcast Solutions: The Complete Guide to Podcasting*. Berkeley, Calif: Friends of ED, 2005.

Podcasting Blogs and Sites

Dan Bricklin's Podcasting Setup
Guide to Buying Podcast Equipment
How to Podcast Blog
Podcast Academy
Podcasting Equipment Guide
Podcasting Tools

The CEO Blogger

There's nothing predictable about Merrill Dubrow's blog. In 10 days' time, his topics included the best date movies of all time, an interview with the president of a leading market research firm, his painful experience taking a Bikram Yoga Class, and a roundup of his favorite board games.

It's not the kind of material you expect to read on a CEO blog, but it works for Merrill. It works very well.

The numbers are respectable: about 900 unique visitors a week. But what's remarkable is the comment activity—an average of 47 per week. Some posts draw 40 or more comments. The feedback energizes Dubrow, who is president and CEO of MARC Research, a 100-person market research firm in Irving, Texas.

"It's led to speaking engagements, new hires, and proposals for work," he says. "When I'm at a conference, 10 or 15 people will come up and comment about the blog."

Conventional wisdom says you shouldn't run a blog this way. Blogs are supposed to be focused and professional, full of insight on topical issues. The reason Merrill Dubrow can get away with his approach is that he's, well, Merrill Dubrow.

"I'm a connector," he says. "I know a lot of people, and I'm extremely visible in the market research industry. I help people connect with each other."

He's also got a style that people find appealing, and the blog reflects his personality. It's an approach to blogging that can be enormously effective if you have a voice to make it work and you're not afraid to hang it out on the edge a little.

Dubrow describes his voice as "Sincere. Opinionated. Goofy. Crazy." The blog, whose rather prosaic title is The Merrill Dubrow Blog, "is stuff about life. It's Seinfeld-esque," he says, citing the hit TV show that was about nothing in particular.

Dubrow and his associates are serious about measuring response, though. In addition to standard Web metrics, the company measures the average length of comments (106 words), the total number of comments (1,700 in a little more than 18 months), and the number of people who have contributed more than four comments each (115), among other factors. Dubrow also tracks his performance on Google searches, keywords, and RSS subscriptions.

The ROI? It's uncertain, but the value in name recognition and reader affinity has been well worth the modest cost, he says.

The CEO takes a disciplined approach to his task. He posts new entries on Monday, Wednesday, and Friday and generally keeps them under 400 words. He actively encourages visitors to comment and has used marketing tactics like a stock market guessing game and a book club to stimulate repeat traffic. Tried-and-true topics like a face-off between Yankees and Red Sox lovers are guaranteed hits. Offbeat subjects like his skydiving experience also work. He frequently crafts his content in the form of questions to the audience. "If you love to watch people, where is the best place to go?" asked one recent entry. Twelve people answered him.

It's not all just fun and games, though. Dubrow leavens his content with discussions of new trends in market research, profiles of industry colleagues, and interesting findings from his company's own research. This is, after all, an executive blog.

The following are some of the secrets that Dubrow has learned from more than 18 months of active blogging:

• Start slow and don't try to post every day. Make sure you respond to reader comments.

• Have an objective in mind. Are you trying to promote a book? Get a job? Generate business? Tell the world about your vacation? Your content strategy starts with your goal definition.

• Don't go it alone. Have a partner to brainstorm topics, proofread copy, and help with technical glitches.

For executive bloggers just starting out, he recommends the following:

• Be creative. Look at what is working for other bloggers and adopt the techniques that are most comfortable for you.

• Be personal. A blog should reflect your personality and give readers a sense that they know you. The more you personalize the content, the more successful you'll be.

• Do what comes naturally. Dubrow doesn't speak on many webcasts because he likes to engage with an audience interactively. He loves getting comments, and so he structures his blog as a conversation rather than a lecture. This won't necessarily work for you, but whatever you choose, it should fit well with your style and voice.

Dubrow says the power of the blog never ceases to amaze him. It hits him every time conference-goers say they came to his session because they'd read his blog and felt compelled to meet him.

"Your words are very powerful now," he says, "more powerful than they've ever been."

6

Customer Conversations

"People on MySpace aren't running away from pedophiles and stalkers. They're running away from marketers and advertisers."
— Giovanni Gallucci, cofounder, Dexterity Media, <u>in an interview</u>
<u>on IT Conversations</u>

With 11 million registered members, 30 million monthly unique visitors, and over one billion photos, <u>Flickr</u> is the 800-pound gorilla of photo sharing communities. Its members upload more than 1.5 million photos per day and they actively seek out and comment on each other's work. Professional photographers put their entire portfolios on Flickr, and the site's 500,000 groups are a hive of activity.

There's a Flickr group for almost anything you can imagine. For example, <u>Urban Nature</u> has images of nature in an urban context, while the <u>Bacon Group</u> is full of pictures of, well, bacon. Members of the <u>Starbucks group</u> post photos of their favorite stores and merchandise. The nearly 900 members of the <u>Mini Cooper group</u> have uploaded 6,000 photos of their petite automobiles.

It's not surprising, then, that the marketers at camera maker Nikon saw opportunity when they waded into Flickr in 2006. Dozens of Nikon enthusiast groups already existed, some with several thousand members. People were sharing all manner of tips about their equipment and techniques. To Nikon, these were the proverbial fish in a barrel.

The company loaded up its marketing budget and fired. It contracted with Flickr owner Yahoo! to place Nikon branding on some Flickr groups and launched a new site called <u>Nikon Stunning Gallery</u>, where the best photos contributed by Nikon enthusiasts on Flickr were featured. When the company introduced its D80 digital cameras, it gave

16 of them to active Flickr users. Those enthusiasts' best work was featured in a three-page advertising insert in *BusinessWeek*. The campaign was a godsend to the photographers, who constantly struggle to promote their work. It was a no-brainer for Nikon, which was eager to ally itself with quality amateur work.

Today, there are more than 50,000 members of various Nikon groups on Flickr. A Yahoo! executive called the Stunning Gallery campaign the most successful Flickr promotion of 2006.

Social Networks Come of Age

Nikon's experience is about as good as it gets in the fledgling world of social network marketing. The whole field is so new that few best practices exist. It's not that online communities are a new thing; discussion forums were one of the first uses of computer networks and the earliest branded communities date from 1995. But the exploding popularity of these online gathering places has made them *the* force for marketers to reckon with since 2007. Global advertising spending on social networks was $1.2 billion in 2007, according to eMarketer, and it was expected it to increase 75 percent in 2008.

Secret: Social networks can dramatically cut membership development costs.

One reason social networks can be a great opportunity for businesses is that they eliminate one of the most onerous costs of online marketing: building a community. There are more than 100,000 members of various Starbucks communities on Facebook, for example, and none of them are sponsored by the coffee retailer. Community is a powerful attraction for users and a tempting target for marketers. "The main selling feature of [Facebook game] Scrabulous for me is the fact I can play it within Facebook. If it were on an external site, I would have to search for my friends all over again," says Facebook member Karl Savage in an article in <u>Knowledge @ Wharton</u>.[1]

However, social networks are so new and untested that many marketers are wary of making big bets. That's one reason they've been dis-

---

[1] Scrabulous was one of the great early Facebook viral hits. The story is told in Chapter 11.

appointing as advertising vehicles. In cutting its 2008 social network ad spending projections from $1.6 billion to $1.4 billion, eMarketer noted that the leading networks are still struggling to come up with a viable advertising model. The research firm now expects U.S. social network ad spending to grow to $2.6 billion in 2012, which is barely 5 percent of the online ad market.

Online marketing firm Prospectiv reported that 87 percent of the more than 3,000 social network users it polled said that few or none of the ads they see on those networks match their interests. However, respondents did indicate receptivity to more targeted advertising.

Google reported lower-than-expected earnings in the fourth quarter of 2007 due in part to disappointing results from social network advertising. "Social networks have some of the lowest response rates on the Web," said *BusinessWeek* in a January 2008 article. "Marketers say as few as four in 10,000 people who see their ads on social networking sites click on them, compared with 20 in 10,000 across the Web."

> **Secret: Social networks resist marketing messages and they are currently some of the least effective social media marketing platforms.**

Part of the problem is that people use social networks to connect with people, not brands. They resist or openly resent efforts by marketers to intrude on those conversations. "[Social networking sites] are primarily organized around people, not interests," noted Danah Boyd and Nicole Ellison in their research paper, "Social Network Sites: Definition, History, and Scholarship," published in the *Journal of Computer-Mediated Communication*. They concluded that "social network sites are structured as personal networks, with the individual at the center of their own community." That people connection is sacred.

Personal connections are one of the most appealing aspects of social networks. However, they also make these places a marketing minefield. On the one hand, members willingly share more information in social networks than they have ever shared in any other online forum. But they want to control who sees that data and what they can do with it. In a notable incident in late 2007, Facebook was forced to withdraw and revamp a service that revealed the purchasing decisions people reported to their friends. More than 75,000 members signed an online petition against the service, which was called "Beacon." The incident was widely regarded as a symbol of the limitations of marketing through social networks. People like sharing information with friends and colleagues but resist sharing with institutions. This makes social networks a slippery slope for marketers.

Categories of Social Networks

There are social networks for nearly every age group, special interest, and geographic region. There are groups for restaurant reviews, local events, medical conditions, and sports teams. There are at least four networks that primarily deliver how-to videos by members. There are social bookmarking networks where people recommend websites to each other. There are networks oriented toward different kinds of media, such as video and books. New networks are launched almost daily, driven by the plummeting price of technology and availability of cheap network bandwidth. Trying to throw a rope around all of them would be a book in itself, so I'll focus on the most prominent brands and what they do right. But first, let's look at the phenomenon from a higher level.

Social networks can be broadly grouped into the following areas:

General purpose—Massive sites like MySpace and Facebook specialize in connecting people across a wide variety of interests. With memberships numbering in the tens of millions, there's something for everyone. For big brands, a presence on general purpose networks can deliver the largest possible audience but not necessarily the most discerning buyers. Outside of the two gorillas in this market, no one has more than 2 percent share of total traffic, which is why the market began consolidating beginning in late 2007. However, some of these smaller networks have greater reach overseas than they do in the U.S.

Vertical networks—These focused communities serve people with specific interests ranging from physicians (Sermo) to personal finance (Wesabe) to shopping (ThisNext). They have fewer services than general purpose sites, but what they do have is richer content, and their smaller communities are often highly engaged.

Vertical networks are proliferating, presenting choices but also creating a bit of chaos. In the area of health, for example, there's Care-Pages, Wellsphere, Patientslikeme, RevolutionHealth, and iMedix. Seniors can choose from Elder Wisdom Circle, Grandparents, Tee-BeeDee, and Multiply. Mothers can sign up for Cafemom, Mothers-Group, MomJunction, and MothersClick, among others.

Many of these networks may be attractive marketing venues. Don't let the small memberships fool you. Scan the groups, discussion topics, and participants and look for content profiles that match your market. Marketing costs are generally lower than those of the big social networks and the audiences can be far more targeted.

Social media marketer Jeff Greene of Gold Group in Clark, New Jersey prefers the more intimate and involved environment of special interest communities to the vastness of YouTube. "Some of the viral video sites where you'd expect to have the most control are actually the worst in terms of influence," he says. For a Lipton Iced Tea promotion that involved a series of humorous videos, Gold Group had more success on special-purpose sites like LiveVideo and DailyMotion. Friends networks are stickier on those sites, he said, meaning that a "favorite" vote can drive more traffic than there than on YouTube.

Social bookmarking—This is one of the largest categories of social networks, encompassing massively trafficked sites like Digg, del.icio.us, Sphinn, reddit, Propeller, and Shoutwire. Members share and comment upon interesting websites and compete to boost their profiles based upon the quantity and quality of their recommendations. Their primary value to marketers is as traffic-driving engines. A mention on the front page of Digg, for example, can deliver tens of thousands of visitors to a website in a single day.

Recommendation engines—Players in this relatively new category take many forms, from the straight-up review sites like Yelp and

Links indicated in the text above may be found at SSMMBook.com | 99

Going to services that map content to specific tastes. Recommendation engines share a lot in common with social bookmarking sites. StumbleUpon, for example, was one of the earliest and most popular examples of this genre. It delivers recommended websites identified by members to others with similar interests. Matchmine lets users describe the entertainment they enjoy and presents them with recommendations based upon other members' input. Scouta has a similar approach. Criticker is a community film recommendation engine while Loveth.at has members recommending ads to each other.

Social shopping—One of the newest and fastest growing social network categories, these recommendation engines indulge people's inclination to treat shopping as a group event. Stylehive, Kaboodle, and CrowdStorm build upon Amazon's model by organizing communities that deliver feedback and reviews to help people choose products of all kinds. Kaboodle is the early traffic leader, but this market is young and highly fragmented. Social shopping sites have great potential, as evidenced by a September 2007 iCrossing study titled "How America Searches: Online Retail," which found that 63 percent of consumers frequently research purchases online. Social shopping sites are finding ways to connect businesses with positive reviews for instant ordering.

Horizontal networks—These sites serve broad interest areas like travel (TripAdvisor), real estate (Zillow), life skills (Only Human), dating (Match), and business development (LinkedIn). They vary widely in membership size and scope, as well as in their value to marketers. Audience interest can be quite intense, since members are often contemplating major investments or life decisions.

Secret: Photo- and video-sharing sites are some of the most fruitful sources of enthusiastic customers.

Photo/video sharing—People use these sites to exchange and comment upon their own work and the work of others. Sites like YouTube and Flickr are gargantuan in scale and can deliver millions of viewers. YouTube has almost single-handedly driven some of the Internet's most successful viral marketing campaigns. These are a great resource for marketers to repurpose campaigns and test new messages, although the communities' blunt and sometimes offensive commentary can be offputting.

Virtual Worlds—Second Life is the poster child of these visually rich environments but many others exist, including Gaia, There, and the gaming-oriented Everquest and World of Warcraft. These communities have great audience appeal—eMarketer says about a third of the more than 34 million child and teen Internet users in the U.S. visit them at least monthly—and they've had success as the gathering places for virtual events and stores. However, their overall effectiveness as marketing venues is vigorously debated.

Mobile—Twitter was one of the hottest social networking stories of 2007, and it presents one of the most intriguing marketing opportunities. These group instant-messaging services have an appeal that's baffling to the uninitiated, but which has sparked a rabid following. Dozens of services have emerged that mimic or build upon the Twitter platform, including Jaiku (now owned by Google), Utterz, Pownce, and Seesmic.

> Secret: The most popular social networks in overseas markets are almost unknown in the U.S.

International—Services that dominate the U.S. market rarely have the same appeal overseas. Google's Orkut, for example, has been a nonstarter in the U.S. but has a huge following in Brazil. Cyworld is popular in Korea, while Hi5 has a big Latin American membership. In Japan, Mixi is the largest social network. The Swedes love Lunarstorm, and the Poles take to Grono. Different countries also embrace different features. The QQ instant messaging service has a huge following in China, where cell phones are the dominant computing device. Any company with international reach should look at the opportunities in their overseas markets.

Primary Reason that US Adult Internet Users Have Contributed to a Social Networking and/or User-Generated Content Web Site, April 2007 (% of respondents)

Feel part of community

31%

Recognition from peers

28%

Participate with characters or brands I like

9%

Make money

6%

Recognition from colleagues

4%

Other (share with family or for fun)

22%

Note: ages 18+
Source: IBM Institute for Business Value, "US Consumer Research: Digital Entertainment & Media, April 2007" conducted by Zoomerang Market Research, August 2007

086777   www.eMarketer.com

Common Characteristics

Each social network has unique features, but most have a few things in common. One is *open enrollment*. Most make it easy to join with little more than a name and e-mail address. This tends to fill the membership rolls with large numbers of casual and one-time visitors, but it can also build very large communities quickly. Services usually know little about their members at the outset but rely upon community dynamics to coax engaged members into giving up more information.

Members usually have access to a *personal space*, where they can specify their interests, background, personal websites, favorite entertainment, and other information. These details may be shared generally or only with selected members.

Connections between members are essential to social networks. These relationships go by various names, such as *friends*, *followers*, or *connections*. In some cases, these relationships are created by mutual consent, such as Facebook's "friends" or LinkedIn's "connections." In other cases, a member may unilaterally elect to follow another unless blocked by that member. An example is Twitter's "followers." Friends networks are a key appeal of social networks. Forrester Research says 86 percent of members say they participate in networks "to see what my friends are up to."

An increasing number of social networks support *software applications*, most of which are provided by third-party developers and marketers. This trend was given momentum in early 2007 when Facebook opened up its programming interfaces with great success. A year later, there were more than 15,000 third-party Facebook applications. Others quickly followed, with Google attempting to trump

Facebook with OpenSocial, a set of software hooks that developers can use to build applications that run across many networks. Google has had reasonably good success with OpenSocial, but Facebook continues to be the leader.

Software applications are an intriguing marketing opportunity. The most popular ones have been adopted by hundreds of thousands of Facebook users, who measure their taste in movies or music against their peers' or play multiuser trivia games. These applications have succeeded because people want to use them. In that respect, they are some of the best examples of new age marketing through customer engagement rather than interruption. On the other hand, the vast majority of social network applications have adoption rates in the hundreds or less.

The sociology underlying friends networks is complex. Some people set out to accumulate a large number of friends in hopes of driving up their visibility and influence in the network. Others insist that friendships should be intimate and selective. Super-blogger Robert Scoble's roster of almost 5,000 Facebook friends and 14,000 Twitter followers has been a source of vigorous blogger discussion, with some people arguing that such networks trivialize the friends concept.

Regardless of member motives, friendships are essential to effective marketing with social networks. These relationships are necessarily personal, which means that companies need to bring individuals from their organizations into the networks to facilitate friendships. We'll go into more detail in Chapter 9.

Friendships often carry with them a level of information access that can be valuable to each partner. Facebook members, for example, are granted additional information about a friend's interests, memberships, and connections. LinkedIn members can tap their connections to introduce them to other members. People can also ask direct questions or announcements to their universe of friends or engage in activities such as games and contests.

These personal relationships are also one of the most challenging issues for marketers. Most social network members view friendships with corporate entities as being a contradiction. The essence of these friendships is the sharing of information that may be intensely personal, and few people trust corporations to handle that relationship responsibly.

As a result, it's essential that marketers learn how to tap into the dynamics of these relationships as partners rather than sellers. There are notable examples of user communities welcoming marketers with open arms if the value they bring to the group is consistent with social norms. For example, Dell Computer conducted a successful campaign using Facebook's Graffiti Wall in early 2008. Members were asked to illustrate what "green" meant to them, and 7,300 did. Entries received more than a million votes and the Dell profile was "friended" 1,300 times. For Dell, which has made environmental awareness a selling point, the brief event fit perfectly with a branding campaign for its ReGeneration.org site.

Communities can be powerful sources of feedback and even profits. Candy maker Cadbury reintroduced the Wispa chocolate bar in late 2007 after tens of thousands of fans on social networks launched campaigns demanding its revival. Facebook still lists more than 500 Wispa groups, some with more than 10,000 members, and Wispa TV commercials from the 1980s began appearing on YouTube. "We get letters about the Aztec bar and the lime barrel in the Dairy Milk tray. But this is on a whole different scale," a spokesman told the Telegraph newspaper. "This is the first time we are going to give the Internet a chance to prove itself and see whether it is all hype or genuine."

Writing on iMediaConnection, marketer Matt Heinz of HouseValues, Inc noted, "The social networking phenomenon is teaching us… that people desperately want to share things about themselves. They want others to know what they like, what they don't like, even (thanks to services such as Twitter) what they're doing at this very moment."

Heinz cited music-sharing platforms like Apple's iTunes, Lala, and Pandora as examples of services that add value by enabling people to share richer information with their peers. "These companies can then use that shared information to target products and services back to their customers," Heinz wrote. "And when offers are made with this deep level of relativity and context…they're rarely perceived as marketing."

Groups are another essential element of many social networks. An evolution of the early online model of discussion forums, groups are self-organized collections of members who share similar interests. They almost always feature discussion forums, but may also include video-, photo-, and music-sharing as well as collaborative or competitive applications.

Groups are generally easy to set up and join, which is why so many of them are dormant. Search for your brand or category in Facebook, for example, and you may be surprised to find how many groups already exist. You may also be surprised at how many of them haven't been updated in months or have just a few members. Facebook lists more than 500 groups about the Apple iPhone and more than 250 that cover bowling balls, but most have fewer than 100 members. These groups generally aren't worth your time. Look for the groups that have growing member bases and active discussions. Very often, your constructive participation will be welcomed.

> **Secret: Most social network groups are too small to be worth your attention.**

As a member of a network, you're free to set up your own groups. When done well, these campaigns can cost little or nothing in insertion fees. Tax-preparation giant H&R Block ran a social media campaign on YouTube, Facebook, and MySpace that included games and videos about a tax-obsessed character named Truman Greene, according to a *Wall Street Journal* account. The content was posted using only the free group features on those networks. Be careful of taking advantage of free services, though, for many social network operators are struggling with business models and may resent your creativity.

When interacting with members in groups, be careful to observe the following unwritten rules:

Always disclose your affiliation. Failure to do so puts you at risk of being "outed" and charged with insincerity, deception or worse.

Offer something of value. This incentive could simply be information, access, or a new promotion or video. Put yourself in the shoes of your prospective members and ask what would entice them to join a network. Then try to deliver along those lines.

Persist. I mentioned that a lot of groups go dormant. Don't let yours become one of them. It's a bad idea to start a group just to deal with a point problem or a single promotion. You should have a strategy to grow and expand your charter.

Have fun. In the case of lifestyle networks like Facebook, MySpace, or <u>Bebo</u>, games and contests engage members. These don't have to be complicated. Victoria's Secret's Pink group on Facebook, for example, featured a discussion thread in which women were asked to guess the height and weight of the member who had posted just before them. More than 350 members engaged in a spirited and fun discussion within the first month. The idea not only generated activity on the site, but helped members meet each other.

Use digital branding devices. One of the hottest Web concepts of 2007 was widgets, which are small graphical badges that link to other sites or provide information. Widgets are just one kind of digital eye candy that can dress up your group. Others include wallpaper, promotional or user-generated video, photos, and trial downloads. You can learn more about widgets in Chapter 14.

Why Social Networks? Why Now?

Online discussions are as old as computer networks themselves, having their origins in the early Internet newsgroups and private networks like CompuServe and The Well. So why has their popularity suddenly exploded?

Technology developments are certainly are a factor. The pervasiveness of low-cost broadband networks, cheap hardware and open source software have made it possible for entrepreneurs and enthusiasts to launch services at a fraction of the cost of just a few years ago. Add to that the availability of inexpensive multimedia such as online video, photos, and voice chat, and you have a much richer environment in which conversations can take place.

In a 2007 interview on the National Public Radio's "TechNation," Silicon Valley legend Guy Kawasaki told how his Web venture Truemors was launched for just $13,000 with a staff of three contractors. Three years ago, such a venture would have cost up to half a million dollars, he said. Open-source software like mySQL and Ruby on Rails has fundamentally changed the economics of software development. No longer do entrepreneurs need to spend hundreds of thousands of dollars on software licenses and custom programming. Most of the necessary software is now free and highly functional.

However, it was innovations in the design of social networks over the past few years that turbocharged this phenomenon and transformed social networks from a niche market to a mainstream lifestyle. For kids, in particular, social networks have become the online equivalent of the local mall. My 16-year-old daughter, Alice, sums it up this way: "If you're a teenager and you don't have a MySpace account, there's something wrong with you."

The revolution in social network design sprang from the concept of personal spaces, which are now indigenous to nearly every online community. On networks like MySpace and Facebook, personal spaces are rich multimedia diaries that define the passions, needs, and even fears of their creators. Network providers often have fun with these personal home pages. Yelp, for example, invites members to reveal the first concert they ever attended and complete the sentence, "Don't Tell Anyone Else But…" Events network Going offers "I'd max out my Card at…"

People used to fret about publishing personal information online, but today they reveal remarkably detailed data in their profiles. The ability to share this information selectively and to create and enhance relationships because of it is one of networks' important appeals. Personal spaces are also a foundation for building influence and status in the community.

Most social networks tie a member's activity back to a personal profile. The more the member contributes to and interacts with the community, the more influence she gains. This has its downsides. In the summer of 2007, *The Wall Street Journal* analyzed Digg and reported that a very small number of members made decisions about the articles that made it to the Digg front page: "At Digg, which has 900,000 registered users, 30 people were responsible for submitting one-third of postings on the home page," the newspaper reported. "At Netscape, a single user...was behind fully 217 stories over the two-week period, or 13 percent of all stories that reached the most popular list."

Scores of bloggers have written treatises on how to game various services to promote their content. Many of these tactics actually work well, but the risk of being discovered is high and marketers should avoid them. The traffic they bring can also be of marginal value.

Just as each network's services differ, so do members' motivations. Research has demonstrated, for example, that people use Facebook primarily to maintain existing relationships, while they use LinkedIn to form new ones.

Some people are also motivated by personal gain. For example, some self-described experts have posted advice on how to use StumbleUpon to vote randomly for other people's sites in hopes that they'll return the favor. Bloggers have written 3,000-word essays on how to angle content, write headlines, and time postings to maximize traffic from Digg (hint: create content that builds on demonstrably popular topics). LinkedIn has a feature that awards members points for giving useful answers to other members. Some people say these rankings have helped land them jobs and consulting contracts.

The secret is to understand what motivates the members of each site and to choose the networks that most closely match your own objectives. You don't want to promote a product to members who are mainly interested in finding jobs, or a travel destination to people who are looking to buy a home. Now let's take a look at what people of all ages find so attractive about social networks, after which we'll look at the ones that matter most.

What Motivates Social Networkers

For Chuck Hester, it's a way to get business done more efficiently. For Maureen Gray, it's a lifeline to friends and business colleagues who otherwise might fall out of touch. And for Katie McDonald, it's a way to meet future classmates.

Everyone derives different value from social networks—and some see no value in them at all—but a few threads run through stories told by active users. In researching this book I asked dozens of people about the personal and professional value of services like Facebook and LinkedIn. I also interviewed a handful of people in-depth. My conclusions: People of all ages find similar value in social networks, but kids are more creative and resourceful in unlocking their potential.

Expanding Networks

One clear fact is that social networks are good for keeping up with acquaintances. Whether used personally or professionally, everyone appreciates the efficiency that they bring to maintaining relationships.

When I was a kid in the 1970s, I could count my close friends on two hands and my acquaintances in the dozens. Today's social networkers still have only a small number of close friends, but their acquaintances may number in the hundreds.

For adults, the discovery that scores of friends from current and past lives are already online is eye-opening. Seeking out a Facebook group from a high school class or past workplace can re-establish relationships that have been dormant for years.

Social networks bridge gaps of distance and time. We've all had the experience of losing touch with people who may have once been close friends, but who have become separated from us by relocation, marriage, or job change. Social networks allow people to connect across this void.

"I keep in contact with people that I rarely see, or at least I know what they're up to," says Heidi Lemarr, an account executive at Javelin Direct in Dallas.

Katie McDonald, a 21-year-old, recent college graduate, agrees. "The biggest value to me is keeping in touch with people I wouldn't talk to that often."

Social networks also enrich the value of casual contacts or acquaintances. An acquaintance may be someone who has shared a classroom or attended a party, but who isn't a close friend. While the relationship may also be distant, it's worth maintaining.

Telephone and e-mail contact can do a lot to sustain relationships, but they take time. Social networks make connections a by-product of everyday activities. Whenever people answer a quiz, upload a photo, write on a virtual wall, or post an update of their whereabouts, an entire network of associates may be notified. These indirect contacts are what make social networks so efficient.

Search engine marketing specialist Stephanie Faskow says MySpace and Facebook have played a big role in helping her to stay in touch with friends. "I moved 1,200 miles after college and owe a lot of my continued friendships to these networks," she says.

Maurene Caplan Grey describes herself as a "people person." As a former analyst at the technology research firm Gartner, and now as founder of her own firm, Grey Consulting, she has been working from her home office for eight years. "Social networks allow me to stay connected; I don't feel so alone," she says.

Grey finds value in contact management services like Plaxo and LinkedIn, which automatically distribute updated contact information whenever people move or switch jobs. "I know people who have moved to five different companies in five years," she says. Online services keep her current on their whereabouts.

Independent graphic designer Lori Anne McKague shares Grey's view that social networks are a lifeline to workplace interactions that self-employed or remote workers miss. "Online networks allow me to experience 'inter-office' networking virtually," she says. "So much of a workplace is social. Now I no longer miss that." She adds that Facebook's photos also enable her to "see" faraway clients.

Career Move

For some people, social networks have been a career-transforming experience. Publicist Chuck Hester has focused his energies on becoming an expert at LinkedIn, where he's assembled a carefully cultivated strategic contact list. "It's built my reputation nationally," says Hester, who works at Durham, North Carolina-based iContact, an e-mail marketing service. "I've been interviewed in the media and gotten speaking invitations. I can think of at least eight publications or blogs that have covered iContact as a result of my reaching out to them [through LinkedIn]."

Hester uses the service to set up meetings during his frequent travels. He's arranged dinner events for bloggers and reporters who are LinkedIn contacts and hosted "LinkedIn Live" events in the Research Triangle area. "I got tired of doing coffee one-on-ones, so now I can get everyone in one room," he says. The events have raised his profile as someone who can make relationships happen. "I'm known now as the Kevin Bacon of Raleigh," he smiles. "If I don't know a person, I probably know someone who does." His success at finding jobs for friends through LinkedIn contacts has further elevated his profile.

Hester is a big fan of LinkedIn Answers, an application that enables members to seek out experts to answer questions. In his professional capacity, it helps him to find reporters looking for sources. Personally, it positions him as an authority in his field.

I can endorse that approach. All but one of the people quoted in this vignette came to me through LinkedIn Answers or Facebook posts.

The Youth Factor

Given the ubiquity of MySpace and teens' overall comfort level with electronic relationships, you'd expect that young people would use social networks very differently than their elders. You'd only be somewhat right.

In interviewing teenagers and polling several college classrooms, I expected to find that social networks were at the center of many young people's lives. In fact, I concluded that kids don't use these services all that differently from their parents. Like adults, they see them as an efficient way to maintain large networks of acquaintances.

"It's a great way to keep communication with people you don't see a lot," says Olivia Cutitta, of Wayland, Massachusetts. At 15, she already has more than 550 Facebook friends.

Not surprisingly, kids' interactions are structured more around leisure time than work or homework. And their network of friends can be very large. Michelle Alter, a 19-year-old University of Massachusetts student, has nearly 1,000 Facebook friends.

However, both Cutitta and Alter said that only about a third of their contacts are true friends. Most are casual acquaintances, or what one college student referred to as "the people you say 'Hi' to in the hall but wouldn't necessarily stop to talk to."

The applications they use also reflect teens' digital lifestyles. When Alter and her friends return from a trip, they upload and share the photos they took. That's a way of keeping in touch indirectly. Even if she never interacts with the photographers, Alter says, she feels like she's keeping in touch.

Like many young people, 21-year-old Katie McDonald is an avid user of instant messaging (IM). "I've gotten so used to talking to my friends over the Internet that I don't think I would pick up the phone," she says. "When I use the phone it's to send a text message."

Some adults cringe at that kind of talk, believing that it confirms their suspicion that kids are forsaking meaningful person-to-person contact in favor of idle online chatter. Kids don't see it that way, though. In their view, IM is simply a more efficient way to carry on conversations. They may have six chat windows open and engage with their friends sporadically over a period of hours without the overhead of telephone small talk.

In fact, they would argue that instant messaging actually promotes relationship building. "IM's a good way to communicate with people who aren't best friends," says Olivia Cutitta. "If I'm not comfortable calling someone, I'll talk to them by IM."

My interviews also belie the common perception that young people are replacing personal relationships with one-dimensional online interactions. In fact, I asked two college classes totaling more than 50 students if anyone had formed meaningful relationships solely through online contact. Only one hand went up. And while several young people I interviewed for this vignette told me that they have initiated friendships online, they wouldn't consider someone a true friend without face-to-face contact.

Anticipation

My interviews did turn up one important distinction between the way kids and adults use social networks. Young people are more likely to employ them as a way to anticipate future relationships. Alter notes that there was a flurry of Facebook activity in the summer months before college classes began. Matriculating students were searching out people they expected to meet on campus. "I know people who have chosen roommates through Facebook," she says.

Recent college graduate McDonald echoes that opinion. "In classes with 30 people where I don't know everybody, having seen their face makes me more comfortable," she says.

And not all young people are social network fans. John T. Gallant, a 20-year-old student at Endicott College, doesn't belong to any of the major networks. He's a gamer, and while he's got plenty of online gaming pals, they usually talk to each other over the background noise of virtual gunfire. Different strokes.

Twittering in the Baja

The Baja 1000 is a punishing road race, a 24-hour marathon off-road event that takes competitors driving vehicles ranging from motorcycles to tricked-out trucks through some of the most desolate land on earth. It takes place in terrain so remote that competitors literally disappear from view for hours at a time. So it seems an odd venue in which to promote whiskey.

But for Beam Global, the makers of spirits such as Makers Mark and Knob Creek bourbons, Laphroaig scotch, and Courvoisier brandy, the Baja 1000 turned out to be not only a branding bonanza but also the test bed for a new kind of media campaign.

Beam Global's Jim Beam brand sponsors Robby Gordon, a NASCAR veteran known for his toughness and individuality. The company wanted to do something out of the box for the Baja, so it gave the project to publicity firm Doe Anderson, which handed it to Jason Falls, its chief social media strategist.

Falls knew the Baja's isolated location was a negative to race fans. Few media organizations had either the resources or the inclination to cover the entire event, and the lack of cell phone towers or even power lines meant that fans had to live with their favorite drivers being out of view for hours at a time.

Recently, Falls had been playing with a new service called Twitter, which enabled users to post short blog entries as cell phone text messages. He had a brainstorm: Perhaps Twitter could be used as a medium to cover the entire race.

Filling a Communications Gap

The Baja actually has a rudimentary communications network called Weatherman that consists of spotters who use satellite phones and a modified form of CB radio to track the competition. The network exists almost entirely for the safety of the drivers; it was never meant to be a broadcast medium. Falls figured that by equipping the Gordon crew with the technology to deliver regular updates on their own man, and by listening in to Weatherman, he could use Twitter to send updates to eager fans. The Beam Twitter Tracker was born.

Several members of Gordon's 70-person team were equipped with satellite phones to report on their driver's progress. Falls also tapped into other electronic networks that were already in place. He hadn't counted on staying up for 36 hours straight, monitoring a phalanx of radios, video and global positioning system feeds, and texting more than 400 messages to an audience that grew by the hour. But as it became evident that his Twitter feed was becoming the world's most reliable news source about the progress of the race, he sensed that he was on to something big.

Falls knew that it was important that he not use his position to shill for Robby Gordon or Jim Beam, so he made every effort to deliver as comprehensive an account of the action as time and technology permitted.

"People use services [like Twitter] to get away from marketers, so we needed to get a brand in front of them in a way that was useful," Falls says from his home office in Louisville, Kentucky. "We wanted to do something branded with Beam that gave off-road racing fans something they weren't going to get anywhere else."

They did just that. Fan bloggers for other racers had noted the effort and were pointing their readers to the Twitter feed on RobbyGordon. com. "We were the Baja ticker for all intents and purposes," Falls says.

As the race proceeded, more fans began to talk about what was going on with the Robby Gordon Twitter feed. A message board on a racing fan site began to fill up with comments. "The Twitter Dude ROCKS!!! Funny as hell and very informative," wrote one participant. "E-mailed Jim Beam last night and told them what a great job twitter dude has done," enthused another.

The folks at Beam Global were pleased as well. An analysis of online chatter obtained by tracking firm Radian6 showed that in the two-week period surrounding the race, the Baja 1000 was mentioned in almost 360 blog or forum posts. Robby Gordon was mentioned in two-thirds of them and Jim Beam in more than half. In contrast, race winner Mark Post got fewer than 20 mentions. Both Beam Racing and Robby Gordon are looking to incorporate Twitter-like feeds into their 2008 campaigns.

The Beam campaign exemplifies the new power that social media gives marketers. With creative thinking and some inexpensive tools, it's now possible for businesses to become media operations. By delivering a valued service to a receptive audience, they can cast a brand in the most positive possible light.

7

The Social Network Gorillas

The war for social network supremacy that began in 2006 ended nearly as quickly as it started. By early 2008, a handful of major properties dominated the landscape and consolidation had set in among the also-rans. Most of the winners are still struggling to figure out a revenue model, but that doesn't change the fact that millions of visitors a day are flocking to their sites.

These sites may not be the best targets for marketing dollars in many cases, but they are the trendsetters. Concepts adopted on Facebook or YouTube spread quickly to sites of the same genre. While there is no guarantee that these early winners will survive in the long term, it's important to understand what they're doing, if only because everyone else will be doing it a short time later.

It would be impossible to deliver an exhaustive survey of a market with more than 2,500 players, so we'll profile some of the largest sites in this chapter and then look at a handful of smaller, more specialized competitors. The goal is to give you an overview of the most common features and formats so you'll better understand how to navigate the options.

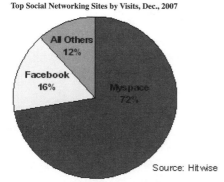

Top Social Networking Sites by Visits, Dec., 2007

Source: Hitwise

MySpace

Adults need not apply. After briefly flirting with an opportunity to become the mainstream network for users of all ages (an October 2006 comScore survey reported that more than half of all visitors were 35 or older), MySpace seems to have ceded the adult market to others and settled into being a place where teenagers have to be. Membership was reported to top 130 million in early 2008, but that figure isn't audited and the large number of spam and abandoned profiles indicates that the actual number of active users is much lower. Still, MySpace's reach into its target audience is awesome. It logs over 70 percent of visits to the top ten social networks and has great reach into entertainment and consumer-product markets. If you're a band, record company, or movie producer, you have to have a profile page there.

MySpace wasn't the first service to incorporate the concept of friends, but it was the first to take it mainstream. Successful MySpace campaigns are often defined in terms of the friends lists they assemble, and some music groups have accumulated more than 100,000. That makes MySpace more of an advertising medium than a social network. The site's young members aren't as socially aware as their grown-up counterparts on Facebook, and they're more inclined to align themselves with brands and organizations. "Facebook is a place to strengthen relationships and make new business connections. MySpace is more of a general branding site," says G. Kofi Annan, owner of Annansi Clothing, which uses both networks to promote its goods.

Anyone can have a profile page or a group. MySpace offers sponsored pages that give businesses the leeway to eliminate contextual ads but little additional

Secret: When marketing on MySpace, get a kid to help.

functionality. The company keeps its marketing opportunities close to the vest. That's partly out of protectiveness for its young audience. All members can blog and share photos, calendars, and videos as well as post music samples. A limited number of applications are available for now, although MySpace has announced support for Google's Open Social specification.

If you're going to build a presence on MySpace, get a kid to help you. That's no joke; the language and ethos of MySpace is so specific to the under-20 audience that anyone who doesn't instinctively talk the talk may look foolish.

Marketing on MySpace can be labor-intensive. You need to build a visually and contextually compelling profile, keeping in mind that a homepage design or blog entry that appeals to a professional colleague will do you no good with a 15-year-old. Then you need to accumulate friends. The safest way to do this is by sorting through groups and available profiles of members with similar interests and sending invitations to the members you find there. Forming friendships gives you permission to contact people, which you should do sparingly and only with information that helps and interests them. Sending ads or overt promotions can get you kicked off the site as a spammer.

Successful MySpace promotions usually combine fun, competition, and bragging rights. They give kids a sense of achievement and the chance to become famous.

Coca-Cola used MySpace in a relaunch campaign for its Cherry Coke and Cherry Coke Zero brands in 2007. Recognizing that the profile pages that members design are often atrocious, the company built a short-duration campaign around a set of branded design tools for personal spaces. It also negotiated a novel deal with MySpace owner News Corp. that provided for the top-voted contest submission to become the MySpace home page for a day. This played well to the young audience's thirst for bragging rights. Coke also cleverly built viral marketing into its promotion. It helped promote the contest through music visualization widgets that members could post on their personal spaces.

"MySpace said if we got 2,000 submissions, we would be successful," says Josh Mooney, chief marketing officer for JUXT Interactive, which managed the campaign. In the first 24 hours, though, Coke logged 32,000 friends and 30,000 submissions. The final tally reached 40,000 submissions and 60,000 friends.

Because MySpace members are in such a vulnerable age group, the service controls privacy tightly. Many profiles and groups are private, and members are given limited tools to reveal personal information. The site fights a constant battle against "address bots" that harvest member profile information and it seems to be having some success in the fight.

Facebook

Until recently, this social network was just a Facebook in the crowd, a little-known community that was popular among college students but closed to the general public. But in late 2006, Facebook opened its doors and found an audience that had been craving a MySpace for adults.

That move made Facebook *the* social network story of 2007. Membership more than quintupled to 50 million in the 12 months after the doors were flung open. Unique visitors doubled to over 20 million from early 2007 to early 2008. Forty percent of members are over 35 years old, and the audience is more affluent and better educated than the MySpace community. New members typically say they're amazed to learn how many of their friends are already members. When I signed up for Facebook in early 2007, I immediately found more than 40 close friends and business contacts in my network. I was sold, as many others have been.

Facebook embodies an overwhelming number of social network elements, from personal profiles to movie reviews to photos and calendars. Since the last half of 2007, thousands of application developers have streamed in to add their own tools and games in hopes of catching the viral wave. Applications run the gamut from speed dating to throwing office equipment at one's friends. Few have gained much of an audience, although the really successful programs have been adopted by millions.

Facebook continues to be a closed network that is invisible to search engines, save for a small number of public listings that members volunteer to make public. This exclusivity is one of the features members like about it. Facebook supplies various levels of privacy control within its walled garden to insure that private conversations will, to some degree, stay private.

Facebook still has a rabid following among college students, but adults use it to keep up personal acquaintances and to deepen relationships with business colleagues. The "News Feed" strip in the middle of a member's home page has been compared to personalized information services like MyYahoo!, the difference being that the news is provided by friends instead of a wire service. That feature in itself is enough to keep members engaged, and if a network's value is a function of its active membership, then Facebook's position atop the social network hierarchy seems secure for the foreseeable future.

Friends on Facebook can easily keep track of each other's activities. Members' activities, from changing an address to completing a game to signing up a new friend, can be automatically shared with other members on their personal network. This has high utility for busy people, since it can significantly reduce the need to proactively keep others informed.

Facebook is the most marketer-friendly of the major social networks, perhaps because it needs to sustain its lofty $15 billion valuation. The site offers sponsored groups, demographic profiling, and targeted advertising, among other products. However, it has recently pulled back on the utility it offers to sponsored group pages. It has numerous imitators, including Xanga, Bebo, and Orkut, but none appears likely to eclipse Facebook's impressive reach, at least not in the U.S. The biggest threat to Facebook's hegemony may be the limitations of its business model. As I mentioned, advertising has not performed well on social networks so far and the "killer app" for the business hasn't yet been found.

Secret: Few Facebook groups have many members.

Facebook groups are a mess. They're simple to start, and just as simple to forget. This has led to thousands of empty and abandoned groups. Facebook provides no advanced search for groups, meaning that marketers may have to navigate hundreds of them to find truly active communities. The site does offer sponsored groups that provide marketers with considerably more variety and flexibility than the fixed format of standard groups. However, not many companies have taken advantage of group sponsorship. Perhaps that's because of experiences like that of Dell Computer. Its sponsored Facebook group was quickly used by dissatisfied customers to host a discussion of reasons to hate Dell.

Those companies that sponsor groups generally use them as accompaniments to their websites and as an efficient way to tap into Facebook's vast membership. Victoria's Secret and Southwest Airlines are two of the more popular sponsored groups. Even some grass-roots groups can grow very large, though. An independent Starbucks fan community has more than 50,000 members. "Friending" on Facebook also enables sponsors to gain some visibility into the members who choose to share personal information, making it a useful market intelligence tool.

LinkedIn

LinkedIn is the social network for businesspeople, and it enjoyed a rush of popularity beginning in late 2007. The site works on the six-degrees-of-separation principle. Members find and connect to known business contacts and then use those people's connections to find other members who aren't in their Rolodex. Members can also maintain detailed résumés, write recommendations for others, and easily keep their networks updated on job changes and new projects.

LinkedIn has become the leader in its category, which also includes Plaxo, Xing, iHipo, and Visible Path. Many small-business professionals swear by it as a way to find jobs, business partners, and employees. The site reported 21 million members in April of 2008 and was adding one million members every 25 days. In the same month, Nielsen/NetRatings reported that LinkedIn's audience was primarily composed of 41-year-old business decision makers with household incomes of $110,000, a better demographic profile than *The Wall Street Journal*'s online audience. In late 2007, LinkedIn announced that it would follow Facebook by accepting third-party applications, although few are available.

One of the more interesting applications actually appeared not on LinkedIn but on *Businessweek*.com, where users could click a LinkedIn icon to see how they were connected to the company being reported on in the story.

LinkedIn and similar services can greatly streamline the process of tracking contacts and maintaining business relationships. When members update their profiles, that new information is available to everyone simultaneously. Members can choose to make their profiles public and searchable, making LinkedIn an effective way to find experts. The degrees-of-separation principle amplifies the value of contacts. A person who has only 100 direct contacts, for example, may have indirect access to over a million others through the indirect network. The process of requesting an introduction to an indirect contact is simple, although success isn't guaranteed. Premium members can use the service as a mailing list manager.

Secret: LinkedIn's Answers feature is a great way to show off expertise as well as to find quick answers to business problems.

One of the most successful LinkedIn features is Answers, a discussion forum where people can ask questions and invite contact from members. Active contributors are ranked according to the quantity and quality of their answers. Members can gain visibility and win business opportunities by promoting their expertise in this way. Some members answer as many as 200 questions in a week.

When I was writing this book, I twice posted queries on LinkedIn Answers and received valuable advice both times. Some reporters now use Answers instead of comparable services from public relations wire services because the quality of contacts is so much better. The site also maintains a useful advisory blog.

LinkedIn's business model is built around premium memberships, corporate recruiting solutions, job postings, and advertising. Marketers can target ads based on the latest profile data members share in their profiles. Advertisers include Dell, Microsoft, HP, Porsche, Brooks Brothers, and BMW.

Southwest Airlines CEO Gary Kelly used LinkedIn to post a question asking, "How can an airline make you more productive?" He got 167 answers in a week.

In March of 2008, LinkedIn added company profiles constructed from LinkedIn profile data. Users can see how they are personally connected to a company, who recently joined the company, where employees typically worked before being employed at a new firm, and other aggregated information.

In addition to its appeal as a means to target affluent professionals, LinkedIn is also a great utility for finding contributors and influencers. The Answers feature can also be used to gain feedback on new initiatives. It's also a great recruiting source.

YouTube

The hottest social media property of 2006 went mainstream in 2007, establishing itself as the place for businesses and individuals to post viral video. Members upload an average of 65,000 videos to YouTube every day, and the site's impressive speed as well as its utility as a way to distribute videos to other websites and blogs has solidified its popularity. MySpace actually claims to host the largest number of videos, but YouTube has seized mindshare in the category. It boasts 55 million unique users per month, with its largest user populations in the 35-and-over category. Google saw the value, and acquired YouTube in November 2006. YouTube has struggled to create a sustainable business model, however, in part because its infrastructure costs are so high.

The popularity of online video has created a raft of followers, including <u>Revver</u>, <u>Blip</u>, <u>Stickam</u>, and <u>Joost</u>. In addition, most social networks and all the major search engines support video. YouTube continues to lead the pack despite its relatively stingy 10-minute limit on video length.

All marketers should be familiar with YouTube, even if they don't produce video themselves. At the very least, the site is an effective place to retire television commercials or internal productions after their run is through. Many consumer products companies do just that. Anheuser-Busch posted its 2007 Super Bowl television ads on YouTube and a handful of other video sites and got more than 22 million downloads in just a few days. This was purely bonus visibility for ads that otherwise would have gone in the archives. Blendtec, a Utah-based maker of high-end blenders, quintupled its business in a year on the strength of a hugely successful viral video campaign.[1] Procter & Gamble extended its popular "Talking Stain" Super Bowl campaign with a YouTube contest that had consumers creating their own variations of the TV ads. YouTube also offers sponsored spaces where businesses may showcase videos and accumulate friends. Many movie producers use it for that purpose.

> **Secret: The humorous videos that people produce for internal company meetings can often find a broad audience on YouTube at no cost.**

---

[1] Blendtec is the subject of a Vignette profile following Chapter 13.

But even companies that don't contribute to YouTube can discover valuable information about their businesses and customers there. IRobot, a Burlington, Massachusetts-based maker of industrial and home robots, was surprised to find that its customers had posted more than 300 videos of its Roomba vacuum cleaner on YouTube, demonstrating a level of enthusiasm and affection for the appliance that the company didn't previously know existed. A search of your brand on YouTube may turn up a surprising number of fan videos.

YouTube offers all of the standard social network features, including personal spaces, playlists, friends, and discussion. Members who post repeatedly about particular topics may be valuable influencers. YouTube is also a good place to find content for a business blog or presentation.

When investigating YouTube videos, look for a few key metrics. Highly rated videos and those with a large number of views are good candidates to go viral. Also, read comments to assess member opinions. A large number of views isn't necessarily good if the comments are negative and the ratings low. When investigating contributors, look for those with a large number of uploads, views, and "favorite" votes. These are people who have established a following. They may be important to you as influencers or contributors.

Secret: Photo-sharing sites are one of the great underused resources for finding influencers and groups.

Flickr

Flickr is a leader in online photo sharing, a large category that also includes PhotoBucket, Shutterfly, Smugmug, and Snapfish.[2] Most of these services support a common set of social network features and maintain large and active groups. Some sites target casual snapshot-takers and position themselves as sharable online file cabinets. Others, like Flickr, appeal more to professionals and amateur enthusiasts, with community features that enhance the value of sharing. These are the more interesting opportunities for marketers.

Photo sharing sites can be an outstanding resource for companies whose products and services have a strong visual component. In addi-

---

[2] A list of popular sites is here.

tion to identifying influencers, photo sites can be a source of inexpensive images for branded promotions and a way to identify applications of the company's product that aren't otherwise obvious. People like to document their own innovative ideas, and photo and video sites are a popular way to show off their inventions.

Marketers can create groups for free or sponsor branded groups. Purina's Do More For Pets gallery on Flickr is part of a larger branded Yahoo! initiative targeting pet enthusiasts. Printer maker Hewlett-Packard sponsors HP Resolutionaries, a Flickr group that it describes as being about "compelling imagery that captures power, serenity, devotion and shocking interpretations." Each day, members vote for the 12 best submissions of the past 24 hours.

Alicia Dorset, who edits the General Motors blogs, started cataloging photos on Flickr out of convenience. "I did it because I didn't know where to put photos we already had," she says. But then she realized there was an opportunity to reach out to enthusiasts and showcase the best work they've done on their GM automobiles. She began to post a featured photo of the day and to ask auto enthusiasts to submit their own best work. "At any given time, I usually have about 2,000 photos to pick from," she said. "We're way past 100,000 views."

Photo sharing sites are often underappreciated as marketing vehicles, particularly if marketers don't believe that their products are visual. However, the potential is greater than it may appear. Many people communicate better with photos than they do with words, and concepts like "beauty," "efficiency," "color," and "cool" may lend themselves perfectly well to visual expression. Photo contests are easier to run than video or even written competitions, so consider ways to use them.

When investigating photo sharing sites, be on the lookout for tags. These descriptive labels applied by photographers to their own work, as well as by others, can reveal trends and perceptions that aren't intuitively obvious. For example, photos of a Canadian resort that are also tagged "skiing" and "snowboarding" may reveal that skiers are a prime market opportunity. Some profiles may also contain tag clouds, which reveal a photographer's interest by the prominence of various terms. A tag cloud can be a quick way to identify someone who's an enthusiast and prospective influencer.

Secret: Use Twitter to broadcast limited-time specials like temporary discounts.

Twitter[3]

One of the most unlikely social network successes of 2007 was Twitter, a free service that lets people communicate in real time to groups of friends using any one of a number of devices, including cell phones. Twitter is basically a form of group instant messaging and it has built a devoted following. Marketing pundit Joseph Jaffe calls Twitter, "Real-time word-of-mouth."

Many people don't understand Twitter the first time they see it because its short-text interactions (messages are limited to 140 characters) are often about mundane things like going to work, sitting in meetings, and the weather. But Twitterers also send "tweets" about weightier topics, such as what a speaker just said at a conference or a business problem they're confronting.

The instant feedback that these messages generate is one reason that Twitter has become so popular. PR blogger Josh Hallett tells of being marooned in Washington D.C. during a string of thunderstorms. He Twittered a call for help and had three offers of a place to stay within 10 minutes.

Several enthusiasts I spoke to at one social media conference said they routinely send 30 or more tweets a day. Forrester Research estimated in late 2007 that 6 percent of U.S. online adults already used Twitter regularly. Mashups have emerged that aggregate Twitter activity, including Twittervision and Twitterverse. News of natural disasters has tweeted users hours before it hit the mainstream media. By one estimate, more than 100 services have sprung up that imitate or build upon Twitter. Utterz, Seesmic, Qik, and others are embellishing the basic service with audio and video capabilities, making Twitter a bona fide platform, which is a good thing to be.

---

[3] Portions of the Twitter profile originally appeared in *BtoB* magazine, ©2007, Crain Communications

This service addresses people's fundamental needs for connectedness and immediacy in a way that other mobile information services haven't. While cell phone companies do a good job of delivering headlines and sports scores to portable devices, none has enabled customers to tap into networks of like-minded peers. It turns out that people like sharing with their friends, even if they're talking about nothing in particular. Members can designate themselves as "followers," meaning that they can listen in on messages broadcast by other members, unless blocked by those members.

Twitter doesn't yet have a business model and doesn't reveal membership figures, but independent sources estimated that the service was approaching one million members by its first anniversary in March 2008. Users have discovered they can use Twitter to organize meetings and pinpoint the location of field representatives. Marketers are jumping on board. Media organizations like NBC and *The New York Times* are broadcasting updates on Twitter. Dell Computer's outlet store uses Twitter to broadcast promotions and specials. "A year after we launched… we found that 22 percent [of followers] said they weren't aware of Dell Outlet before finding us on Twitter," says Dell's Ricardo Guerrero.

Businesses in time-sensitive markets that need to communicate quickly with customers should take a hard look at Twitter. At the moment, the service is free to all.

Twitter's Quirky Appeal

Laura Fitton is a Twitter master, an independent consultant whose two young children create some lifestyle choices. She wants to work, but she needs to do that mainly from home.

Twitter has become Fitton's business network and support group. She has collected an entourage of more than 3,500 followers, and she has established relationships that have led to new business, speaking invitations, and personal friendships.

Fitton Twitters constantly at twitter.com/pistachio, describing professional and life experiences in 140-character bursts. She supplements her text posts with live video streams from <u>Qik.com</u> and short recorded videos from <u>Seesmic,</u> an instant video messaging service.

The length limitations of Twitter messages require a different approach to blogging. Entries are composed as a sequence of miniature thoughts and observations, each expressed in the unique language of a space-limited medium. Twitter has effectively sparked a new style of writing. People cover hour-long conference keynote speeches as a sequence of Twitter messages. Frequent users have learned catch phrases that prompt the largest possible response.

Twitterers are exhilarated by the idea of making connections. To them, the service is a lifeline to people they'd never otherwise meet, and that serendipity is one of the service's principal attractions. Twitter embodies the Web 2.0 concept of "presence," meaning that people make themselves available to converse by whatever means is at hand.

The immediate feedback is a powerful concept and Fitton crystallizes that with an example. One day she was pondering what to make for breakfast for her kids. She Twittered "pancakes or waffles?" to her followers and within two minutes had 10 responses. While I was interviewing her, she pulled out a small video camera and recorded me describing an idea I had outlined to her earlier. While we were speaking, she posted the video using Seesmic and Twittered her followers. Within 20 minutes, there were a half-dozen comments about my ideas.

One of Fitton's Twitter friends is Guy Kawasaki, a venture capitalist and Silicon Valley cultural icon. Their online exchange led to a lunch meeting and access to Kawasaki's vast Bay Area network.

The trend of "pitching" bloggers as if they were journalists has even trickled into the Twittersphere. Fitton receives 15 to 30 requests a week to post a link to someone's site, post, or project. Using trackable URLs from Tweetburner.com, she's found that those links can sometimes get hundreds of clicks. I've seen this power personally. When promoting a free preview for this book, I learned that a single tweet to my modest network could deliver 30 registrations in minutes.

Twitter users constantly point out interesting online resources to their followers. One Twitterer proposed that in this respect the service is becoming an alternative to daily newspapers. Newspapers have long provided guided discovery to information identified by editors. Twitter does the same thing with information identified by trusted sources. The two approaches fulfill a similar need. They just do it in different ways.

Del.icio.us

The granddaddy of social bookmarking sites has managed to overcome a dense user interface (redesigned in mid-2008), unpredictable performance, and limited functionality to remain atop the heap in its market. Del.icio.us defines one of the largest categories of social networks (Digg is a derivative) and offers marketers a valuable opportunity to peer inside the minds of their constituents.

A social bookmarking site is simply an extension of the bookmarking capability that has existed in Web browsers since the earliest days, only the bookmarks are saved to a Web server instead of to a local computer. Once posted online, members can tag their bookmarks with descriptive terms, append short commentaries, and share the bookmarks with other users. Tags can be used to organize like material into groups, and one web page may have dozens of tags. Looking at a user's profile on Del.icio.us, you can quickly see what interests them by viewing their tag cloud, making this service a good place to find influencers. Del.icio.

us has personal spaces, but they consist solely of a user's bookmarks and comments. Anyone can see anyone else's profile. Members can choose to subscribe to others members' bookmarks.

> **Secret: Think of social bookmarking sites as human-powered search. Every page in its database has been chosen by a person.**

This relatively simple concept actually has powerful utility. For example, going back to our Canadian travel resort example from Chapter 3, a del.icio.us search on *québec + resort* turns up a list of 74 items, many of which are directories or travel guides. A marketer may wish to contact these sites to be listed in their database.

There is also an assortment of personal sites maintained by people who may be influencers. Where pages have been tagged by multiple users, you can click on the "saved by" link to see who's tagged those resources and what they say about them. If the link is to your own site, it's often revealing to read the comments and to note the other tags that users have applied to your content.

Bookmarking sites are also useful personal productivity tools. When I was writing this book, I saved hundreds of bookmarks using a service called Diigo, which I like better than Del.icio.us. I would tag each entry with labels like *social_networks*, *case_study*, *social_media_research*, and *blogging*, highlight interesting passages, and append my own comments. When the time came to fold this background information into the book, I was able to easily search and sort my bookmarks by tag and to recall comments I had made months earlier.

Social bookmarking is a foundation for some of the most popular social networks. Popular services like StumbleUpon, reddit, Ma. gnolia and Digg are derived from this concept. Even if you don't use Del.icio.us yourself, it's in your best interest as an Internet marketer to understand how it works.

Digg

Getting mentioned on Digg.com can be the best or worst thing that ever happened to you. This powerful social bookmarking site can send tens or even hundreds of thousands of visitors to a website or video with just a single link on its storied homepage. It can also turn a corporate misstep into a global embarrassment with stunning speed.

Digg is social bookmarking on steroids. With more than 26 million monthly visitors, it has awesome power to drive awareness of online content. Members submit items that they find on the Web to a community voting process. Items that accumulate a large number of favorable votes, or "diggs," move up the popularity stack. Negative votes, or "buries," counterbalance positive ones. Digg keeps its vote-weighting algorithm proprietary, in large part to discourage scams.

In early 2008, Yahoo! launched a Digg competitor called Yahoo! Buzz. The service raised eyebrows by showing the potential to drive nearly as much traffic as Digg in just its first few weeks. Whether Buzz develops the personality and throw-weight of Digg is still to be seen, however. The early success of Buzz, though, was evidence that demand for these kinds of referral sites is insatiable.

There are a few examples of businesses benefiting from Digg's largesse. When 7-Eleven dressed up some of its stores to imitate Kwik-E-Marts for the opening of *The Simpsons Movie*, a related Flickr photo essay made it to page 2 of Digg's Entertainment section. Blendtec's destruction of an Apple iPhone in one of its blenders was one of the most "dugg" stories of 2007. When Coca-Cola teamed up with Apple to give away songs on iTunes, the story got more than 1,400 diggs. Breaking the 1,000-digg level should be considered an accomplishment, with handsome rewards in the form of traffic.

Secret: A small number of Digg members can exert disproportionate influence. This is a good place to become a power user.

Examples of successful marketing campaigns are scarce, though. Digg thrives on the bizarre, the political, and the techie. Stories about Apple Computer are a favorite. The site's snarky attitude and somewhat juvenile tone make it a generally inhospitable place for marketers. Alternative social news sites like Propeller and Sphinn are aimed at a more mature audience, with Sphinn targeting marketers directly.

Digg can provide a minor traffic lift from just a few votes. You'll get the best results with content that's novel and funny. It can't hurt to list on Digg, but the chance of getting huge viral traffic is limited.

Digg's more important contribution to social media may be its popularity engine. There are no editors at Digg and the management insists that its tiny staff never makes decisions about content, other than to remove objectionable items. Members submit content for consideration by the community. Most stories go nowhere, but a few take on a life of their own and can quickly develop considerable momentum. This technique has been embraced in a more business-friendly manner by other services, like Dell's IdeaStorm.

Digg fights a constant battle against people who try to beat the system by creating dummy accounts or even paying others to vote for them. Numerous blog entries have appeared advising marketers on how to improve their rankings (this comprehensive guide is one of the better ones). This process is known as "linkbaiting," and it can be quite effective in a limited way. However, tricks are no substitute for innovative content. It's useful to learn how to optimize social news sites, but don't linkbait to rescue bland material.

Second Life

No social network has been more revered, reviled, and debated than Second Life. The poster child of a new breed of online communities that have their roots in virtual-reality gaming, Second Life inspires a fanatical following of loyalists and an equally outspoken cadre of critics who call it over-engineered, baffling, and mostly deserted. As with most controversial issues, there is truth to both sides.

Second Life attempts to mimic the real world through a three-dimensional experience in which the user's character—or avatar— walks, runs, and flies between destinations representing different communities of interest. Characters can interact with each other through instant messaging and voice and can even control their body language and facial expressions. In this respect, Second Life comes the closest to resembling genuine human interaction. There's even a native currency that can be converted into real money. The visually rich environment can be mesmerizing, although the technical resources it requires can sometimes slow performance to a crawl. This is one reason Second Life has such a high attrition rate. More than 10 million people have signed up for the service, but less than 10 percent reportedly visit it regularly.

Second Life certainly has its enthusiasts. IBM, CNN, Sun Corp., Adidas, Sears, Cisco, Coca-Cola, and General Motors are just a few of the major companies that have constructed "islands" there. IBM has been so taken with its experience that in late 2007 it announced a partnership with Second Life developer Linden Lab to collaborate on core technology for virtual worlds. The CEO of Linden Lab predicted at a July 2007 conference that virtual worlds would be more prevalent than the Web itself within a decade.

Michael Azzara, a veteran technology publisher, wrote a white paper in late 2007 praising Second Life's utility as a b-to-b marketing instrument. Business media is "all about connecting buyers and sellers," he wrote. "Virtual worlds eliminate all the real-world pain-in-the-neck barriers to face-to-face meetings, and replace those barriers with an easy-to-scale learning curve…Second Life…is an open virtual world platform that supports rapid and inexpensive innovation."

Yet a scathing article in *Wired* magazine just a few months earlier painted a different picture:

> *Once you put in several hours flailing around learning how to function in Second Life, there isn't much to do. That may explain why more than 85 percent of the avatars created have been abandoned. Linden's in-world traffic tally, which factors in both the number of visitors and time spent, shows that the big draws for those who do return are free money and kinky sex. And even when corporate destinations actually draw people, the PR can be less than ideal. Last winter, CNET's in-world correspondent was conducting a live interview with Anshe Chung, an avatar said to have earned more than $1 million on virtual real estate deals, when Chung was assaulted by flying penises…*

Second Life unquestionably has value as a medium for virtual meetings, where presentations can be combined with discussions and ad hoc groups can form. The site has even shown value as a treatment for autism in children. More than 50 other virtual worlds have sprouted up around the Internet. While many are aimed at children and gamers, some sites like There target adults.

Event organizers claim that virtual trade shows can deliver outstanding lead generation at a fraction of the cost of physical events. A late 2007 study by market researcher FactPoint Group of 200 virtual events managed by Unisfair found that the average virtual event registered 3,102 people, nearly half of whom actually attended. Sponsors generated an average of 348 leads per event, while attendees stayed an average of two-and-a-half hours. Those numbers are particularly impressive given the cost-efficiency of virtual events.

For now, virtual worlds remain in the experimental stage, but a few early successes indicate they merit watching.

Wikipedia

This phenomenally successful community-edited encyclopedia deserves inclusion in this roundup only because it's such a tempting target for marketers. And why not? Wikipedia's breathtaking scope, impressive traffic (with an estimated 300 million daily page views, it's the ninth most visited website, according to Alexa.com), and strong search engine performance make it appear to be a natural venue for promotion. Many companies may be surprised to find that Wikipedia entries already exist for their brands, so why not adjust what's there to cast the brands in a positive light?

In general, this is a bad idea. Wikipedia's gates are guarded by an elite militia of volunteers who scrub entries for any sign of guerrilla marketing. Suspect entries may be slapped with one of the more than 100 disclaimers that the site employs to designate content that doesn't meet its standards for impartiality. What's more, flagrant violations may leak into the media, with embarrassing consequences. And once you get disclaimed, it can be very difficult to earn back your good name. Wikipedia's elite editors are mostly anonymous and can be all but impossible to track down for discussion. A Wikipedia entry may also backfire if your company is at the center of a controversy. Once you're listed there, critics may add accounts of your missteps and embarrassments. Wikipedia users don't care whether the news is good or bad as long as it's useful and relevant.

Although Wikipedia never trumpets its value as a traffic driver, anecdotal evidence suggests that it is substantial. Rand Fishkin of SEOmoz told attendees at the 2007 Search Engine Strategies conference that his company's inclusion in Wikipedia's

> **Secret: Wikipedia can outperform even the first page of Google results, but be sure to play by the community rules.**

"search engine marketing" entry outdrew its first-page ranking in Google results for the same term. Don Steele of Comedy Central said Wikipedia delivers about $20,000 worth of traffic per month. And consultant Jonathan Hochman, who is a Wikipedia editor, said the site's traffic often converts better than Google's paid search advertising.

Wikipedia has value to marketers, even if their brands are never mentioned. Nielsen Online executive vice president Peter Blackshaw uses the site to assess what he calls "counter-advertising." That's the process of comparing the Wikipedia description of a brand against the brand's own positioning. If the two aren't in synch, the brand has a problem, he wrote on ClickZ. Blackshaw said he also has text-mining gurus run a yearly analysis of Wikipedia to see what bloggers are linking to. "I treat it as a leading indictor of what consumers want or their unmet needs. What people look for and link to on Wikipedia is powerful and better than a focus group," he wrote.

Be careful about messing with Wikipedia. Stick to the facts. In fact, including some not-so-positive information about your company can actually work in your favor. If your entry is flagged as advertising, don't get rattled, but try to address the issues earnestly. Better yet, hire a freelancer to create a balanced story without your direct oversight. The risks of a negative backlash outweigh the upside of a few positive words.

8

Niche Innovators
Profiles by Dana Gillin

While Facebook, Digg, and YouTube are the undisputed giants of the social network world, their sheer size and scope can appear daunting. That's why the action in the market is increasingly moving to smaller, more specialized communities. With nearly every online publisher adding community features to its services, the distinctions between what social networks are and what they aren't is becoming fuzzier. The following snapshot profiles of some successful, but lesser-known networks should give you a sense of how some services are differentiating around the basic network constructs.

Gather

Gather is the social network for National Public Radio types. In fact, it was created by an NPR executive who saw the opportunity for a community built around the worldly interests of the public radio audience. Gather caters to people who are, according to *BusinessWeek*, "over 35, highly educated, and keenly interested in the political and cultural world around them."

Gather's home page has choice picks ranging from cooking to family activities to politics to health and money. A member's page can be populated with friends, groups, video, photos, and articles, as well as activity on the site.

Ad revenue is partially dispersed among the most active Gather members, according to whether they recruit members, write regularly, or search and read articles on the site. Most rewards consist of credits with Gather partners, although finding the partner can take some detective work. Because of Gather's strong demographics, the service has attracted blue-chip advertisers like Volvo and Charles Schwab—

this despite the fact that the overall membership was below 100,000 as of early 2008. As they say in publishing, it's all about focus.

Jigsaw

Jigsaw lives where social media meets old-time baseball card collecting. It's one thing to list 350,000 members' business cards, complete with name, e-mail address, phone number, title, company, and work mailing address; it's quite another to treat those members' 7 million business contacts like they were Mickey Mantle's 1951 rookie card. But that is precisely the concept upon which Jigsaw was built.

Jigsaw's directory is expanded when each new member dumps his virtual Rolodex into the site. Then other members "trade business cards they have for business cards they need." Jigsaw's founders have a lofty endgame in mind: "To map every business on the planet. Each Jigsaw member contributes to the puzzle. The result is a radically new and more effective way to gather and maintain corporate information."

Members are rewarded for updating incorrect contact information with additional contacts and penalized if they submit incorrect information. The Jigsaw market works two ways: A contact is given for a contact received, or a paid membership ($25/month buys 25 contacts/month).

Salespeople should find this site valuable, since it cuts down on cold calls. Directors and managers, however, may want to make sure their company has implemented Caller ID, since Jigsaw does not require a contact to give permission to be listed on the directory.

Jigsaw claims the information is already "out there" and the site just aggregates it. Also, the site lists only business information; no personal information is allowed. Non-members can also update their entries by specifying how and whether to call them as well as write a note to members who might buy their business cards in the future.

Privacy experts are less than enthralled with Jigsaw. Annalee Newitz, vice president of Computer Professionals for Social Responsibility, claims Jigsaw also provides a "stalkers' paradise," not to mention a fertile field for identity thieves and spammers.

Meetup

Founded in 2002, Meetup exists so that people can use the Web to get off the Web. It strives to connect people in their geographic area who share similar interests or hobbies using the old-fashioned way—in person.

In a world in which many people work from home, Meetup is a charming throwback to the front stoops of years gone by. The more than 4.6 million monthly visitors can choose from 37,000 local groups. Everything from local craft groups to political debate groups to book clubs is represented. The objective is to make it easy to create physical get-togethers.

In the summer of 2005, Meetup started charging group moderators a monthly fee to run a group, a controversial decision. However, committed moderators are forging ahead, asking members to pay a portion of the fees.

The 2004 Howard Dean presidential campaign gave Meetup national prominence by serving as a tool for campaign organizers. Supporters of candidates John Kerry and John Edwards have also put the service to good use, making politics a Meetup standout. Meetup continues to be a worthwhile resource for political candidates at all levels.

Marketers can use Meetup to target specific interest groups by advertising on the group landing pages. There's also no restriction on businesses using Meetup to arrange events. Expect to attract a lot of Web 2.0 types. For intimate gatherings centered around special-interest topics, though, the audience is vast and attentive.

Photobucket

Founded in 2003, it took Photobucket only two years to be named the fastest growing site of 2005 by Nielsen/NetRatings. As of March 2008, Photobucket had 34.6 million unique visitors a month worldwide, making it the most popular online digital photo conglomeration site in the U.S. Flickr is still considered the gold standard for hard-core photographers.

Members can choose from free or paid plans to post and share pictures, slideshows, and videos and be connected to other people in a friend network. With a $25 annual paid account, users can get away from the free account's image size limits and get 5GB instead of 1GB of storage, as well as a 10 percent discount on prints. Photobucket also lets users download images from their cell phones and browse other people's photos on their phones. Photobucket has contracted with TiVo so members of both services can view their online photo and video albums on their home television sets.

Photobucket was acquired by MySpace for $250 million in May 2007, at which point the site had 40 million registered users. It primarily earns money through paid accounts and advertising. Photobucket has a wide variety of marketing programs. Sponsors can buy such programs as custom image editors, custom albums, and even tie-ins to tagging and e-mail notifications.

Propeller

Owned by America Online, Propeller is a reborn and rebranded version of AOL's experimental Netscape community news service. AOL has positioned it as kind of a Digg-like social news site for grown-ups. Like Digg, users can vote stories up and down the popularity stack, but Propeller also has a team of "Anchors" who monitor the site to remove tasteless material and spam. Propeller also employs "Scouts" who submit stories and maintain link integrity. The look and feel of the Propeller content is serious, with many stories addressing national affairs and politics.

Reddit

See Digg. With some small differences, reddit, founded in 2005, is basically Digg with a different spelling. (There is a veritable cheerleading squad of popularity sites on the Internet—from Digg to Propeller to Yahoo! Buzz to reddit. It's a popularity contest among sites that are themselves popularity contests.)

Membership for the two sites is generally the same type of crowd, but the top Diggers are not the top redditers, and vice versa. There is a little bit of snobbery among the memberships; each pumps the value of its own brand.

The differences? Submitting to Digg is a bit more cumbersome than submitting to reddit—the former provides checks and balances to make sure the site has not been dugg before, requires a thumbnail for news stories, and provides a user with more categories from which to choose. reddit's story order comes only from people voting on the story; good votes move it up the list, bad votes move it the other way.

Digg's algorithm, as noted in Chapter 6, is deliberately mysterious and may involve such factors as variety and the status of individual voters. Digg also has richer profile and social interaction mechanisms. In contrast, interaction in reddit basically consists of commenting on someone else's pick. Some people say Digg is more mature, while reddit is more streamlined.

Sermo

Founded in late 2006, Sermo seeks to connect doctors across the U.S. in an advice network. Because the site is user-moderated, advice given by fellow doctors must be taken with a grain of salt.

Sermo blends anonymity and personal details in whatever combination the user wishes. All that's displayed to other members is a screen name and specialty; the rest is up to individuals to disclose in an optional profile. This is mainly a professional networking site.

Instead of letting pharmaceutical companies have their way with the members of Sermo, the site sells access to the anonymous comments to financial institutions, health care organizations, and government bodies. The idea is that the thoughts of this highly qualified, physician-verified audience will have special value to those institutions. Sermo even passes along some rewards to members who offer "astute observations and clinical insight" that is "highly relevant and valuable." Sponsors can also post questions, to which doctors can respond. One sponsor is the American Medical Association, which offers Sermo members access to exclusive content material like the *Journal of the American Medical Association.*

Squidoo

In an effort to cash in on the nomenclature karma of sites like Google and Yahoo!, author/blogger Seth Godin teamed with four other people to create Squidoo in 2005. The concept is fairly simple: Users (called "lensmasters") register and create a page (or "lens") about an area of interest and expertise. The site provides a loosely organized template with categories that the lensmaster can rename and populate as he or she wishes, with no input or editorializing by Squidoo. Why not just Google your query? Godin calls Google "too good," meaning that it provides too many search results; Squidoo can sort through those results for you and pull out the most relevant.

Each section of a lens can be several different things: a text module, Amazon module, RSS feed, link list, or Flickr module. Squidoo actually encourages people to creates lenses based purely on their personal agendas, online stores, or blogs. It's a free-for-all, but if you search for your favorite keywords, you'll probably get a well-rounded set of results.

One of the shortcomings of Squidoo is that a single topic may be called several things and have several different lenses. For example, "Barack Obama Shirts" and "Barack Obama Tees" have similar goals and content, but are owned by two different lensmasters. Members have to choose their lenses carefully to attract search traffic and may have to create multiple lenses for the same topic.

Why bother? Because not only does Squidoo share profits from ads and other paid links with each lensmaster, but it gives an automatic 5 percent of its profits to charity. Godin estimates that about half of its lensmasters also give their 45 percent share of lens profits to charities instead of pocketing the cash.

Squidoo is marketer-friendly. Not only can anyone create a lens to promote expertise, but advertisers can align their promotions with specific topics. Squidoo also provides helpful advice about internal and search engine promotion.

Spotting a good idea, Google announced in late 2007 that it is working on a similar service called Knol. Some cynics suggest this project may be one reason that the performance of Squidoo lenses dropped sharply in Google search results in mid-2007.

StumbleUpon

This popular social bookmarking site, launched in 2002, simply states its goal as being able to "help people discover interesting or informative web content that they wouldn't have thought to search for." It does this through the use of a StumbleUpon toolbar, which a registered user can install on Firefox or Internet Explorer. Members can use the toolbar to immediately flag interesting sites. Selections and descriptions go into a common area where members can see what other members have chosen and why. As others vote for the same sites, those selections rise in the StumbleUpon hierarchy.

A user can select categories of interest and click the "Stumble!" button to be taken to random sites recommended by other members in those favored categories. Sites that have been favorably reviewed are more likely to turn up in random "stumblings."

It's perfectly okay for members to tag their own sites as stumble-worthy. This isn't gaming the system, because that selection only becomes important if other people vote for the site as well. If nobody else finds the page interesting, nothing much happens, but if a page attracts enough interest, it can draw an astonishing amount of StumbleUpon traffic.

Users like StumbleUpon because of the unique discovery experience. Not only is there an element of surprise, but the sites are almost always relevant.

Web auction giant eBay bought StumbleUpon in May 2007 for $75 million. Google, which was rumored to be interested in StumbleUpon itself, later added similar functionality to its toolbar. StumbleUpon's unique advertising model inserts sponsors' pages in its lineup of random stumbles. No ad copy is required. Advertisers can guarantee that their pages are seen by a certain number of members who meet specific demographic criteria.

You don't need to buy an ad to submit a page, though. Clever, well-executed content marketing campaigns should be submitted to StumbleUpon as a matter of course. There is no downside and the traffic benefits can be impressive.

ThisNext

A venture-backed site launched in 2006, ThisNext is a social shopping service where members can recommend favorite products and help others to discover little-known gems. Users can search a directory of more than 100,000 products by category and get listings of options ranked by ratings from other users. A unique feature is "shopcasts," which are essentially lists of favorite products published by members. The site has generated extensive media coverage and some positive press from boutique product makers who have had success there. Marketing opportunities at this point are limited to banners and badges. The company has so far refused to allow marketers to align themselves with favorable reviews.

Utterz

Utterz' favored platform is the cell phone, which can be used to capture photos, audio, video, and text into a media mashup that can be cross-posted on popular blogging software like Blogger, WordPress, Typepad, and Twitter. While Utterz is a popular add-on for Twitter users who want to add multimedia to their "tweets," its service can be used with many other publishing platforms. Utterz entries can also be created and posted online with a webcam and a microphone.

Limitations of the service include cell phone overhead charges and the fact that text-only services like Twitter can't accommodate multimedia. In these cases, the visual and audio aspects of the post are lost, although links are preserved.

Utterz users are able to form networks with other Utterz users and follow those friends' posts. So, a podcast published on Utterz can be advertised to a specific group of people, in addition to being posted on any or all blogs of the podcaster's creation.

Visible Path

Visible Path was born out of perceived weaknesses of LinkedIn. Instead of listing every contact equally, Visible Path provides several layers of affiliation and differentiation based on a member's personal knowledge of a contact. According to TechCrunch, "You have to exchange e-mails, carry out meetings, or provide a deep level of contact information on their vCard to show a real relationship." There are two uses of Visible Path—the free version connects individuals to individuals and leaves the responsibility for finding contacts in the users' hands. The paid corporate version can monitor a company's Outlook calendars and e-mails and continuously update the interaction proximity of each user on the network, in addition to any individual contacts made outside the company.

Visible Path was founded in 2002. Rumors circulated in late 2007 that the company was being bought by "a multibillion international company," but that the service will continue to operate.

Yelp

When the Yellow Pages concept met social media, Yelp was born. The site is organized by U.S. city, from Park La Brea, California to Burlington, Vermont, and contains prolific member reviews of restaurants, hair salons, night clubs, and any other local establishment. The site is known for the quality and honesty of its reviews, both pro and con. And all aspects of shopping or dining are welcome—from parking to selection to customer service.

Only registered members can post reviews, but those reviews are searchable and accessible by any visitor. Multiple reviews are aggregated and averaged, yielding an overall rating from one to five stars. In fully populated categories like restaurants, the ratings can separate the wheat from the chaff. In niche categories, like religious institutions, the lack of activity makes the ratings suspect.

The Yelp staff pulls out members who contribute particularly helpful and readable reviews for designation as Elite Yelpers. They are invited to special events at nightclubs, restaurants, and cultural activities in San Francisco, Seattle, New York, Boston, Los Angeles, Washington D.C., and Chicago.

Yelp is mainly useful in and directly around cities. Suburban towns and rural areas are the next logical coverage areas but are as yet only spottily covered. The site's membership has been criticized for not being evenly distributed among the major markets it claims to serve; the company was started in San Francisco and still has its stronghold there. More than half of all Yelp members are between the ages of 25 and 36, which gives the site a decidedly youthful and nightlife-oriented tinge.

Yelp currently earns revenue through advertising, and has pulled in about $15 million in venture funding. Advertisers can buy sponsored placements atop search results as well as standard ad units. Yelp is a great place for local businesses to monitor customer feedback, and a string of good reviews can be good marketing fodder. Beware, though: A couple of negative reviews in a lightly covered market like Stockton, California can have a disproportionately depressing effect on overall ratings.

Two former Paypal engineers formed Yelp in July 2004, making Yelp the granddaddy of social networking. The site has many competitors, including Yahoo! Local, Plazes, and CitySearch. However, none have yet garnered the buzz of Yelp.

Zillow

Started in 2005 by two former Expedia.com employees, Zillow has strived to become a resource where real estate agents and homeowners can access the kinds of statistics and tools to which only real estate agents were once privy. It has raised $87 million in venture capital funding. Zillow creates a mashup of each home in its database by using public information such as satellite images, street maps, and real estate records to profile millions of U.S. properties. Its "Zestimate" is a current evaluation of the home's worth. Zillow also hosts more than 6,500 neighborhood profiles that include statistics on crime rates and resident data, figures with which real estate agents are seldom forthcoming. The Zestimate does not include neighborhood factors like quality of schools or remodels, but there are places in a home's profile to include comments on these.

Zestimates, however, are a source of some controversy. They've been criticized as being untrustworthy and some real estate agents worry that Zillow is horning in on their business. Zillow disclaims the absolute accuracy of its estimates. A *Wall Street Journal* article gave reason for doubt. It documented a case in which Zillow had estimated a home's value at $660,000, whereas the home actually sold for $2.7 million.

The site features a wiki where members can list their own homes, upload photos, and specify a "Make Me Move" price, which is the point at which they would be willing to accept an offer even if the house isn't on the market.

Zillow has also recently gotten into the lending business. Mortgage lenders can now "obtain free, instant, and unlimited access to Zillow consumers who are shopping for a loan." Zillow also makes money the old-fashioned new media way—by selling advertising.

Self-Appointed Celebrity

Veteran real estate professionals will tell you that their business is not about selling property as much as it is about building relationships. Customers often deal with realty pros at times of upheaval in their lives—changing cities, switching jobs, and forming new social circles—and they come to rely on them for much more than just a roof over their heads.

Rebecca "Reba" Haas is a born networker. A former technology salesperson, she maintains 1,500 contacts in her address book and takes pride in helping her clients get anchored in new locations. Over the course of her career she's helped at least 20 clients and colleagues find jobs. She's been in realty for the last five years.

Rebecca "Reba" Haas.

"People are always asking realtors for help," she says. "You have to be good at learning the community and drawing information out of people." Not surprisingly, social networks are a natural tool for Reba Haas.

In an industry where only about 2 percent of professionals even maintain blogs, Haas' Team Reba throws off the average. Not only do they blog, but Haas herself uses more than a half-dozen social networks for various business-building practices.

Reba Haas has successfully positioned herself as an authority on the Seattle area, not only touting it as a good place to own a house, but also as an entertainment destination. It's paying big benefits. She entered a field in which first-time brokers usually close less than a half-dozen deals their first year and sold 17 properties in 12 months. After less than five years in the business, her practice is included in the top 2 percent of RE/MAX agents internationally; her offices are often cited as the number one or two broker in the area's multiple listing service.

Relationships are a big part of that success, and Haas uses online resources liberally to maintain them. Her favorite tools include:

TeamReba blog—The frequently updated group blog has plenty of valuable advice for buyers and sellers. Topics have ranged from trends in rental prices in the Puget Sound area to advice on decommissioning oil tanks to advice on changes and regional multiple listing service financing forms. Articles are written to help and inform buyers and sellers, not to push properties.

Like many good business bloggers, the TeamReba blog mixes in an assortment of less serious content, such as restaurant reviews, bargain shopping opportunities, and fun and interesting websites. The blog address goes on every piece of e-mail and collateral the team distributes and blog feeds appear on Facebook and syndicated sites.

LinkedIn—This professional networking service is where Haas keeps a directory of contacts who can help people with legal advice, jobs, financial assistance, and other practical concerns. "It's where we show our credentials in a big way," she says. Now, instead of rifling through address books to answer clients' questions, she sends people to LinkedIn to look up her contact list and offers to connect them to reliable professionals. This means she serves more clients in less time.

Judy's Book—This site specializes in highlighting deals and reviews

---

Rebecca Haas' Secrets:

☞ Find as many outlets as possible for your content and re-purpose existing content into new venues. RSS feeds are an easy way to do this. Facebook, for example, can import blog posts automatically.

☞ Point customers to information online that helps them with their questions. When possible, direct them to areas where your content is featured. This enables you to maintain more relationships in less time and showcases your expertise.

☞ Become an expert in a few specific topics and build on that profile to achieve prominent placement in relevant online forums.

---

of local merchants and services. "It's allowed me to give back to the community," Haas says. But it's also positioned her as an expert on the locale. "I've written copious reviews of shops, restaurants, and other places to help clients get situated. It's also good because clients then write stellar reviews about us."

Zillow—This consumer realty site enables buyers to find homes and owners to estimate the value of their property. It's been somewhat controversial in realty circles because some agents believe it is a potential competitor, but "We're going full tilt with it," Haas says. "We contribute to the Q&A sessions and list our properties there. We'll re-purpose material from the blog and get the benefit of a national audience."

Facebook and MySpace—The team maintains personal profiles on these services with Haas' younger staff members maintaining most of the relationships there. "We use it to show that we're real people with interests outside of just selling real estate," Haas says. She's also used Facebook to build support around a favorite charity.

Haas estimated she's closed over $3 million in business as a result of her online promotion, with another million in the pipeline. She's also convinced that the relationships that she's developed have been critical to the team's success. The practice closed 25 deals last year. It does almost no print advertising.

9

Learning from Conversations

"The question that so many marketers and PR professionals think they face today is giving up control of their brand. The truth is they never had it. The brand has always resided in the hearts and minds of our consumers. What has changed is that we no longer control the message."

—Duncan Wardle, vice president, Global Public Relations, Disney Parks & Resorts, speaking to Bulldog Reporter's Media-Relations Summit 2008

The Guild of Madison, Wisconsin, represents about 1,200 artists who handcraft everything from furniture to paintings and jewelry for sale to an upscale and discerning customer base.

The 22-year-old company has its roots in business-to-business markets, but The Guild has had designs on the home market for years. An early Internet effort ran up against the bursting of the dot-com bubble, forcing the business to retrench. In 2004, the original owners bought back the firm from the bankers and relaunched it as The Artful Home, channeling most sales through a Web catalog.

Business was good, but managers argued about buyers' motives for coming to the website. "We had a lot of debate on this," says Toni Sikes, founder and artistic director. "I assumed people wanted to know about the artists we represented. Others thought visitors were looking for famous artists. And there were still other people who said the core customers were consumers who were making their homes more artful."

The question was critical. In the market for big-ticket items, a couple of points' improvement in conversion rates can be a big boost to the business. A year earlier, The Guild had conducted focus groups and in-depth phone surveys at a cost of about $25,000. The results were inconclusive.

As Sikes was pondering 2008 priorities, she bumped into Dan Neely, an entrepreneur who specialized in customer intelligence. At that time, Neely was launching Networked Insights, a company that would build customer communities. He offered to build one for The Guild, and also to outfit it with new software that Networked Insights had developed to let business owners discern insights from discussions going on in their customer communities.

Sikes has a master's degree in market research, so she knows a few things about how to mine information. Instead of posting an online survey, she recommended organizing the site's discussion areas around the various customer motivators that were being debated internally. She figured that activity within those areas would give clues about what customers thought was important.

It didn't take long to get an answer. Within a few weeks, it was clear that activity was clustering around home decoration topics. "All kinds of people were answering questions, sending photos, and offering advice," Sikes says. "It became clear that the primary reason people were coming to us was to look for ideas to create a more artful home."

Question answered, strategy defined, and The Guild entered its 2008 planning cycle with a clearer idea of how it would structure its site and promotions.

Analysis of the conversations also yielded other insights. Staffers were surprised to learn that 60 percent of the visitors had never done business with The Guild before. They also discovered that once people registered for the community, they converted to customers at a 12 percent rate. "If we had a rate like that for our entire site, I'd be on cloud nine," Sikes laughs.

It's still early to measure results, but The Guild is putting far more wood behind the home decorating arrow than before it began monitoring conversations. And rather than a point-in-time survey, it now has ongoing discussions it can monitor for new insight. Which all proves that sometimes it pays just to listen.

Stories like these are sweeping the business world and catalyzing a new industry built around customer conversation analysis. Drawn by the opportunity to gain rapid, actionable feedback from dedicated customers, businesses are increasingly tapping in to focused communities that have sprung up online or even creating their own branded and gated forums. The market is still emerging, but more than 100 "white box" community hosting services have popped up, most of them in the last couple of years. And the success stories are breeding excitement.

Secret: Don't just listen to what customers say about you. The other topics they discuss can yield segmentation insights.

For instance, there are stories like that of a large pet products maker, who prefers to remain anonymous, that wanted to learn more about how people in different age groups perceived their pets. In the process of mining communities of pet lovers for insight, the firm's strategic partner, Umbria, turned up an unexpected but more intriguing thread: People were frustrated by the hassle of traveling with their pets.

Pet owners weren't stating this frustration explicitly, but references to the topic kept cropping up in discussions on travel sites and blogs, says Howard Kaushansky, president of Umbria. "No one was looking at travel discussions for pet-product ideas," he says. "If we had asked focus groups about their challenges, this might not even have come up." The client quickly went to work on a line of travel-friendly products for pet owners.

A Revolution in Research

Umbria and an emerging class of new-age market intelligence firms are building upon traditional research tools like focus groups and surveys by mining unprompted comments that customers post to their friends' networks or by creating feedback loops of very large customer groups at a fraction of the cost of traditional telephone and face-to-face interviews.

Conversation monitoring has caught fire in the last couple of years. An early 2008 survey by Aberdeen Group, which was underwritten by several conversation monitoring companies, as well as the Word of Mouth Marketing Association (WOMMA), said that top-performing companies were nearly seven times as likely as poor performers to use social media monitoring tools to predict customer behavior. Nearly two-thirds of the top performers had formal monitoring programs in place and 42 percent were actively listening to detect early warning of threats to their brands.

Businesses are beginning to fund these new research channels as the cost-benefit equation becomes more apparent. U.S. firms spent $40 million on research using customer panels in 2007 and that figure was expected to grow to $69 million in 2008, according to Inside Research, a firm that tracks market-research spending.

> Secret: Private online communities often need nothing more than regular company interaction to stay active.

One of the appeals of community research is time-to-market. Because feedback is immediate and conversations are ongoing, businesses find they can substantially reduce the time needed to get a fully baked idea to market.

Del Monte Foods used a handpicked community called "I Love My Dog" to test ideas for a new breakfast treat for dogs. The feedback from the 400 members was that the product should have a bacon-and-egg taste and a dose of extra vitamins. Del Monte obliged with Snausages Breakfast Bites. It brought the product to market in six months, about half the usual cycle time, according to a _Wall Street Journal_ account. Ideas from customers convinced P&G that its Dawn dish detergent could be packaged in such a way as to make dishwashing a fun activity for kids.

Online Insight

Watertown, Massachusetts-based Communispace is a rapidly growing 200-person company that specializes in creating private communities of customers and prospects who provide the feedback on all kinds of questions.

Founded in 1999, the company originally developed software, but found that there was greater market demand for its skills as a community facilitator. It now recruits groups of constituents to help clients position and market their products as well as to identify new market opportunities. Communities can range up to several hundred members. Communispace actively monitors what members are saying and prompts discussion to keep groups active and creative. The company has created more than 300 custom online groups.

Secret: Regularly scheduled online events keep community members coming back.

The company claims that, on average, 68 percent of its community members are actively participating within 48 hours of joining. It does this with minimal financial incentives. In fact, the greatest draw is often simply the knowledge that their opinions are being heard. "It's very motivating for a lot of consumers to deal with the brand and the people behind it," says Julie Wittes Schlack, a senior vice president. Rituals like Tuesday night chats, weekly polls, shared stories, and shared photos of items that members have in common helps drive return traffic, notes Larry Weber in *Marketing to the Social Web.*

Kraft Foods conceived of the idea for its successful line of 100 Calorie Packs, based in part on Communispace community research. Dialogue with customers uncovered insights such as the fact that people who were trying to lose weight valued portion control more than they valued special low-cal ingredients. As Kraft narrowed the domain of discussion, the company used the group to determine factors like maximum fat and calorie counts and the types of snacks to produce. It then distributed samples and showed prototype advertising to the group. The 100-calorie snacks rang up $100 million in sales in the first year.

GlaxoSmithKline Consumer Healthcare used Communispace groups to closely define the customer base for its new line of Alli weight-loss products in mid 2007. Glaxo marketers knew that Alli wasn't for everyone. In fact, customers who failed to lose weight after using the product could potentially generate damaging negative word-of-mouth. Private online groups helped identify the characteristics of the target market: people who were willing to take responsibility for their own weight loss and to accept slow progress in return for long-term results. Glaxo sold $155 million worth of Alli in its first six weeks on the market, and the company has kept the conversation going through Communispace research and an advisory blog.

Community analysis can also be used to identify new segments. Umbria used its text-mining technology for an apparel client to segment the target audience into groups with playful labels like "Fit Finders," "Self-

Expressives," "Bargain Seekers," "Label Whores," "Style Gurus," and "Dissenters."

Fit Finders, for example, are Generation X consumers who want jeans that complement their changing physiques. Self-Expressives want the control to customize their jeans by distressing them or

> **Secret: Conversation analysis can reveal new customer segments.**

adding patches and embroidery. The apparel maker used these insights to design and market products to each group.

A similar project for a packaged food company analyzed female bloggers to identify women's needs and interests at different times of the day. The analysis identified afternoon as "Connect Time," or the period when women share stories and experiences with their friends. "Me Time" is early morning, when women seek control over their busy schedules.

Products and promotions were then mapped to these time-based segments. For example, calendars were distributed with times blocked out for "Me Time." A line of stimulating teas was targeted for early-morning consumption.

Public or Private?

Private branded communities are one of the fastest-growing areas of social media. They are also one of the least publicized, in part because the companies that commission them discuss confidential topics like new product plans and marketing proposals behind closed doors. The so-called "white box" social network providers offer a wide range of options ranging from software to fully moderated groups.[1]

There are a variety of ways to mine special-interest communities. Some companies use conversation monitoring services like the ones listed in Chapter 3 to simply keep an ear to the ground. Others prefer to build their own product support communities, as technology companies have done for years. Still others outsource the process to professional facilitators. Within each option, there are a variety of sub-options. For

---

[1]Forrester Research's Jeremiah Owyang has assembled an impressive list of these providers.

example, a branded public community may focus strictly on product development or may encompass other professional or lifestyle issues.

Canadian electronics retailer Future Shop is using customer conversations not only to learn more about its customers but to help sell and support products. The company, which is Canada's largest consumer electronics retailer, is built on a high-touch model in which sales associates are taught to be valued customer advisors. The company has come up with a strategy to duplicate the real-world experience online.

Since mid-2007, visitors to Future Shop's website have been greeted by a video image of a sales associate who offers to help guide their experience. Customers can ask any question of the avatar (he'll even dance for you) and get results from a growing database of advice contributed by sales associates and customers. Future Shop created the video front-end itself and bound it to a community portal from Lithium.

"We're trying to blur the lines between the offline and online experience," says Robert Pearson, Future Shop's director of e-commerce. "Our goal is to become the largest technology community in Canada."

Future Shop is well on its way to achieving that objective. In less than a year, the site signed up 50,000 members, which would be equivalent to about 450,000 members in the much larger U.S. market. But the community isn't just a discussion forum. Future Shop co-developed a ranking system with Lithium that lets customers provide feedback on each other's comments and on the quality of information offered up by sales associates. Customer contributors can earn discounts and status in the community. The most helpful sales associates can earn cash.

Next up: Facebook-like functionality that gives contributors their own personal spaces and ties sales associate profiles to store locations. Success is measured by a survey of customer affinity with the brand. As of mid-2008, the project was too new to yield measurable conclusions, but all the trends were pointing in the right direction. "We're getting about 250,000 visitors a day out of a population of 33 million," Pearson says. "That's many more than come into a store. We actually see people walking in with printouts and asking for specific experts they've met online."

The following are other examples of businesses tying communities into their sales objectives.

• Hair color maker Redken launched Do You Shades EQ? in the spring of 2008 for salon professionals who use one of its product lines. The site has downloadable formulas, video interviews, and a place for hair professionals to upload their own creations. Contributors are entered to win a trip to New York City to participate in a photo shoot for an ad campaign.

• Disney set up the Walt Disney Moms Panel, featuring a dozen mothers who answer questions from prospective visitors about the company's theme parks and vacation resorts. In early 2008, Disney launched the Mickey Moms Club, a gated community capped at 10,000 members. The community has become one of the most frequently visited of all Disney sites, according to Duncan Wardle, vice president of global public relations. Visitors spend an average of eight to 10 minutes per visit, which is more than on any other park's website, Wardle told the Bulldog Reporter's Media Relations Summit. Site visitors also spend more on their vacations than non-members.

• P&G is so bought in to communities that it set up a subsidiary—Tremor—to market word-of-mouth services to other companies. Among the communities P&G operates is Capessa, a site where women can discuss a variety of health, beauty, parenting, and relationship topics without marketing pressure.

Branded communities, whether public or private, appeal to companies that worry about the chaos of public networks. Since there's no way to guide what's said in public forums (Dell Computer's sponsored Facebook group, for example, prominently features a discussion thread called "Why Dell sucks"), private communities enable sponsors to influence discussion more directly. That gives them the flexibility to hear honest comments and to follow up on what ideas have the most potential.

It's not hard to start a social network. Google Groups and Yahoo! Groups are free and easy to create. However, they have limited functionality, can be time-consuming to maintain, and offer little control to the organizer. Free or inexpensive hosted services like Ning, Crowdvine, and CommonGate offer more control but limited customization.

At the high end of the market are companies that run private, branded communities. Their customers are often very large companies that want hand-selected groups of targeted customers that are vetted by professional researchers. These services come at a price, though. Fees run in the low six figures, including a proprietary technology platform and a range of services intended to make the community a turnkey proposition.

Which Community Is Right?

Sometimes you don't even need to build your own community. Some independent groups can become large and successful enough to provide a built-in feedback source for the vendors. SegwayChat is an independent forum with 6,500 members and over 165,000 messages. The independent TivoCommunity is so active that the digital video recorder maker lends it financial support and positions the community as an important source of customer support. In cases like these, brand representatives can tap into an ongoing conversation. The community has already done the heavy lifting for you. "In most cases, you're not creating communities. You're tapping into communities that already exist," says Maggie Fox, a veteran social media marketer.

Tapping in doesn't mean intruding, though. Communities have their own personalities, which often flow from the style of the founders or chief moderators. If you enter these discussions talking like the vendor voice of God, you'll alienate the audience you're trying to reach.

Palm, the maker of the Treo personal digital assistant, had to walk this line after discovering that many of its customers were getting their information from independent online groups instead of from the Palm website. That wasn't necessarily a bad thing, but Palm wanted to entice customers back to its own support resources. It dispatched technical support representatives to engage with people as helpful resources, using the language that was specific to each community. "We approached customers as peers, not as aquisition targets, which helped win their trust," wrote Noah Elkin, vice president of corporate strategy at iCrossing, which consulted with Palm. "Taking an active interest in their communities also helped increase affinity for the brand."

Most organizations don't have the luxury of an active independent user group, so the question is whether a branded community is worth the effort. For most businesses it is. The options, though, are all over the map.

Support forums are a natural option for companies with complex products. They're simple to start and can build enough momentum to become self-sustaining. Customers naturally gravitate toward their vendors for product support, so for most businesses, this is the easiest option.

Special interest groups build cohesion around topics of interest that may not directly relate to specific products but that educate and support target audiences. Procter & Gamble's Beinggirl community for teenage girls is an example.

Customer communities may grow out of successful support forums as members expand their discussion to other areas of common interest. Or they may be branded promotional vehicles. Sheraton Vacation Ideas is a travel advice forum where customers can exchange tips and photos.

Private communities are captive groups that provide businesses with customer feedback, kind of like a giant focus group. This is one of the fastest growing areas of social media, but one that gets little attention because of confidentiality. Communispace and Sparta Social Networks are just two of a growing crop of vendors.

Experienced community-builders offer the following secrets for success.

Know your goals. People join customer communities for all kinds of reasons. Some want to improve their knowledge of products they use, others seek to swap ideas, and still others are motivated to help the company improve products or invent new ones. It's hard to accomplish all three goals with a single group, so know your goals before you invite customers to participate. "If you have the goal in mind, then it's easier to construct the paths to reach it," says Dan Miller, vice president of mobile solutions at Neighborhood America, a developer of online communities. Then demonstrate your commitment to the goal, he adds, "Make it part of the messaging and positioning of the company. Make it integral to the company's value. Integrate the messaging into all of your communications."

Secret: Constantly sub-divide groups to keep them small.

Keep groups small. "As groups become large, participants feel alienated," says Communispace's Julie Schlack. "When the group gets too large, split it into subgroups so that people feel like they aren't part a big mass." Communispace has found that small groups tend to be more interactive. In a 2007 white paper, Communispace documented how postings to a private community maintained by an airline client were longer, richer, and more constructive than those in a public forum about the same topic.

Reinforce the value of membership. This tactic is particularly effective in private or branded communities, where active contributors may be recognized with special attention or access. However, the same principles can apply to any group. The simple addition of a registration form and a password can enhance people's sense that they are being granted access to an exclusive club. Marketers have been doing this with affinity cards for years, and the same concept works online. According to the Communispace white paper, "Branded communities deliver, on average, 5,000 more pieces of new content yearly than unbranded communities."

Secret: Make members feel like they're something special.

Membership tactics work in public communities, too. When people register for a site, they're offering to establish a relationship with a brand. Reinforce that through regular contact. For example, Beinggirl, a community operated by P&G's Tampax and Always brands, sends members monthly samples and mailings to keep them involved.

Be aware that membership does involve some trade-offs. For one thing, search engines can't look behind your membership curtain unless you make special provisions for them to do so. Also, traffic to a members-only site will be only a fraction of traffic to a public website. Think carefully about your strategic objectives before you erect a wall.

Four Secrets of Social Media Marketing (that really aren't terribly secret)

By Maggie Fox

Talking about social media with people who are steeped in traditional marketing usually provokes expressions ranging from bewilderment to panic. There's just something about the topic that makes people react as if it were a minefield on Mars. The irony, of course, is that the primary skills you need to succeed here are the same skills that everybody already has. They're the skills that are essential to a healthy personal life: the ability to talk to and have meaningful relationships with other human beings.

At SMG, we follow four basic steps with each project. Do this and your efforts will succeed:

Listen. You don't successfully join a conversation by interrupting or talking out of context. We conduct research to find out what people are talking about and how our clients can best add value to what's already taking place. (This includes both technology and content considerations.) Talking before you listen is a recipe for disaster, online and offline. On the other hand, knowing what already engages the community makes it much more likely that you'll be welcomed.

Participate. Once you know what people are interested in hearing about and how they're communicating with one another, you can start participating. But this isn't a one-off; you must be committed to an ongoing conversation. The notion of the "campaign" has no place here. Your dialogue with the market may evolve over time, but if you're lucky, it should never end. This may create some short-term staffing and budget issues, but a deep conversation with your consumers will so energize your staff that they'll find the resources you need.

Influence. Once you're participating and adding value to the conversation, you'll begin to earn credibility. This may take a little while or a long time, depending on your business and the conversation you're joining. Be patient. Once you're participating, the real benefits start to accrue. That's when you become a valued member, not just a marketer.

Act. If you take the first three steps successfully, you'll be able to legitimately influence the conversation. If your involvement is appropriate because you're actively listening and conversing, people will listen to you when you take action.

The surest way to achieve success is to review your proposed program against these four steps. If your plans don't include each one, you're missing something.

Above all, **think about how you talk to other people**. How are good conversations made? What creates quality, engaging dialogue? In a fascinating twist, you'll soon realize this brave new world actually abides by the same rules of socialization that have governed humans for thousands of years.

Maggie Fox is the CEO of Social Media Group, the world's largest independent agency helping businesses navigate the new socially engaged Web. SMG's clients include Ford, SAP, Yamaha, and Dell.

Don't build barriers. Lead generation is the enemy of customer engagement. Yes, it's a necessary evil to some degree, but if you let it guide your thinking when you're building a community, you will drive away the people you're trying to reach. Marketers obsessed with lead generation put too many barriers between the customer and the information the customer wants. As a rule of thumb, every additional click you impose doubles attrition. Do you really need a street address or a departmental budget? If the prospect is really interested, he'll give you that information when the time is right.

Learn from the social network model: In most cases, all a person needs to create an account is a name and an e-mail address. If they like what they find at a site, they volunteer more and more information because they want to become part of the community. The model works beautifully. More marketers should adopt it.

Humanize the interaction. People relate better to other people than they do to organizations. Practitioners say it's crucial to expose people in your organization as facilitators to respond to comments and initiate new discussions. Over time, these people become the face of the company, so choose wisely. Make sure they're committed to participating on a regular basis, at least every other day.

This isn't easy to do. In my experience, working with clients on company blogs and customer communities, recruiting internal talent is one of the most difficult tasks my clients face. This is particularly true with senior employees, who often don't believe they have the time to commit to the project. Forcing people to participate is never a solution. You may get a few months of halfhearted compliance, but people will duck out at the first opportunity.

A better tactic is to recognize and celebrate the competence of the few employees who are really committed to the effort. It's also important to stress the career benefits of engaging in public conversations. Although you don't always want to say it explicitly, the visibility enhances people's marketability both inside and outside the company.

Remember the "99:1" rule. Whether statistically valid or not, the accepted rule of thumb is that only about one percent of visitors to

Secret: A tiny percentage of your members will contribute most of the content.

public forums contribute 99 percent of the content (the dynamics are very different in private communities).

Forrester Research has estimated that only about a quarter of U.S. online adults are what the firm calls "creators" or "critics:" in other words, people who actively author or comment upon online information. Nearly half are characterized as "spectators" or "inactives," meaning that they contribute nothing or don't even participate. Author Clay Shirky has observed this in wiki environments, where he notes that the number one contributor is about twice as active as the number two contributor, three times as active as number three contributer and so on. Don't be rattled by this. Most people come to open forums through search queries and only stay long enough to get their questions answered. The one percent who do contribute actively are your MVPs, and they deserve as many favors as you can throw at them.

Involve the people who actually make the products. Online discussions are just as useful for feedback on existing products as they are for identifying new opportunities. Developers and engineers have to tune in. This isn't easy. Engineers often believe that they know better than customers what the market needs.

Once developers start listening to feedback, though, the effect becomes "intoxicating," says Communispace's Schlack. The Fiska-

Secret: Marketers do best when they get out of the way and let developers talk directly to their customers.

teers experience outlined at the beginning of Chapter 1, for example, completely changed the perspective of the company's engineers. It's thrilling to hear customers rave about a product, but there's also nothing like negative feedback to motivate developers to fix a problem. Companies can't respond effectively to feedback if market-ers are the only people listening.

Developer Serena Software institutionalized a practice it calls Facebook Fridays. The company's 900 employees are encouraged to go to its group profile on Facebook and talk with customers. Serena also uses Facebook for hiring. "Students aren't going to go to a company where there is a huge wall where they can't communicate with anyone," a senior vice president told *Network World* magazine.

Don't be a control freak. Avoid the urge to dominate the discussion. If participants believe they can't talk freely, they'll run away. Forrester Research analyst Jeremiah Owyang cited control issues as the greatest obstacle businesses have to building successful communities in a February 2008 report. "Let go…and act more like a host than a policeman," he wrote on his blog.

However, not being a control freak doesn't mean giving up control entirely. Online communities are fragile things, and they can easily be co-opted by spammers and bullies. Many investment-oriented message boards, for example, are now dominated by loudmouths who beat their chests and pick fights with others. Ordinary investors have been scared away from these places. Many Usenet newsgroups are little more than spam buckets at this point. You don't want your brand to be associated with that. If you sense that extremists or spammers are trying to take over your community, step in and admonish them. If they do it again, block them. This is your turf on the Internet, after all.

Forrester Research tells of Procter & Gamble's experience with its Beinggirl site for teen girls, where teens were posting inappropriate comments. The company stepped in and started screening all comments. Prospective new members were required to read relevant articles before their membership was accepted. The quality of discourse improved dramatically after that, to the point that almost all posts are now user-generated.

> **Secret: Ask questions creatively; use photos, quizzes, and story-telling to address awkward or difficult topics.**

Be inventive with questions. Professional researchers know that people don't always say what they really think, even on anonymous surveys. Focus groups tend to be influenced by one or two outspoken members.

Quantitative surveys force respondents to choose responses that may not reflect their real opinions. These tools are valuable, but imperfect.

Sometimes you can get better response by asking indirect questions. GlaxoSmithKline used this approach when it was trying to get at self-image issues with overweight people, according to Communispace's Schlack. Community members were asked open-ended questions like, "When you talk to yourself, how do you refer to yourself?" and members were prompted to post photos showing what they most regretted about their obesity. Their choices indicated that people were frustrated about being excluded from everyday activities, a sentiment that Schlack believes would not have turned up so vividly on questionnaires.

On the other hand, sometimes it pays to be direct. When one Communispace client wanted to understand why African-Americans weren't using its products, the moderators recommended they just ask the question flat out. It worked. The difference? People often have trouble responding to abstract concepts and so need to use pictures or stories to relay their feelings. However, members of private communities in particular can be quite forthcoming when they believe their remarks will have an impact.

Close the feedback loop. The fastest way to strangle community interaction is to let ideas go unacknowledged. When a company representative requests feedback, she needs to respond to comments and promise action, even if that action is only to take the recommendations under consideration. This doesn't mean committing to implement ideas. People don't expect that. They do expect that their contributions will be taken seriously.

Involve C-level executives. The prospect of interacting with the chief officer of a company that community members care about is a powerful incentive to drive participation. If you're fortunate enough to have a top executive who believes in the value of these networks, convince her to log on once a quarter for a chat and promote that event to the community. For many CEOs, the opportunity to hear unvarnished customer feedback is invigorating.

Use incentives, but sparingly. If you're building a private network or a community of elite customers, small enticements like t-shirts, tchotchkes or even badges to display on their blogs can help make members feel like they're truly part of an inner circle. You don't need to go overboard. In fact, being too generous with incentives can make members feel pressured to contribute when they don't have much to say.

Involve members in product development. As cited in the sidebar to this chapter, customers can often be valuable sources of ideas for new products and markets. Acknowledge their contributions by citing them in press releases and advertising. Some companies have actually staged contests where members come up with new product ideas, with the winners having their contributions developed as products.

Mix it up. Good social networks use all the tools available to them: discussion, chat, webcast, video, photos, animation, podcasts, polls, games, and virtual worlds. People interact in different ways, so give them as many tools as you can. This stuff isn't all that expensive to develop any more. Much of it can be delivered by software-as-a-service providers or contracted offshore at low cost.

Customer-Assisted Development

In 2000, newly appointed Procter & Gamble CEO A. G. Lafley stunned the business world by announcing a bold goal: Half of all new P&G products and technologies would come from outside the company by 2010. As of this writing, P&G was more than halfway to its objective. Whether the company achieves the 50 percent target is inconsequential. Lafley legitimized what has become a hot new trend: outsourcing innovation to customers.

As documented in *We are Smarter than Me*, a 2007 book by Barry Libert and Jon Spector, the company has put its money where its mouth is:

P&G put together a global community made up of high-tech entrepreneurs and open networks such as NineSigma, and including the retired scientists and engineers of YourEncore and the marketplace for intellectual property exchange called Yet2.com. P&G has also gone to Innocentive, a network of 120,000 self-selected technical people from more than 175 countries who receive cash awards if their ideas prove out.

In seeking help from its extended community, P&G submits so-called "science problems" for solutions. Sometimes the problems come from in-house R&D, representing blind alleys those researchers have come up against. Sometimes the company asks its online partners for help in adapting a feature of a competitor's product to one of its own. The right answers have greatly benefited P&G. In the case of Innocentive, for example, a third of the dozens of problems posed have been solved. One crisp example of an early crowdsourcing triumph: When the company was stymied for a way to print messages on its Pringles potato chips, the development community found a bakery in Italy with a little-publicized process that could do the job.

As rising research and development costs challenge resource-strapped businesses, some are finding that by tapping into communities of highly engaged customers, they can come up with better ideas than they could develop internally.

Big companies are adopting this approach enthusiastically. Dell Computer has IdeaStorm, a website where people can submit their suggestions for new products and services and have them voted upon by others. As described by Forrester Research, "After barely three months of existence, the IdeaStorm website proudly reports the submission of more than 5,000 ideas, over 20,000 comments, and north of 350,000 idea endorsements. The site is such an overwhelming success for Dell that a staggering 100,000 people responded within days when the company took the bold step of announcing new machines running the open source operating system Linux, instead of Microsoft Windows."

Here are four companies that have turned customer inventions into profitable business:

Wash 'n Wear Innovation

Threadless, a Chicago-based clothing maker, epitomizes the culture of customer involvement. Founded in 2000 with $1,000 in seed money, the company invites visitors to submit their own T-shirt designs and pays prize money for entries that become products. The company was on track to sell $20 million worth of T-shirts in 2007.

Threadless effectively outsources its product development to a community of enthusiasts. Every week, six new designs are chosen from the roughly 700 entries submitted by customers. The community votes on the winners, who receive $2,000 for a winning design. The voting gives Threadless a kind of built-in market research panel and it seems to work. The company produces between 500 to 1,500 of each new design a week, at an average profit of more than $10 each.

The company is a master of community maintenance. Weekly winners are spotlighted on the Threadless website and an alumni club showcases past winners. Visitors can upload photos of themselves wearing the company's products and earn a discount credit, a brilliant marketing idea at almost no cost. A promotion called Street Team deputizes members to refer customers to the site and rewards store credits for every sale. The online store's language and design reflect the hip irreverence of the founders. A weekly newsletter goes out to nearly 400,000 customers, about three-quarters of whom read it, <u>according to a profile in Business 2.0</u>.

The Little Vacuum That Could

The Roomba was a milestone in its market. Released in 2002, it was the first successful robotic home appliance, a squat, disk-shaped vacuum cleaner than can be programmed to live under a sofa or in a corner, periodically emerge and vacuum a room, and then return to its charging station.

Developer iRobot Corp. of Burlington, Massachusetts, expected consumers to love their Roombas, but they didn't expect how much they would love them. So executives were surprised when customer service reps began reporting that customers were talking about the devices in the same language they used to talk about family pets. "Consumers were referring to them as 'he' or 'she,'" says Nancy Dussault, iRobot's VP of marketing. "Many had names for them."

Not only that, the Roomba had aroused the inventive spirit in some technically inclined customers. These customers had figured out how to hack into the robots, which were never designed for programmability, and teach them to perform stunts and play games. Videos began to show up online of people playing with their Roombas like they would with the family cat.

Some companies might have been alarmed by this development. Toyota, for example, has struggled with customer hacks that have hiked the mileage of its Prius automobiles to over 100 miles per gallon. But the engineering-driven iRobot had few of those liability or safety concerns. People there saw an opportunity, and iRobot took steps to encourage customer innovation.

The company contracted with SkinIt, a developer of designer covers for a variety of devices, to create a line of

Roomba Skins. More importantly, iRobot released a version of the Roomba engineered exclusively for developers. Customer inventions were showcased on a website and the company offered a $5,000 cash prize for the best ideas.

By harnessing the enthusiasm of a customer community, iRobot effectively outsourced part of its research and development. The company has recently introduced robots that clean pools and gutters, as well as take on heavy shop-floor dirt. It's even come out with a virtual visitor. When customer innovation is used well, the sky's the limit.

Bottled-Up Innovation

Sigg USA, a manufacturer of eco-friendly aluminum water bottles, used a social network to help with product design. Sigg makes containers that customers can reuse, instead of throwing plastic bottles into a landfill. The company wanted its customers to identify more closely with its products. Working with the Gold Group, a boutique social media marketing agency, it created a contest called "What Does Eco-Friendly Mean To You?" to challenge customers to create a new bottle design.

The agency targeted its promotions to eco-friendly specialty sites like Hugg, a Digg-like social bookmarking service for eco enthusiasts. It also bought a sponsorship at InHabitat, a community for design and architecture professionals with interests in eco-friendly trends. The presence on InHabitat was noticed by ecology bloggers, leading to more than 100 online mentions of the contest. This also improved search engine performance. Entries were judged by Sigg employees and people recruited from other eco-friendly brands like Patagonia.

Over 160 entries rolled in. The winner's design became part of the Sigg product line. "We got in the neighborhood of 8,000 to 9,000 unique visitors over a little less than two months," says Jeff Greene of Gold Group. "It may sound like small numbers, but it's such an engaged audience that they tell their friends."

Cashing in with Contests

Computer programmers love to write code and they take special pride in figuring out creative new ideas to solve problems or make programs run faster. Paradoxically, software developers are notoriously expensive to hire and retain, but they're more than willing to give away their best work for free.

TopCoder, a software development firm that does custom projects for big organizations, understands this, and it's turned to a growing community of participants in its programming forums to help it lower its costs and build its business.

The company runs regular contests in which members compete against the clock and each other to solve thorny programming problems. The contests have become so popular that today some generate more than 1,000 submissions. Cash prizes are awarded for the best solutions and some developers earn six-figure annual sums from the contests. TopCoder licenses the best ideas for use in its custom development projects at costs that are far below that of hiring full-time staff.

"We primed the pump with cash, but now it's about competition and maintaining ratings and rankings," says Rob Hughes, chief operating officer at TopCoder. "Contestants learn a lot and they become better at coding." Prominent contestants can leverage their success to land lucrative consulting assignments with other companies. Winning a TopCoder competition has become a resume item.

A key success factor has been tying contestants' achievements to personal online profiles. Member spaces include information on performance in past competitions and running point totals. TopCoder continues to run contests and award cash prizes. Special events challenge members to solve thorny algorithmic problems or create innovative website designs. The TopCoder Open is an annual live event in Las Vegas where programmers compete for $250,000 in prizes.

TopCoder now has a library of more than 1,100 reusable software components that it can deploy as needed for customer engagements. "We're at a point where the capacity to develop code is at a pace that outstrips out clients' needs," Hughes said. TopCoder has even run custom competitions for big technology companies. About 60 percent of the competitors come from outside the U.S., with Chinese and Eastern European developers doing particularly well.

The idea won't work in every industry. For example, lawyers and accountants usually aren't as generous with their ideas as programmers. But for people who are passionate about their work and who like basking in the light of peer recognition, TopCoder has mined a vein of community innovation.

Candid Conversations

Plop down in an airport gate area during a long flight delay and you'll invariably hear people begin to swap travel horror stories. Travel is an intensely personal experience for most people, and seemingly minor experiences—both good and bad—can affect customer loyalty.

That's one reason hospitality companies sweat the details. They know that the chocolates on the pillow or the free tube of toothpaste can turn a drive-by lodger into a loyal fan. Hotel chains use every type of market research to measure customer satisfaction, but traditional metrics have been weak at uncovering stories, which are the most powerful form of word-of-mouth marketing.

Hilton Hotels Corp. (HHC) understands the limitations of traditional research, but until about two years ago it had few ways to tap into those all-important client experiences. "We had done a lot of traditional qualitative research, such as ad testing and intercept interviews, but we'd never engaged in ongoing, vibrant three-way communication," says Christine Hight, HHC's director of customer research. The company's use of a full-service online community provider transformed its approach to measuring and understanding customer satisfaction. Company policy prohibits HHC from identifying the vendor.

The Hilton family's hospitality portfolio encompasses nine brands, ranging from the mid-scale, traveler-oriented Hampton chain to the luxury Waldorf-Astoria Collection line. Customers of each franchise have different needs, but they all have one thing in common, Hight says: "They enjoy talking to one another and to us."

Professional Help

Although initially cautious about the high fee structure for a full-service online community product—the provider not only hosts customer communities but actively manages them—the Hilton Family took the plunge on a test project in 2006. It turned out that the advice of professional moderators was useful. The community company's researchers helped recruit current guests, frame questions, jumpstart discussions and invent novel approaches to probing for information. Today, the insight gleaned from customer conversations underlies much of the traditional market research that the Hilton Family still uses.

One of those benefits is speed. Quantitative surveys and focus groups can take months to field and interpret. In contrast, customer conversations may materialize within minutes of a catalyst event. Hight cites the example of the Transportation Safety Administration's 2006 decision to ban liquids in carry-on airline baggage. The day the policy was announced, a member of the Hilton Family's 300-person community initiated a discussion. Comments quickly established that the ban was going to be a source of pain for frequent travelers. Hotels could help by providing items that were no longer allowed on flights as in-room amenities. Some members also pointed to accommodations already being made by Hilton's rivals. That was a valuable bit of competitive intelligence about a rapidly developing issue.

Hilton researchers regard community members as kind of a standing focus group that can be tapped by different brands for different reasons. Membership is controlled and profiled. In the spring of 2008, researchers added an enhancement that enables them to aim certain questions at female travelers, for example, or those who stay in both its business and luxury hotels. Members are awarded points in the Hilton HHonors affinity program, or an online gift certificate, but overall incentives are nominal.

Person-to-Person

Another unique characteristic of communities is peer-to-peer discussion. Hight notes that members frequently use the network to initiate their own conversations without prompting. But they can also be tapped for direct feedback on issues posed by the company. For example, when rival Marriott banned smoking in its hotels, a community member started a discussion on the issue the same day. Hilton asked members if its brands should follow suit. "Within 10 hours, we had a lot of feedback," she says. Hilton learned that while many guests would like to have a smoke-free hotel experience, others were concerned about smokers' rights and comfort. They raised questions about the possibility of alienating long-time loyal guests, and how a hotel could reasonably police such a policy. Using input from the community and other sources, Hilton Family decided not to establish a smoke-free policy in all its hotels, although it periodically revisits the issue.

There have been other benefits. In an effort to gain insights about the stays that guests book using Hilton HHonors points, the company asked members to upload pictures and descriptions from their recent reward stays. In another exercise, members were asked to share examples of pre-arrival communications they received for other products and services that they reserved in advance. "It was like a scavenger hunt for grown-ups and they enjoyed it," Hight says.

Hight offers the following tips for success, based on her nearly two years of experience:

• Think of it as qualitative research. Feedback from the community can be a useful foundation for quantitative surveys, but the value is different. Member stories can often be effective accents to statistical findings when used in executive presentations.

• Don't let the pool get too big. The strength of the community is its intimacy. If the Hilton Family follows through on a proposal to ramp up its customer group to about 400 people this year, it will probably also split the membership into smaller subgroups to keep conversations small and relevant.

• Listen and acknowledge. Members can be incredibly generous if they believe their comments are being taken seriously. Conversely, failure to respond can quickly alienate people. "We don't just ask a question; we often frame it in the context of decisions we're trying to make," Hight says.

• Make it a dialogue. Let members know what actions are being taken as a result of their input.

10

Basics of Social Media Content

At the Clutter Control Freak blog, you can find all kinds of useful ideas for organizing your home. One article offers a list of one-minute projects that can be done whenever you have a spare moment. Another tells how to rescue items from a junk drawer and make a wreath with them. A third offers tips for organizing a woman's purse.

Is this the work of a fastidious homemaker? A Martha Stewart wannabe? Actually, Clutter Control Freak is operated by Stacks & Stacks, a distributor of organization products for the home and business. Launched in August 2007, the site was drawing a healthy 1,500 daily visitors in just four months. Content is provided by a team of unpaid bloggers who contribute to the site in exchange for recognition and the occasional gift certificate. Visitors are encouraged to submit their own ideas and to vote on each other's contributions, with the winners picking up vouchers good for merchandise.

Clutter Control Freak is one of a series of successful blogs conceived by B. L. Ochman (see page 32), a New York-based social media marketing specialist. Her previous hit was EthicsCrisis.com, a site sponsored by SRF Global Translations that encouraged visitors to share anonymously their ethical transgressions for evaluation by other visitors.

Another project to promote a book called *Wife in the Fast Lane* asked people to complete the sentence, "I knew I was living in the fast lane when…" People submitted more than 750 one-liners, essays, and videos, ranging from hilarious to poignant (the winning one liner: "I looked down at the dog bowl on the floor to see it full of my two-year-old son's cereal, milk, and a spoon. I then looked at the breakfast table to see my son curiously tasting his 'breakfast.'"

All three efforts were runaway hits that cost nearly nothing in content development, Ochman says. In the case of the volunteer bloggers, "The incentive was to broaden their audience." EthicsCrisis "went viral," meaning that by the time the site had run its course and was discontinued in early 2007, nearly all of the content was coming from visitors. By that time the blog had racked up more than 850 links on Google for SRF, a company that previously had no Web presence at all.

Secret: Even bland content can be made interesting if approached in an original way.

An Overlooked Essential

Content is undeniably the most important element of a successful social media campaign, yet it is one of the most mysterious and least understood. With the Internet unleashing a torrent of free content, it is increasingly difficult to come up with creative and sustainable campaigns. Business blogs are full of mundane, undifferentiated, or impenetrable prose that could often be made more compelling simply by changing the approach.

If businesses put more thought into what they were going to say before they started talking, they would reduce their staff workload, improve search engine and inbound link traffic, and have more fun. With millions of blogs and hundreds of social networks already established, distinctive content is vital. As we'll see in a moment, this isn't as difficult as it may seem.

Should You Bother with Social Media?

Before you start to use social media channels at all, you need to decide if that's a good idea in the first place. For some businesses, it isn't. Not everyone is online-savvy. Large swaths of the population barely even know how to conduct a Google search, much less join a Facebook group. While the majority of citizens in most developed countries are online, fewer than 1 percent of them have ever posted content to a blog, discussion group, or social network. Of those people who use the Internet to make buying decisions, most go online for research or to consummate a transaction they've already decided to make. Your social media efforts will probably miss this audience entirely, which means that if those are the people you're seeking, you'll be wasting your time.

So the first step is to understand your audience and objective so you can decide whether social media will work. In some markets, such as personal finance, technology, automotive, entertainment, and consumer packaged goods, there is already ample evidence that bloggers and online communities are important sources of influence. You need to be there.

In other markets, though, you may be able to wait. Heavy industry, agriculture, manufacturing, and some b-to-b markets have considerably less active online cultures. It pays to check, however. Recently I did some work for a client in the trucking industry. I expected to find a few online influencers for them to watch, but I was surprised to discover that truckers are actually very active bloggers. Apparently the long hours on the road give them plenty of time to think and to unload when they get to their computers!

What's the Objective?

Let's assume you've decided that social media marketing has value. Your choices now range from influencing bloggers to starting your own community. You need to work backwards from your objective. In some cases, that's easy; you want to make a sale. Often, though, it isn't that simple. Few people purchase cars or houses online, so a more realistic objective for an automotive manufacturer or real estate agent might be to convince a customer to join a mailing list or request a call. People don't make college enrollment decisions online, either, so a college admissions director might set out to encourage a prospective student to download an application or set up a call with a recruiter.

The following are some possible objectives of your online campaign:

- Make a sale
- Request a sales contact
- Request more information

- Download an informational white paper
- Download product specs
- Create awareness of a new product
- Renew awareness of an existing product
- Identify new prospects
- Inform existing customers of an upgrade
- Create or alter a brand image
- Counteract negative publicity
- Deposition a competitor
- Generate advertising revenue
- Raise awareness with investors
- Raise awareness with the media

Each of these goals demands a somewhat different content strategy. A blog, for example, can be an effective way to create awareness or brand image, counteract negative publicity, or to deposition a competitor. However, it may not be as effective for driving sales as, say, a contest which takes players to a landing page with special "winner" discounts.

Many social media are flexible enough to adapt to many objectives, depending on how you deploy them. For example, social networks can be used for brand-building if the members are given an educational or entertaining experience. But they may also be used to generate leads or even sales if activity in the network is linked to offers.

Campaigns may also tie together multiple social media channels to reach buyers at different stages of the process. A YouTube video may be the hook that brings buyers to a page where they can download information. A video series may address buyers at different stages of the buying cycle. Some may actually contain incentives or rewards for completing the series.

Content strategies are all about understanding who you're trying to reach and at what stage in the buying process. This also drives the promotional channels you use. In many cases, you'll want to have several different classes of content to reach buyers at different stages of the buying process. You need to create different content, keywords, and promotional strategies to reach each group.

For example, a new product announcement may contain details that are mainly of interest to existing customers, or it may target a larger audience of people who are interested in that category in general but who haven't yet made a decision. The content and the promotion strategy differ with either approach.

This book doesn't attempt to cover search engine marketing, a vast topic with which all marketers should have at least a working familiarity. *Search Engine Marketing, Inc.* by Mike Moran and Bill Hunt is an exhaustive reference in this area that should be on every online marketer's bookshelf.

What Is "Going Viral"?

The pinnacle of social media marketing success is considered to be a campaign that "goes viral." This means that the promotion—which is usually, though not necessarily, visual—takes on a life of its own, spread by e-mail forwards, blogger links, and shared bookmarks. Several of the campaigns spotlighted in this book have achieved such greatness, including Eepybird's Diet Coke/Mentos experiments, Jonah Peretti's Nike sweatshop story cited in Chapter 1, and Blendtec's "Will it Blend?" (Diet Coke and Blendtec are profiled in detail following Chapter 13.)

Marketers and academics vigorously debate the question of whether it's possible to design a campaign to go viral. No one has figured it out yet, and I don't personally believe anyone ever will. There are too many factors at play and the very definition of the phenomenon is debatable. In my view, the issue isn't one of viral perfection, but rather using word-of-mouth to achieve maximum reach at low cost.

In theory, a message or story goes viral when one person tells, on average, at least two other people about it. This creates exponential growth which can reach a very large number of people in a short time. If each person tells exactly two others, then by the 20th telling, more than a half million people will have heard the news. That number rises to nearly 17 million by the 25th telling.

The real world doesn't work that way, though. Some people may pass along the message to six others while other people don't pass it along at all. Or, each person may pass along the message to less than one other person on average, resulting in a message chain that eventually dies out. I don't see why this should be a disappointment. A viral chain that spreads by only 1.5 people per telling still reaches 2,200 people after 20 cycles and nearly 17,000 after 25. It isn't technically viral, but it isn't bad, either.

A theory proposed by influencer contrarian Duncan Watts (see page 64) is that viral marketing works best when given an occasional push by conventional marketing. Periodically revising a classic campaign can spark a new wave of contagion. The program may never achieve viral nirvana, but the jump-start is quick and fairly cheap. If you've had a winner at some point, it doesn't hurt to dust it off now and then and remind people of why it was so good.

The fastest way to narrow down the long list of options is to decide what the objectives are for each buyer and each stage of the process. Modularize your campaign to keep it manageable.

Secret: You're a publisher now. Think like one.

Old Habits

Social media marketing demands a different approach to customer interactions, one that stresses engagement over interruption. Traditional marketing relied on intercepting the customer, usually when they were doing something else, and attempting to deliver a grabby message. This hit-or-miss approach emphasizes brevity and catchiness: the "elevator pitch," tied to the free trial. It works for catching attention, but it has no staying power. Social media content should combine the best of the elevator pitch with a dialog that is sustainable and interactive. These latter skills are more characteristic of publishers than of marketers, but if you're going to succeed in social media, you can't think of yourself as just a marketer any more.

This point is absolutely essential: *In order to succeed in social media, you must think of yourself as a publisher.* This is, in my opinion, the single greatest disruptive effect of the new Internet. Anyone can now be a publisher, which means that successful practitioners must learn from the tactics that publishers have used to engage their audiences for more than 200 years.

Here are some of the secrets of publishing:

- Identify an audience that has a compelling and ongoing need for information and money to spend.
- Develop a distinctive voice and authority about one or more topics that are of compelling interest to that group.
- Stay relentlessly focused on the needs of the audience and advocate for the interests of that audience. Keep marketing messages separate and distinct.
- Seek continuous feedback on how you're doing at meeting the audience's needs.
- Continually adjust content to meet changing needs.
- Be consistent and persistent. Authority takes time to develop.

That last bullet point can be dispiriting for marketers who are trained to think in terms of short-term campaigns and immediate results. If you're going to do this right, however, you need to take a long-term view. Remember that publishing is one of the most sustainable businesses on the planet. When you think of the number of publishing brands that have lasted for more than 50 years, you can see the value of doing this right.

Secret: Engage, don't sell.

Ditch the Pitch

The first thing you need to do is stop pitching. Not only are customers no longer listening, they're sneering at sales pitches. The new style of marketing is about engagement, and that means throwing out the elevator pitch and the 30-second spot. It means forming a relationship with a prospect through the exchange of useful, meaningful information. It's about forming relationships that lead to long-term repeat business as opposed to making a sale. Long-term relationships invariably pay off better than one-off transactions.

Pitches are hard to give up. They're comfortable and we know how they work. For many years, we've crafted pitches with the knowledge that even though they were ungodly expensive, we could at least get a reasonably predictable response.

But today, customers are not only good at screening out pitches, but they're sarcastic and cynical about sound bites as well. As Joseph Jaffe, author of *Life After the 30-Second Spot* points out, today you aren't guaranteed of getting 30 seconds with the customer, but you have the chance to get hours.

It's hard to ditch the 30-second pitch, but the new economics have made it essential. Communications with the customer isn't expensive any more, so we no longer have to compress message into sound bites constrained by economics. In remarking on the fact that Google, which does no advertising at all, is nevertheless the world's most powerful brand, Umair Haque wrote:

> *For the economics of an industrial era, branding made sense. Interaction was expensive—so information about the expected benefits of consumption had to be squeezed into slogans, characters, and logos, which were then compressed into thirty-second TV ads and radio spots. The complex promise of a Corvette, for example, was compressed into shots of cute girls, open roads, and lots of sunshine.*

But cheap interaction turns the tables. The cheaper inter-action gets, the more connected consumers can talk to each other—and the less time they have to spend listening to the often empty promises of firms.

In fact, when interaction is cheap, the very economic ratio-nale for orthodox brands actually begins to implode. Informa-tion about expected costs and benefits doesn't have to be com-pressed into logos, slogans, ad-spots or column-inches—instead, consumers can debate and discuss expected costs and benefits in incredibly rich detail.

In other words, many of our assumptions about marketing and ad-vertising are based on the assumption that it's almost impossible to get the customer's attention, so you'd better sell hard while you have the chance. To create content for social media, you need to first reject these traditional marketing assumptions.

There's nothing about social media marketing that we don't al-ready know. It's merely the art of conversation and relationship-build-ing taking to a new medium. You have all the tools, but you need to think differently.

Think of the new form of engagement in terms of a cocktail party. When you arrive, you might know just a few people in the room. You greet and chat with your friends and they eventually introduce you to new people. Your first contact with these new acquaintances may be awkward, but in most cases you eventually find common ground and strike up a conversation.

We all know the rules of good conversation. It needs to be a back-and-forth in which both parties contribute. Good conversations are about respect and people helping each other. They're about active lis-tening and feeding back and building trust. We all know how we feel when we meet someone who only wants to talk about himself. We call that person an asshole. It's impossible to have a discussion with someone like that. Yet many of our traditional marketing principles are grounded in that very approach.

Here's a soapbox sermon based on personal experience. For two years, part of my business has been creating custom webcasts and podcasts for technology marketers. These events were basically discussions structured in a Q&A format, and they were the perfect opportunity for conversation marketing. I recorded more than 100 of these events during a two-year period.

Most marketers I worked with understood that these conversations were intended to convey useful information to the listener, yet a surprising number still used the opportunity to deliver sales pitches. They invoked ambiguous superlatives and sound bites as if that were expected. They used meaningless terms like "state of the art" and "leading edge," which mean nothing to anybody. At times, it was almost embarrassing. If they could have put themselves in the customer's shoes, they could have perhaps understood how silly they sounded. But I don't believe that thinking like the customer was part of their job description.

In the two years I worked on those programs, not a single customer set up a place to invite customer commentary or feedback. The objective was to get the customer to download a white paper and drop a lead. It was just more one-way conversation.

Secret: Plan for success. Think of how you'll handle a surge of traffic and discussion.

Campaign Basics

Think long-term. Engagement takes time, so marketers have to start thinking past the 30-second spot and the 13-week campaign. Very few social media campaigns will be successful in the first 13 weeks, even if there are ready-made audiences available. On TV, you can hit 50 million viewers with one ad during the Super Bowl. Online, you have to build audiences by word-of-mouth, search-engine performance, e-mail promotion, and what bloggers call "link love." A successful campaign may run for years. At the very least, plan on a one-year horizon.

Maggie Fox learned this lesson the hard way. Her young agency had taken on a campaign by Harlequin Publishing to promote the horror novel *Blood Ties*. Her agency built a MySpace group that generated quite a following. Until the 14th week. That's when the budget ran out, new content wasn't generated and the program's momentum ground to a halt. "It just faded," says Fox. "The content dried up and there was no one tasked with ongoing engagement."

Successful campaigns require care and feeding to make them self-sufficient. The good news is that a popular community site may run for a long time with little need for additional creative content. But even then, it's important that the host make occasional appearances to remind people that their contributions are appreciated. Visitors may even come to anticipate new installments, so you don't want to disappoint them.

OfficeMax ran a holiday campaign called ElfYourself in 2006 and again in 2007. Visitors were invited to invent their own versions of the company's holiday elf mascot. Traffic more than quadrupled the second year as the promotion went viral. In six weeks, the site had over 193 million visits and over 123 million elves were created. OfficeMax was ready. The 2006 campaign had created advance buzz that OfficeMax was unable to satisfy, a spokesman told MediaPost. "We received millions of hits to a dead site before launch." The next year, OfficeMax had the program ready as it launched an off-line campaign that included in-store displays and placement in a print catalog. The secret, an agency spokesman said: Keep it simple, make it personal, and give people a reason to pass it on.

Photo galleries can be almost self-sustaining. Shoe maker Converse encourages customers to upload photos of the company's Chucks sneakers to a community website. Activity was still brisk more than a year after launch, with little promotion or attention from Converse. Communities that need no care and feeding provide very good ROI indeed.

Search engine performance is central. If you're older than about age 25, you probably completed high school before using a search engine. You were probably taught some tricks for effective writing: Use catchy titles, start with an anecdote, incorporate elements of surprise, and learn how to turn a phrase. It's all good advice, but it's all completely useless in a search-driven world.

Secret: Optimize everything for search. Search engines don't appreciate a well-turned phrase. They compare queries with information they collect from crawling the Web and deliver the results that match most closely. Period. It's boring and mechanical. It's also incredibly effective.

Consider the headline that ran on the front page of *The Boston Globe* (and online at Boston.com) when the Red Sox won the 2007 World Series: "The Best!" Now consider another approach: "Red Sox Sweep Colorado Rockies to Win 2007 World Series." Which headline is going to perform better on a Google query for "Red Sox 2007 world championship?" Like it or not, the second, much more boring headline is far more effective. We'll look at search in more detail in the next chapter.

Online marketing won't work if people can't find your content, but many marketers do a lousy job of maximizing discoverability. This often torpedoes corporate blogging initiatives. Companies conceive of a good idea and generate internal enthusiasm, but contributors don't write in the terms their customers use. They don't tag or cross-promote or submit their work to recommendation engines. Results disappoint and contributors lose interest. The easiest part of creating a blog is the most often overlooked.

Google rarely discusses its proprietary search algorithm, but in an April 2008 interview in *Popular Mechanics,* Udi Manber, Google's vice president in charge of search quality gave some clues:

> *I wish people would put more effort into thinking about how other people will find them and putting the right keywords onto their pages. The content provider should think about how users will look for their content...Very often people make the mistake of using a search engine as if they are talking to another person. They use all sorts of words that a person will understand, but are not going to be in the content they are searching for. You should think about what you expect to see in the actual page and search for that.*

By "think about how users will look for their content," Manber is advising businesses to put themselves in their customers' shoes. Don't think of how you want your customers to find you; think of how they are most likely to find you. These are the keywords to use.

Secret: Basic search strategies aren't complex or expensive to master.

As was mentioned earlier, *Search Engine Marketing, Inc.* by Mike Moran and Bill Hunt (IBM Press, 2006) does a fantastic job of unraveling the mystery of how search engines work. Blogs like Search Engine Watch and Dosh Dosh also provide a steady stream of advice and news about this topic.

The fine points of search engine performance can encompass volumes, but the essential element is to use the language that customers use. This seems simple enough, but it actually goes against the grain of the way many marketers work. We are taught to use vague descriptors like "market-leading," "best-of-breed," and "breakthrough," which are words that have little meaning to customers. In fact, I guarantee you no customer of yours has ever searched Google looking for a "breakthrough" product.

All online marketing content, regardless of format, should incorporate terms that customers use in search engines. This means writing in simple, declarative language with lots of facts and few meaningless modifiers. It doesn't mean that you can't be creative and have fun, but somewhere in that text, preferably near the top, you need the right keywords.

Content should also capture customers at different stages of the buying cycle, or what the authors of *Search Engine Marketing, Inc.* call "primary demand" and "selective demand." They cite the example of a company that makes snow blowers. A primary demand customer is someone who doesn't yet know that she needs a snow blower. She might search on terms like *snow removal* or even *snow shovel*. The snow blower maker needs content that will match these terms.

A selective demand customer knows that she wants to buy a snow blower but doesn't know which features or brands to look for. She might query on *snow blowers* or *best snow blowers*. The company needs content for these searches, too.

"Studies show that searchers tend to click a result that contains the exact query words in its title and snippet," the authors say. That seems intuitive enough. But are you creating content that way?

Author David Meerman Scott loves to beat the drum on this point. In 2007, he took a good-natured stab at dramatizing the pointlessness of PR-speak with "The Gobbledygook Manifesto," an analysis of press releases that looked for common, yet meaningless, superlatives such as "flexible," "robust," "world class," "scalable," and "easy to use." He partnered with Dow Jones' Factiva service to analyze 388,000 press releases and discovered that nearly 20 percent of them contained one or more of the offending words. These releases were intended for journalists (who don't read them, anyway) but totally missed the much bigger opportunity to pick up customers using Google. He wrote:

> The worst gobbledygook offenders seem to be business-to-business technology companies. For some reason, marketing people at technology companies have a particularly tough time explaining how products solve customer problems. Because these writers don't understand how their products solve customer problems, or are too lazy to write for buyers, they cover by explaining myriad nuances of how the product works and pepper this blather with industry jargon that sounds vaguely impressive. What ends up...is a bunch of talk about "industry-leading" solutions that purport to help companies "streamline business process," "achieve business objectives," or "conserve organizational resources." Huh?

Much of the gobbledygook problem can be resolved by eliminating superlatives. What, exactly, makes a product "industry leading"? How, precisely, does the product help "achieve business objectives"? How many person-years of effort went into this "groundbreaking" technology? Spending a little more time with the people who built the product or defined the need for it usually unearths these gems. It will certainly make your words more compelling.

The point is that in the new world, human beings no longer make all the decisions about what information people can consume. Increasingly, search engines fulfill that role, working from words that the information consumers themselves specify. Google doesn't fundamentally distinguish between an article you write and an article in *The New York Times*. The best way to take advantage of that great level playing field is to use the terms your customers use. Consider the following ideas:

> **Secret: Google is the great equalizer. You are potentially as important a source as *The New York Times*.**

Make it human. Good writing is conversational. It uses terms like "I" and "you" and speaks in declarative terms. Most corporate communications organizations aren't trained to talk that way. Their communications are cleansed of personality in favor of a detached third-party dialect. That works okay for a 10-Q statement, but not when the name and face of the author appears alongside the content. When you talk to your constituents online, write like a person.

> **Secret: Write like you speak. Dictation software is a good way to create blog entries.**

Social media is, after all, social. People don't talk in passive voice or third person when they're having conversations, so don't do it when the conversations are online. If it helps, speak your words into a voice recognition program and then go back and polish them later. I wrote much of this book that way.

Having a conversation doesn't mean giving up power. Joseph Carrabis, founder of *NextStage Evolution* and the author of more than 20 books on customer behavior, tells how you can keep the upper hand in a conversation without doing all the talking. His advice seems counter-intuitive. By giving up some control, he argues, you actually gain credibility. His secrets are listed in the accompanying box.

> **Secret: Giving up control is the best way to keep the upper hand in a conversation.**

"Power in the blogosphere is about respect. It's about a healthy social setting," Carrabis says.

Joseph Carrabis' Secrets of Conversation:

☞ Give credit where it's due

☞ Admit your mistakes

☞ Be honest

☞ Lead the discussion

☞ Explain everything

☞ Recognize other people's authority and experience

☞ Accept chastisement graciously

☞ Never argue

☞ Be willing to learn

☞ Encourage the discussion

☞ Never cover up

For proof, just look at the work of social media scions like Robert Scoble and Steve Rubel. Their blogs are full of links and acknowledgements of the contributions of other bloggers. Yet they have tremendous authority in their fields. Their influence results from credibility, which is an outgrowth of their respect for other people's expertise.

Be passionate, or at least committed. You need commitment because otherwise you'll run out of things to talk about. Believe it or not, this happens a lot. People launch a blog or podcast series because they feel strongly about a topic but then discover that there's only so much they can say about it. If your topic is too specific, this is a risk. Look for themes that spark passion in others and that generate a steady stream of new material from the news media.

Secret: Find topics that inspire passion. Choose passionate people to lead the campaign.

Passion doesn't necessarily mean products; it can also be conceptual. Abstract themes like beauty, simplicity, color, health, or greatness can be the foundation of great programs that involve employees and customers. Wells Fargo chose San Francisco history as the theme for a blog and podcast series. It shares a passion for its city with a large number of customers. Dell chose green computing for a blog and sponsored a Facebook group. Coca-Cola's first blog was written by the company archivist, who's passionate about documenting the history of the company.

No matter what you decide to do in social media, find someone with passion to lead the charge. Otherwise, you will be at risk of looking contrived, and nothing can kill a campaign faster.

A Worthy Cause Makes Business Sense

Small specialty retailer Annansi has learned that social media + worthy cause = business success. Annansi makes clothing that invokes African culture, even though the products are made in Brooklyn. Founder G. Kofi Annan (no relation to the U.N. General Secretary of the same name) emigrated from the African continent 20 years ago. Annan is proud of his heritage, and he found that U.S. clothiers didn't have styles that expressed that same degree of pride.

Annan started making his own clothing, first for himself and then for sale. He also tapped in to blogging, online video, and social networks to talk about African culture. His Annansi Chronicles blog presents "the African point of view" on topical issues, he says. Annan wasn't trying to promote the business. Things just turned out that way.

"Most of my clothing has a story behind it," he says. "I started Annansi Chronicles to record conversations and research. People started coming to the site to read the African point of view. They'd go to the About Us page and learn more about the company."

One of Annan's causes was "Bling is Dead," a campaign to dissuade people from buying diamonds from companies that exploited African miners. He created logo clothing and a MySpace page to promote the cause and partnered with a musician and filmmaker on an art video. "It showed that we're about more than just being fashionable or trendy," he says.

Annansi's clothing website is a far cry from the standard retail fare. Its simple home page features a black-and-white art video of a handsome, young black man. "We shot the video to show what the African experience abroad is about," Annan says. "It shows a distinct identity of who our customer is and how they would use the clothing in everyday life."

Annansi is a small company; sales were about $300,000 in 2007, but business is growing briskly. Annan has never spent money on marketing. He can't afford to. "There was no way we could have built our brand without the website and interactive tools," he says. "We gave people a message and just watched everything happen. Not enough companies engage with people after they make first contact."

11

Picking Your Spots

The next two chapters will explore the finer points of content: how to express yourself in words and images. We'll then briefly touch on the new opportunities that social media has opened in the area of contests, games, and reviews. These chapters should help you decide how choose a topic and communicate about it with clarity.

I'll deal with words at some length because 20 years of writing and managing writers has taught me a lot about the craft. I've also taken and edited enough photographs to have an appreciation for visual expression. The finer points of video production and programming are best taught by others, but I'll pass along wisdom that experts have shared with me.

No matter what medium you use, there are five essential considerations in creating distinctive content: *Objective*, *Topic*, *Voice*, *Approach*, and *Medium*. Let's look at each in turn.

Objective

We noted in Chapter 2 that a business objective should precede selection of a communications tool. The same goes for developing content. Is your objective to raise awareness of your company? Highlight a problem your prospects don't know they have? Generate sales leads? Address a customer perception problem? Support existing customers? Build channel awareness? Your content may run the gamut from funny to authoritative to skeptical to hip to sympathetic depending on the objective of the campaign. The same tool may be used to achieve different purposes depending on this factor.

For example, let's look at three very different uses of blogs:

• Microsoft used blogs to fight an image problem: It has long been widely perceived as a ruthless corporate predator. In

2004, it began hosting employee blogs (it has more than 5,000 of them today) and a video archive called Channel 9. Both initiatives exposed talented individuals within the company and helped establish Microsoft as interesting, approachable, and fun. In this case, the blogs were used to make the company appear more human. As none of Microsoft's top executives were bloggers, Microsoft wanted to take the spotlight off its top executives and train it on the thousands of people who built, sold, and maintained the company's products.

• The American Society for the Prevention of Cruelty to Animals (ASPCA) needed to grow membership. The company knew that each new registrant on its website was worth about $25 in donations, and it used its blog effectively in 2007 to drive registration numbers. That was a big year for animal cruelty stories, unfortunately. There was a large recall of Chinese pet food and a dog-fighting scandal involving Atlanta Falcons quarterback Michael Vick. The ASPCA discovered that it could use its blog to convey frequent commentary and advice on both topics. By educating its target audience, the ASPCA enhanced its authoritativeness. Traffic spiked, and so did memberships.

• General Motors was fighting the image of being slow-moving and out-of-step with trends in its markets. Executives felt the company wasn't getting a fair shake in the media and that its message was being filtered by biased influencers. The new GM Fastlane blog takes the automaker's message directly to its constituents. It highlights cutting-edge work being done in the development labs and GM's commitment to energy conversation and environmental causes. It has been enormously successful in reinvigorating GM's public image.

In each of these cases, and in dozens more like them, the programs worked because the companies had clear goals in mind. On the flip side, companies that launch social media campaigns, because the CEO or VP of marketing thinks it's a great idea, almost never succeed. If the business goal isn't defined and employees are coerced into participating in a project that has no relevance to them, their contributions will reflect their confusion and disinterest. Or worse, people will actively undermine the whole effort.

Topic

In my days as a chief editor, I often worked with a wonderful journalism coach named Don Fry. Don has a gift for coaching young reporters, who often get bogged down in the minutiae of their work at the expense of the big picture. One of Don's favorite questions is "What's the story *about*?" It seems a simple enough request, but it can stop journalists dead in their tracks. They're so busy assembling facts that they've lost sight of what they're trying to say.

Secret: Post a picture of a typical member of your audience on your office wall. Repeatedly remind yourself of that person's information needs to keep yourself on track.

If this question baffles professional journalists, it's no wonder that marketers have the same difficulty. They can become so lost in the details of execution that they forget what the business purpose was in the first place.

Focus is the key to success in any content initiative. Lose track of your audience's needs and your own objectives and your campaign runs off the rails. The Internet seems to be overrun with people talking about nearly everything, but that's actually not the case. Some topics are heavily covered—entertainment, sports, health, the environment, etc.—but some very large markets actually have little activity. For example, the data-mining software business is a multibillion-dollar industry, yet there are only a handful of regularly maintained blogs about the topic. You can find many blogs about civil engineering, but almost none of them are active. With the right topic focus, you can become prominent in your field very quickly.

Selecting a topic is a matter of balancing the needs of the audience, available information, and your own comfort level. Just because there is a lot of activity in a particular topic area doesn't mean opportunities don't exist. If you

Secret: Even popular topics can be addressed distinctively by varying voice, approach, and medium.

combine the five essential elements in the right way, you can almost always carve out a niche.

Pick a subject that you know a lot about and then start searching to see who else is out there. If there's a lot of competition, start narrowing your options. Your goal shouldn't be to identify an area that's completely uncovered (you'll actually want to reach out to other people for ideas and reciprocal links) but to stake out a niche where you can spread your wings and find an audience without running out of things to say. Don't be disappointed if your initial searches turn up a lot of other options. You may discover that those sites are infrequently updated or even abandoned. In fact, if lightly tended sites perform well in your search results, it's probably an even better opportunity for you.

Even crowded markets have attractive niches. Take marketing, for example. It's one of the busiest topics of conversation, so you need to specialize. Perhaps your opportunity is in direct marketing, e-mail marketing, viral marketing, or marketing to certain verticals. Or you could specialize in customer research, website design, user interaction, or marketing careers. There are plenty of ways to approach the market if you come at it from an angle rather than head on.

A topic should be a starting point and not a pair of handcuffs. As you start engaging with your audience, you will find that certain subjects evoke a stronger response than others. Let those be your guide. The focus of your blog, podcast, or community may be entirely different six months after you start, and there's nothing wrong with that as long as the guidance comes from the people you're trying to reach.

Secret: Choosing a distinctive voice is the single most important element in differentiating content.

Voice

In my opinion, voice is the single most critical element to publishing success. It's a mix of style, variety, media, personal style, and attitude. It can help you stand out even in a market that's full of competitors. TechCrunch, for example, was a late entrant to a market that was stuffed with blogs about Silicon Valley companies. But it displayed a unique voice: a combination of hip insiderism and smooth confidence. That, combined with the fact that blogger Michael Arrington is an insightful and prolific writer, enabled it to burst out of nowhere to become a major media outlet.

Voice may be unique to an individual or an organization. In the case of a site with multiple contributors, voice should persist even as employees come and go. A voice is like a personality, and it is an essential part of your social media appeal.

Voice is a matter of personal style, but it works best when it reflects the values of an organization. Take Woot.com, for example. This quirky retailer, which sells just one product each day, communicates with customers largely through a blog, podcast, and FAQ page. Its voice is playful, iconoclastic, and even sarcastic. "If you buy something you don't end up liking or you have what marketing people call 'buyer's remorse,' sell it on eBay," the site says. "It's likely you'll make money doing this and save everyone a hassle." This voice wouldn't work for everyone, but it meshes well with Woot's cyberpunk audience. It says, in effect, "We're so busy saving you money that we can't take the time to be nice." But it says it with a wink.

Many marketers struggle with issues of voice. After all, they've grown up in the homogenized language of press releases and annual reports. This corporatespeak may be appropriate for institutional investors, but it doesn't work very well in conversations. Since social media is all about people, establish a voice that sounds like speech.

A good example of this is the blog written by danah boyd, a Ph.D. student at Berkeley. Boyd has written extensively about social media in academic papers, using the weighty, authoritative tone that those documents require. Yet **Secret: Humanize the social media experience. Write in personal terms. Tell stories.** her blog reads like a conversation: informal and spontaneous. One subtle tactic she uses is to write mostly in lower-case, a mark of nonconformity that's also a back-handed tribute to the style of the Internet. Boyd walks the line between her twin roles as researcher and blogger with great success.

Social media is an opportunity to break ranks with the buttoned-down voice with which most businesses communicate, and it can be even more effective when the contrast with the corporate style is incongruous.

A good example of this is IBM, which used a series of humorous videos that it had originally prepared for internal sales meetings and then posted them on YouTube. "Mainframe: Art of the Sale" features Bob Hoey, the head of IBM's mainframe sales operation, spouting tired clichés and inane sales wisdom with straight-faced earnestness while a tiny crew of sales reps go door-to-door in search of customers. "You have to make sure the customer knows what you said, even if you don't," Hoey deadpans in one scene.

The sheer silliness of the IBM video series may seem baffling, but Hoey had an objective. "We need to…grow out this mainframe platform, which means reaching out to a whole new set of people who may not know the mainframe value proposition," he told *IBM Systems* magazine. "I'm talking about the university students…What we've tapped into…is a valuable resource for finally reaching a younger audience who may not know what a mainframe is and saying, 'hey, the mainframe is still here, it's interesting, and, yes, fun.'"

The program has worked. The first three videos did so well that IBM added six more programs that have logged more than 450,000 downloads on YouTube and a bouquet of positive publicity. Traffic to its mainframe blog grew tenfold and visits to the mainframe section of the IBM website doubled. One reason the series worked so well is that people couldn't believe that such a buttoned-down company could be so playful. The voice was interesting because it was so unexpected.

This doesn't mean that your voice needs to be humorous. It's perfectly all right to take a thoughtful, serious approach when attempting to position yourself or your employees as an authority on a topic. Keep the voice consistent, even if there are multiple contributors involved. And don't neglect the personal angle. Anecdotes, travel notes, and snapshots do a lot to personalize the experience for readers.

I recommend that you document your voice as clearly as possible. Bloggers and community moderators will come and go, but an organization's voice should be fixed and consistent. This document should also be useful in explaining your strategy to journalists.

Approach

Approach is really about packaging. The angle you take when creating any kind of content can make a huge difference in readership. The more provocative your approach, the more appealing your topic will be and the larger the audience

Secret: Magazines in the supermarket checkout line are an excellent example of how to package and promote content.

you'll draw. Much of this is just common sense. Go stand in a supermarket checkout aisle and look at the magazines on the rack. The editors of these publications excel at writing headlines that make you want to take that magazine home with you. You can apply the same principles to your own content.

Let's say you're trying to market a service that helps people better organize their tax records. You want to package the content to reach a consumer audience. Which of the following approaches do you think will work best?

- The Evils Of Disorganization: How Poor Record-Keeping Is Costing Americans Billions In Lost Taxes
- 10 Hidden Tax Savings You Probably Don't Know About
- Mining Gold From Paper: Uncovering Hidden Deductions On Your Tax Return
- Tax-Saving Tips From the Experts
- Organize Your Way to Tax Savings
- Tax-Saving Secrets the IRS Doesn't Want You to Know
- How Much Can You Save On Your Taxes? Take This Simple Test and Find Out.

There is no right answer to this question. Each of these approaches can work for different audiences and situations. A package that works for an individual taxpayer may fall flat for an audience of certified public accountants. The secret is to align your message with the audience you are trying to reach and then deliver on that promise.

That last point is important. We've all had the experience of responding to a sexy headline and then discovering that the article contained no useful information. Piquing your audience's interest and then delivering mismatched content is worse than never getting the audience's attention in the first place.

There's no big mystery to figuring out what approaches work. Think about what makes you stop and take notice. Top 10 lists, little-known facts, counterintuitive wisdom, human stories, contests, advice that speaks to people's pain points, and interesting people are all good attention-getters. The editors of women's magazines probably do this better than anyone. Their business success depends on grabbing their audience in the few seconds of attention that they might get in a supermarket checkout line.

If your culture permits it, do something outrageous. In his book, *Marketing to the Social Web*, Larry Weber tells the story of Genmar Industries, which makes boats that are known for their toughness. Genmar's ad agency got the idea of hitching a boat to the back of a trailer and dragging it through backcountry roads, slamming it against trees. Naturally, the boat still floated at the end. This and other stunt videos got great online viewership and coverage in *The New York Times*. If you're willing to laugh at yourself a little, you can do great things.

Gimmicks aren't appropriate for every audience. In some cases they can actually backfire on you. When I was an editor at a b-to-b Internet company, my staff lived and died by our website traffic. We became very good at using tactics such as contests, reader submitted anecdotes, and lists to pull in visitors. The problem was that we were delivering the wrong people. Visitors were attracted by bright, shiny headlines but the content wasn't helping them do their job any better. They stopped by for a quick look, but few came back. For a company that was trying to establish a serious value proposition for technology professionals, this was precisely what we *didn't* want. Ultimately, we abandoned most of these tactics.

In Chapter 6, I mentioned "linkbaiting," a practice that uses creative packaging techniques to attract attention from people and search engines. Linkbaiting is in vogue today because Internet users tend to "graze" for information. They often make decisions based on nothing more than a few words in a headline. There's nothing wrong with linkbaiting as long as the content delivers on the promise. If it fails that test, however, it can just leave people frustrated and angry.

One of the *New York Post*'s greatest headlines would perform poorly in search engines.

You should also take search into account. While cutesy headlines may attract the attention of the human readers, search engines may not treat them so kindly. Simple, declarative headlines that match the search terms that matter to you will give you better performance over time than a single clever turn of the phrase.

Medium

Today's social media marketers have more choices than ever before in deciding how to engage with an audience. They can use the following:

- Textually through blogs, communities, and even instant messaging
- Audibly through podcasts and webcasts
- Visually through images and video
- All of the above in some combination

The increasingly popular choice from the above is option four, usually in combination with some sort of traditional marketing promotion. Vehicles like blogs and Facebook groups can be thought of as containers. They support every kind of medium and address constituents through whatever means they prefer. Individual elements, like videos, can be hosted on You-Tube and served through a blog. This can deliver double the search engine performance while also enabling the video to live in a branded area on YouTube as well as on the company website. Cross-linking between the hosting sites can further drive traffic and audience engagement.

Secret: If you're using video, post it on a service like YouTube and embed it in your blog or website to double visibility.

Not every kind of content lends itself to every kind of media, of course, and not everyone is equally fluid with speech, text, and video. Start by choosing the medium that best fits the objective. If you want to hit your audience in the gut with something dramatic or humorous, video is a good choice.

To explain a complex concept, text or audio works better. Often these can be combined. For example, a technical white paper can be paired with an audio version of the document or an interview with the author. Video segments can easily be inserted into blog entries and syndicated through RSS to Facebook profiles. In fact, the more media you can find to disseminate a message, the better your results are likely to be.

In the next chapter, we look at the distinct characteristics of each medium and some tricks for working within it.

12

Telling Stories with Words and Images

Professional writers learn early in their careers that readers respond to stories. Anecdotes hit us with a power that all the statistics in the world can't match. If you're old enough to remember Ronald Reagan, you know that he who was often called "The Great Communicator" was a master storyteller. This used to enrage his opponents because Reagan could win over an audience with an anecdote that contradicted a mountain of evidence against his position. But it worked wonders for him.

I once worked with a writing coach named Bill Blundell, who was for many years a feature writer for *The Wall Street Journal*.[1] One bit of invaluable advice he gave me was, "Write in pictures." If you were to **Secret: Write in pictures.** look up any of his work, you'd see what he meant. His stories used powerful descriptive adjectives that created rich mental images, yet his language was compact and spare. He didn't use two-dollar words, but he wouldn't settle for "fall" when "plummet" was more vivid, or "laugh" when "hoot" painted a better picture. He also interspersed quote fragments and brief anecdotes to underscore the key points of his story. Blundell knew that an hour-long interview with a source was worthwhile if it yielded just a six-word quote, as long as those were precisely the right six words in just the place that he needed them.

The people who write for your blog or community forum aren't professional journalists and no one expects them to be, but they can learn from the tactics of professional writers. Social media is about people, so make your contributors human. Publish their photos and bios. You'll find that bios are some of the most popular features on blogs.

A few bullet points to remember:

---

[1] Blundell's *The Art and Craft of Feature Writing: Based on The Wall Street Journal Guide* (Plume, 1988) is well worth reading.

• Write in first person. This drives home the fact that an individual is speaking and it makes the writing more readable. Most content written for social media should be written this way, unless the writer is referring to a group or the company as a whole.

• Tell stories. This may be a personal experience or a retelling of someone else's experience. Stories are most powerful when they have a moral or lesson. We're not talking Aesop's Fables here, but stories are the best way to illustrate a point. Keep them brief and make sure to tell readers what you learned from the story you just told.

• Write like you speak. Much of this book was actually spoken, not typed. I dictated into a speech-recognition program and then revised at the keyboard. Even with extensive revision, the text stays conversational. Different tactics may work for you. Some people like to pretend they're writing a letter to a close friend. Others imagine they're creating diary entries. Use whatever tactic helps you resist the urge to become stiff and formal.

• Keep it brief. It's no secret that people have shorter attention spans when reading a screen than a printed page. If you have to write a lot, use subheads, bullet points, bold-facing, and other text formatting to provide visual relief.

• Cite statistics. This is particularly important if you're trying to argue a point. Statistics shouldn't overwhelm or dominate an argument (there is no faster way to lose an audience, believe me), but they should be summarized and cited selectively to underscore a position. There is so much research available on the Internet for free these days that it's almost absurd not to use supporting evidence.

• Use visuals. Even if you don't have compelling photos, you can usually find a few items of clip art or a logo to dress up a page of text. Always be aware of intellectual property concerns. Artwork that is licensed under a Creative Commons license can usually be used without royalties or legal agreements.

• Keep headlines declarative. In most cases, the headline is the most important part of the article because that's what the search engine cares about the most. Cute headlines may entice readers or help you with linkbaiting, but they won't appeal to search engines. Consider the tradeoffs. Some search engine optimization utilities allow you to use one headline for an article and another for the paper title, which is a good balance.

• Always cite and link to sources. No one knows who first said, "Links are the currency of the blogosphere," but he or she was right. When you comment on another person's words, you should always link to her. It doesn't matter whether you agree or disagree. Linking is a sign that you consider someone else's contributions to be valid. Failure to link is considered an insult.

• Invite response. Social media is a two-way conversation, so constantly ask readers for their feedback, perspectives, and suggestions. Then comment upon what they say. Don't allow comments to just flap in the wind; that's a sign that you don't care about your readers.

Images—A Different Way to Tell A Story

I wish more bloggers would use a camera. It would contribute so much depth to their work. Today's digital cameras offer unprecedented flexibility, low cost, and immediate gratification, so there is no excuse for not being able to take passable photos.

> Secret: When shooting photos, get close up and take advantage of the slight distortions of non-standard lenses.

When I speak to clients about setting up their business blog, one of the first points I make is they should take a camera with them whenever they attend a relevant event. Whether it's a trade show, company meeting, professional conference, or a meeting with a business associate or customer, the opportunity to dress up a story with photos shouldn't be ignored. Photos can also be repurposed in social networking sites like Flickr and Facebook to broaden your audience and they can be tagged for search engine performance. The following are a few tips for getting the most out of your digital camera:

Invest in a good single-lens reflex (SLR) camera—Point-and-shoot cameras are portable and convenient, but they don't capture the quality of images that you can get with an SLR. Yes, SLRs are bulkier and more expensive than the pocket miniatures, but they offer superior quality and interchangeable lenses, which give you many more options for making even ordinary scenes look interesting. Pocket cameras boast incredible diversity in their zoom features, but most of these effects are accomplished digitally. You can't beat a piece of glass for getting the best possible effect. Wide-angle lenses, in particular, are useful for moving in on interesting subjects and capturing close-up detail and background scenery in the same shot. My favorite and most flexible lens is a 28 mm, semi-wide angle.

Get close—Photos work best when they capture an image that the viewer wouldn't normally see. For this reason, landscapes are some of the least interesting scenes. Unless the colors are vivid or the scenery striking, one outdoor photo looks pretty much like any other picture of the same scene. However, there is infinite variety in detail. A photo of a single brilliantly colored leaf is often more striking than a panorama of the New England countryside in the fall. This requires a different approach to looking at scenery. Instead of trying to capture everything in one shot, move in and photograph the small things.

This also works with people. Casual photographers have a tendency to take full-body photos of their subjects. But no one's interested in looking at someone's feet. Move in on the face and capture the expressions and features that define personality. Take lots of pictures. Digital cameras make it cheap to keep shooting until you find the one image that really works.

> Secret: The easiest way to make a boring photo interesting is to shoot from an unusual angle.

Experiment with angles—The least interesting pictures are those taken from a standing or sitting position. That's how most of us view the world, so it's natural that we wouldn't see much novelty in that perspective. You can often make a photo more interesting simply by getting down on one knee or climbing a flight of stairs before clicking the shutter. You can also try shooting from beneath a tree or through a doorway to frame the scene in interesting fashion.

Be conscious of light—Photography professionals are constantly aware of lighting conditions. Light affects color, contrast, and depth of field, making it an essential part of storytelling. There's only so much you can do with overhead fluorescent lights, but if you're shooting outside, try to work in the morning or evening for the best effect. Morning light reveals the most vivid colors and detail, while evening light bathes scenes in a soft glow.

Ditch the flash—You should only use a flash when absolutely necessary. Flash lighting distorts colors, eliminates backgrounds, and replaces eyes with red dots. When you get that nice new SLR camera, the first thing you should do is figure out how to turn off the flash. Fortunately, modern digital cameras enable you to push the film speed to ASA 1600, or even higher, making available-light photography feasible even in lowlight situations. By using a monopod or tripod, or even by bracing yourself against a wall, you can often shoot sharp images at 1/30th of a second or slower. Available light adds a richness and depth of field to images that a flash can never reproduce.

Many good SLR cameras are capable of shooting at three-to-five frames per second. Use this feature to capture the best scene in a motion sequence. If it takes you 50 shots to get the exact right one, so be it. There's nothing lost by keeping your finger on the shutter.

Add people—Even the most prosaic product shot looks better with the inclusion of people. Human figures provide context and expression that viewers can relate to. They also give a sense of scale to the scene.

Audio—The Genuine Conversation

Webcasts and podcasts are a staple of Web marketing. They're time-efficient because they don't require a listener's full attention and they create personality the written word can't match. They can be serialized, just like a radio program, and they can develop an audience that grows over time.

Secret: Podcasts are more effective in b-to-b marketing than in b-to-c marketing.

However, there are some big downsides, too. Two years after *The New Oxford American Dictionary* declared "podcast" its word of the year for 2005, there was still no reliable mechanism for measuring podcast listenership. Most portable music players do a poor job of managing podcast files; some don't even remember where you left off the last time you listened. File sizes are large and subscribing to podcasts using anything but Apple's iTunes is often too technical for the average listener.

All these factors have led some people to discount podcasts as a failed opportunity. That's probably true in business-to-consumer and entertainment markets, but podcasting has shown surprising resilience among audiences that are deeply interested in their content. Business-to-business marketers report more success with podcasts than business-to-consumer marketers, according to "Harnessing the Power of New Media Platforms," a report sponsored by the Association of National Advertisers and *BtoB* magazine which was released in early 2008. In that survey, 21 percent of b-to-b marketers found podcasts to be very effective, compared with only 13 percent of b-to-c marketers.

I suspect that the reason for this is that audiences with voracious information needs and little time appreciate the efficiency of a medium that they can consume during downtime in their day. This should tell you a lot about how to make your own programs successful. Leave the pranks to videos. Podcasts are all about usefulness.

There are three basic formats that work well in audio programming:

1. Presentation—This is the audio version of a standard conference chalk talk. Conference organizers like O'Reilly Media and ad:tech have made great use of podcasting to capture sessions and use them to promote future events.

You need to edit these podcasts pretty carefully to cut out the dead air and inaudible audience questions that typically occur during presentations. If possible, make sure the speaker knows she's being recorded for a podcast and ask her to repeat audience questions. Also, ask her to avoid relying too heavily on PowerPoint visuals. These can frustrate a listening audience.

Secret: The optimal length of a podcast is 15–20 minutes.

2. Q&A—Nearly every one of the corporate podcasts I've recorded uses this format. It's simple, effective, and easy to produce. The accompanying sidebar, "Podcasting on the Cheap," offers a few tricks I've learned along the way. Q&As are an effective companion to other content. For example, you can pair a new white paper with an author interview or summarize a one-hour webcast in a 20-minute companion podcast. Unless you're doing "man on the street" interviews, avoid having more than three voices in the conversation. It's difficult to tell who's talking.

3. Co-hosted—This is talk radio. If you have two knowledgeable speakers who can build upon each other's comments and who have a comfortable back-and-forth style, it's a great approach. It's a good idea to have the speakers choreograph their format and approach so they don't step on each other's words or create awkward pauses.

There are a lot of tricks you can use to dress up podcasts and make them sound more professional. Musical introductions, recorded comments from callers, and sound effects all have their place. Download a few popular programs and listen for ideas.

Podcasting on the Cheap

I produced more than 100 podcasts between 2006 and 2007 for global corporations like IBM, Microsoft, and SAP. Most of these were recorded, mixed, and encoded on a standard desktop computer with less than $200 worth of audio hardware and software. While you can easily spend thousands of dollars on professional equipment, the secret is that you don't have to.

Secret: You can create good quality podcasts for an investment of less than $200.

I recorded the programs using open source audio editing software called Audacity and a $50 Radio Shack microphone. Many of these programs required interviewing speakers by telephone. For that, I used Skype or Gizmo, which enable people to make phone calls over the Internet. Both services are free when parties on both ends use the same software or carry a nominal charge for calls to standard telephones. The audio quality is superb; I've conducted interviews with speakers in India who sounded as if they were in the studio with me. I record the programs with MX Skype Recorder, which costs about $15. Pamela is another Skype recording option.

These programs have the advantage of recording conversations on two separate tracks. This is useful because I can record my own voice locally in Audacity while simultaneously recording the phone conversation with MX Skype Recorder. Afterwards, I simply delete my own track from the call recording and substitute the track I recorded locally. This delivers the best possible sound quality. Audacity makes it easy to edit the conversation and mix in theme music. The whole program is then exported to an MP3 file.

Here are a few secrets that I've learned about successful podcast production:

Choose an articulate moderator. The moderator holds the program together, so you want someone with broadcast or public speaking experience who has a strong voice and the ability to speak in complete sentences. Believe it or not, these qualities are rare. Audio tends to amplify people's speaking quirks. Microphone-savvy people can be found within your organization and they welcome the opportunity to take a spot in the limelight.

> ## Podcast Secrets:
> ☞ Choose an articulate moderator
> ☞ Have talking points, but not a script
> ☞ Keep it brief
> ☞ Don't over-edit
> ☞ Use music
> ☞ Fill ID3 tags

Have talking points, but not a script. This is a delicate balance. If a conversation is too scripted, it sounds wooden. However, if there's no structure at all, it can become aimless. Moderator and speakers should work from talking points, but should take care to speak in their own words as conversationally as possible.

Keep it brief. The most common question people ask me about podcasting is how long a program should be. My response is "as long as it's interesting." I've listened to 75-minute podcasts that were fascinating and 15-minute programs that were excruciating. But if you want a rule of thumb, a podcast had better be pretty good to run over 20 minutes. Remember that many people listen to podcasts while commuting or exercising, so try to keep your program within the limits of a standard workout.

Don't over-edit. You can go crazy with sound editors to the point of removing every stammer or "um" in the conversation. At some point, though, this makes interviews sound unnatural. Take out the most noticeable mistakes, but don't make your speakers sound like they're reading from a script.

Use music. Musical intros and outros lend a professional feel to your podcast without much cost. Look for music that is licensed as "podsafe"

Secret: Always fill in ID3 tags on audio files. That's how search engines find you.

or under a Creative Commons license. It's generally available at little or no charge.

Fill ID3 tags. Digital music files typically include a set of data fields that provide information like the title, artist name, description, and running time. Music players know how to read this information, but audio editing software doesn't always require you to provide it. It's important to fill in these tags, though, so that search engines can find your programs and so people can pick your podcast out of a list.

Video—Make it Compelling

Let's state at the outset that producing good video is hard. Lighting, camera angle, audio quality, storyboarding, titles, background music, transitions, and other details are all important. Also, video editing is much more complicated than audio editing. If you do it right, however, the payoff is impressive. Witness the success of videos like Blendtec's Will it Blend? series or Eepybird's Diet Coke/Mentos experiments (see vignettes following Chapter 13). Viral video offers perhaps the biggest upside in social media.

I don't claim to be an expert in video production, so for this section I spoke with several people who have had success with online video. Their advice can be summed up in what you could call the "AEIOU" rule: *Authentic*, *Entertaining*, *Intimate*, *Offbeat*, or *Unusual*.

Authentic means using real people in real situations. While some professionally produced campaigns by advertisers like Anheuser-Busch and GoDaddy have achieved a second life online after their TV run has ended, most successful online video producers have told me that they intentionally give their programs a bit of a home-video feel. Audiences associate high production value with professional marketing, and that's actually perceived as a negative. Remember that one of the most popular viral videos ever—Gary Brolsma's Numa Numa dance—was recorded on a cheap webcam with the subject sitting in a desk chair.

Entertaining means fun. People like to share content that's good for a laugh and that maybe stimulates a quick e-mail discussion. Weighty videos tend not to perform well virally.

UK-based candy maker Cadbury Schweppes used humor to great effect in a TV-ad-turned-viral-video that <u>became the most-watched YouTube advertisement of 2007</u>, according to the *Financial Times*. The video featured a close-up of a pensive-looking gorilla grooving to the strains of "In the Air Tonight" by Phil Collins. As the camera pulled back, the creature was seen to be a man in a gorilla suit sitting at a drum set. At the appropriate point in the song, the man/gorilla began pounding on the drums in perfect time with the music. The Cadbury logo only appears briefly at the end of the 90-second clip.

The relevance of this image to milk chocolate is hardly apparent, but Cadbury said the viral video, which logged more than 1 million views in four months, noticeably improved candy sales. The head of the agency behind the campaign told the FT, "The link between a man in a gorilla suit and a chocolate bar is the one the man in the street finds easily…when people see the ad they are not scrutinising it for meaning, they are doing the ironing or waiting for the rugby to start. They want to be entertained."

Cadbury was also innovative in limiting branding on the clip so as to make it easy for viewers to download and mash it up into spoofs and derivations. Nearly 30 variations of the gorilla ad appeared on YouTube and the campaign got media exposure in countries where the TV ad never appeared.

Intimate means satisfying people's inner voyeur. Video is the most intimate of all media because it shows the context of a story, including the reactions of other people. Some of the most successful campaigns capture people with their defenses down. For example, Weight Watchers enlisted a prolific video blogger to record her experiences trying to shed pounds under the company's program.

Burger King used this approach effectively with <u>Whopper Freakout</u>, a companion website to a TV campaign in which restaurant customers were secretly filmed being told that the company's signature

Whopper sandwich was being discontinued. The one-minute TV ad was funny, but the eight-minute Web video was more revealing. "What I find most fascinating, is that when customers are confronted with the idea that they can no longer order a Whopper, they immediately recall their childhood memories of Whoppers," wrote Nial McFadyen on Viral Marketing Blog. "The people in this video are still eating at Burger King today, because their parents brought them there as kids." A TV ad thus became an experiment in psychology!

Secret: Want to catch people's attention with your video? Give them something unexpected.

Offbeat and Unusual work together. Surprise and delight viewers with something they don't expect. Being daring or a little risqué can help. Clothing maker Marc Ecko Enterprises conceived of a promotion called StillFree, in which the former graffiti artist was supposedly caught on film "tagging" Air Force One with the words "Still Free" spray-painted on a jet engine. The film was a hoax—Ecko rented an actual 747 for the stunt—but the company claimed more than 100 million downloads of a video that reinforced its anti-establishment image.

Dove's Evolution viral video was offbeat without being humorous. The one-minute clip showing an ordinary-looking woman Photoshopped into a billboard beauty was effective because the storyboarding and technical wizardry were so imaginative. The 1':14" clip also made a statement about Americans' superficial attitude towards beauty. Its goal was to promote the Dove Self-Esteem Fund for young girls. The video was a smash hit, notching more than 10 million views on YouTube, spawning a couple of dozen spoofs and winning a Cannes Lions Live award for advertising. Its global reach extended far beyond its intended Canadian market.[2]

Secret: Make it easy for people to mash up and spoof your content.

The Dove and Cadbury examples illustrate one interesting side effect of viral vid-

---

[2] Dove's parent company Unilever was later a victim of its own success when video mashups emerged showing that its Axe deodorant used advertising tactics that exploited women.

eo: Successful clips are invariably spoofed. To marketers worried about copyright, this may seem horrifying, but it's really a compliment and another avenue to spread the message. Dove made no effort to restrict distribution of high-quality versions of Evolution for mashing up by amateur videographers. Each of the millions of views of the spoof videos was an advertisement for the original campaign.

To the AEIOU rule, I'll add a "B": brief. The longer your program, the smaller your audience will be. Most successful viral videos run under three minutes.

You can do almost anything in an online video format, but programs that "go viral" almost always use humor, absurdity, or a sense of the bizarre. Self-deprecating humor is a great way to disarm critics, although it can be painfully difficult to sell to corporate management.

But even traditionally staid companies are learning to loosen up. When NBC was scored by YouTube members for using the video service to promote its fall lineup in late 2006, the network posted a parody video of "Bill The Promo Guy." Bill asked viewers to go easy on NBC because, "I do some of those promos... NBC is people like me, people trying to put their son through prep school and buy their daughter a horse [that] costs more than a small house." As one blogger commented, "That clip was funnier than all those NBC shows mentioned...COMBINED!"

Video doesn't have to be slick or expensive if the subject matter is interesting. Walter Lewin, an MIT physics professor, has achieved an online cult following for his freshman physics lectures. They're popular because Lewin is a compelling speaker with a knack for theatrics. The most popular YouTube video of all time—Jud Laipply's "Evolution of Dance"—was shot with a single video camera and low production value. It had logged more than 80 million views on YouTube by early 2008.

You shouldn't try to go viral, either. A video that reaches just a few hundred viewers can be called a success if they're the right viewers. Commercial finance company CIT launched a series of edu-

Secret: No one has figured out a formula for "going viral." Don't even try.

219

cational videos on YouTube in the spring of 2007 called "CIT: Behind the Business." They feature interviews with entrepreneurs and CEOs, who talk about the secrets of their success. It's a soft-sell approach that aligns CIT with successful businesspeople, and the videos are easy to produce. This campaign will never achieve viral growth, but it doesn't have to. It aligns well with the company's branding and YouTube gives the videos a longer life than they would have had in a brief TV or direct mail promotion.

13

Engagement through Interaction

The best way to take advantage of an interactive medium is to encourage visitors to contribute their own content. Contests, games, and reviews are three increasingly popular ways to do that. These tools can be very effective if applied appropriately, but they also have the greatest potential to create embarrassment and crushing workloads. Let's take a look at the pros and cons of each.

Contests

Contests work best when they advance the underlying marketing theme and leverage media that are appropriate for the product. They don't need to involve video uploads, user voting, or expensive prizes. They can actually be simple and inexpensive to produce. However, more ambitious efforts can consume significant amounts of time and may yield disappointing results. More on this later.

The easiest contests are simple and cheap. Rocky Mountaineer Vacations, a provider of Canadian train trips and vacation packages, created the Rocky Mountaineer Guest Lounge and invited visitors to share photos and testimonials about their vacations. Prizes were modest—a nice watch, a clock, and a photography book—but the cost of entry was low. People simply had to upload their vacation photos.

Macy's targeted college-age women with a fashion design contest across eight U.S. universities. Entrants were encouraged to submit their own designs to AmericanRagCampus.com, for judging by the company. The winning entry was considered for inclusion in the fall 2007 clothing line. The prize money was a modest $1,000. The campaign was paired with a casting call for a special version of the American Rag catalog featuring real students.

Procter & Gamble used a contest to build upon the popularity of its "Talking Stain" Super Bowl commercial in 2008. The company set up a profile on YouTube and invited submissions, receiving more than 100 entries. The winning ad was to be aired on prime time television. For a relatively modest investment (P&G presumably would have bought the airtime anyway), the company was able to sustain a campaign long after its 30 seconds of fame ended and tap into user innovations that could serve as the basis for future commercials.

Secret: Contests are some of the riskiest and most time-consuming online marketing tactics.

VMware set the bar higher with Become Virtually Famous, a video contest targeting b-to-b customers. The $15,000 first prize was unusually large but probably appropriate in light of the fact that VMWare's customers are busy technology professionals, and server virtualization doesn't exactly lend itself to video artistry. The company knew that customers would need some coaxing to create entries. While the volume of submissions was modest—less than 50—the event generated tens of thousands of downloads from curious visitors.

Contests aren't a slam dunk, though. They've become such popular marketing promotions that some pundits have declared that they're no longer meaningful. The quality of consumer-generated content varies greatly, and most of it is pretty bad. Also, sometimes they just don't generate much enthusiasm. A 1-800-FLOWERS video contest held just before Valentine's Day 2008 got only 14 entries. It's unlikely the company considered that promotion to be a success.

On the other hand, popular contests can generate thousands of entries, drowning marketing and agency staff in work. General Motors' 2006 Chevy Apprentice campaign, in which visitors contributed TV ads assembled from video clips on a website, logged 22,000 submissions. That's over 180 hours of video to view and evaluate. Doritos received more than 1,000 entries to its 2006 contest to create an ad for the Super Bowl.

"Companies have found that inviting consumers to create their advertising is often more stressful, costly, and time-consuming than just rolling up their sleeves and doing the work themselves," wrote _The New York Times_. "Many entries are mediocre, if not downright bad, and sifting through them requires full-time attention. And even the most well-known brands often spend millions of dollars up front to get the word out to consumers."

Contests can also create unintended results. The _Times_ account told of a video contest sponsored by ketchup maker H.J. Heinz that produced some truly bad work. "One contestant chugs ketchup straight from the bottle, while another brushes his teeth, washes his hair, and shaves his face with Heinz's product. Often the ketchup looks more like blood than a condiment."

Beer maker Molson pulled down a photo campaign on Facebook after several Canadian university administrators complained that it promoted irresponsible drinking. The campaign asked students to post photos in a competition for the title of top party school in Canada. Administrators said uncontrollable parties were a big enough problem without getting support from the beer maker[1].

Contests mesh well with social networks because they exploit people's innate competitiveness and give them a chance to become famous, at least in a small way. However, they can be risky. If the brand doesn't stimulate excitement or creativity among customers, or if the customer base doesn't have the time or skill to devote to the effort, contests can be a public embarrassment. There aren't many brands for which customers will spend hours shooting and editing a video, so holding a photo or story contest may be a better bet for those companies.

Games

Top social networks present a tantalizing opportunity to market with games. Online games have been around nearly as long as the Web, but they've been a risky proposition for marketers because of the challenge of raising awareness and attracting users. On social networks, the audience is already in place and a good application

---

[1] The party-school promotion was seen as a black eye for Molson, but the company actually considered the campaign to be a success, according to Dawna Henderson, CEO of Henderson Bas, the advertising agency behind the contest. "We learned a lot about what not to do next time," she says.

is quickly passed from one member to another through built-in invitations.

Secret: Only about 5 percent of computer games make a profit. Keep that in mind if you consider marketing with games.

Of the more than 15,000 third-party applications on Facebook, most involve friendly competition or comparison between members. Flixster's Movies application achieved a 18 percent penetration of the total Facebook audience in just seven months, according to comScore. It lets members compare taste in movies. Quizzes generated a six-figure income in advertising commissions for a 19-year-old Berkeley student in just a few months, according to *BusinessWeek*.

The most notable Facebook game is Scrabulous, a version of Scrabble developed by two Indian programmers. Launched in July 2007, it had a half million daily users by January 2008 and was earning the developers about $25,000 a month in advertising revenue, according to Knowledge@Wharton.

What's incredible about this story is that Hasbro, the maker of Scrabble, demanded that Facebook pull down the application and threatened legal action for copyright infringement. "We have spent many years building the Scrabble brand, and what Scrabulous is doing is piracy," said a Hasbro statement.

Imagine if Hasbro had instead bought the Facebook game, branded it, and used the opportunity to sell its online and retail products. Sometimes, companies just do dumb things.

Games resonate with young audiences in particular. Children's book publisher Beacon Street Girls sells to "tweeners," or girls between the ages of nine and 15. It has built an audience of about a half-million monthly unique visitors without any substantial investment in marketing. The site's key feature is a dress-up game in which girls can outfit models in a variety of fashions and colors and place them in different settings. They can also e-mail each other completed designs.

That e-mail option was the magic formula, according to Bobbie Carlton, director of marketing at parent company B*tween Productions. Because the friend must come back to the site to look at the design, Beacon Street has the opportunity to capture contact information. (The company adheres tightly to Children's Online Privacy Protection Act guidelines.) The dress-up game drives 85 percent of viral traffic. B*tween has invested little in conventional advertising as a result.

Games aren't for everybody. They require technical expertise, creativity, and timing. They are also much more effective with younger audiences. Few publishers outside of the kids market have had much success with games. Facebook does present some tantalizing options for leveraging the power of communities to engage people in friendly competition. However, the vast majority of Facebook games generate little use. In the hit-driven computer game industry, fewer than 5 percent of titles make a profit. About half the industry's revenue goes to the top 1 percent of games published. The same effect seems to be playing out in social networks, which is why games should be approached with caution.

Reviews

Five years ago, no marketer in her right mind would have permitted unscreened customer reviews to appear on a business' own website. But standards are changing and some innovative firms have found that comments—even negative ones—can drive sales.

Consumer demand is certainly there. In a late 2007 report, Forrester Research said user ratings or reviews are the most desired website feature among U.S. Internet users, with 64 percent desiring that function. Special offers and coupons were second at 61 percent, followed by product or price comparisons. Interestingly, games and user-generated content were lowest on consumers' wish list.

Avenue A | Razorfish identified user reviews as the resource that was most frequently used by U.S. online shoppers. And a 2008 survey by eMarketer said that 65 percent of U.S. online buyers read customer reviews before making a purchase decision. They like to write

Secret: Allowing customers to review your products on your website enhances credibility and improves customer retention.

them, too. As Larry Weber says in *Marketing to the Social Web*: "In the new marketing, expect customers to vote on everything from cruise lines to cookware."

Retailers like Toys R Us, Staples, Amazon, Brookstone, and Lillian Vernon use customer reviews to help customers make more informed selections. This is a no-brainer for retailers that sell multiple brands. A more challenging option is for companies to allow customers to review their own branded products. Vendors who have confidence in customer satisfaction find this to be a powerful selling point, however.

Prior to its acquisition by Google, voice mail service provider Grand Central Communications featured a home page link to a section where customers could say whatever they wanted about the product. Thousands did, and their enthusiasm was impressive. In fact, the occasional criticism made the exercise appear more genuine.

Apparel maker Jockey International invites customer reviews on its site, as do Green Mountain Coffee Roasters and LL Bean. Reviews are screened before posting but reviewers don't have to identify themselves. Today, these brand-makers are unusual, though. Most companies are uncomfortable with the idea of exposing their products to such open commentary. However, any company that launches a blog is effectively doing the same thing.

There are good reasons to encourage customer reviews on your website. Unhappy customers who voice their opinions can be contacted and turned into satisfied customers. Reviews also give a company the opportunity to reach out to customers who may have had a negative experience and decide to never come back. And, anecdotal evidence indicates that a few negative reviews isn't perceived to be a bad thing. No company has 100 percent happy customers and those who acknowledge that fact get points for transparency.

If you're confident that you have a good product that delights your customers, why not let them speak for you? It's okay if there are a few naysayers; they actually make your reviews section more credible.

A Roll of Mints, a Jug of Cola, and Wow!

Buckfield, Maine, isn't the place you'd normally expect to find a world-renowned entertainment team. The town of 1,723 inhabitants, which sits astride the unofficial border between eastern and western Maine, has one pizza parlor, a small grocery store, and no stoplights. Its largest industry is a maker of wooden dowels.

But Buckfield also has the Oddfellows Theatre, a small playhouse that has won a following throughout New England for its eclectic mix of offbeat fare. It was Oddfellows that brought together Stephen Voltz and Fritz Grobe, two men who would create one of the greatest viral marketing phenomena of the Internet age.

Voltz and Grobe were both performers by nature. As a boy growing up in San Francisco, Voltz, now 50, had learned to juggle and eat fire, and had performed on street corners near Fisherman's Wharf. In later life, he had put his circus ambitions behind him to become a successful trial lawyer in the Boston area.

The 40-year-old Grobe was that rarest of all artists: a professional juggler. In 1993, he won the International Jugglers Festival individual championships, one of five gold medals he accumulated over several festivals. He now makes a living working with circuses and performing at parties and business events.

In addition to their love of entertainment, the two men were born tinkerers. In the summer of 2005, they started experimenting with a chemical phenomenon known as nucleation. That's the scientific term for what happens when a liquid that's super-saturated with gas comes into contact with an object that causes bubbles to form. Their experimental media of choice were bottles of Diet Coca-Cola and a brand of breath mints called Mentos, produced by a unit of Italian confectioner Perfetti Van Melle. People had known for years that dropping Mentos into a bottle of Diet Coke caused an impressive geyser of foam to shoot several feet into the air. But Voltz and Grobe took the concept a step further. By tinkering with the aperture of the Coke bottle, drilling holes in various places in the candies, and using an assortment of other tricks, they had achieved geysers of 15 feet or more.

In June 2006, the pair decided to show the world their results. Armed with a single video camera, 101 bottles of Diet Coke and 523 specially prepared Mentos, they recorded a display of carbonated wizardry so spectacular that it came to be know as the Bellagio Fountain, a name taken from the dancing water display at the Las Vegas landmark. The synchronized eruption of dozens of Coke bottles was all the funnier because the two performers, clad in white lab coats, uncorked them with such matter-of-fact disinterest. Music by the techno/pop/funk band AudioBody added a metallic backbeat and the three-minute clip ended with Voltz and Grobe choking on an over-carbonated victory toast.

It was funny as hell, but neither performer was ready for what came next.

Inside the Tornado

On June 3, Voltz posted the video on a website the pair named Eepybird.com after a fictional character created by a friend. He sent off a single e-mail to a brother in San Francisco, asking him to take a look. The brother notified Fark.com, one of the top linklogs on the Internet. Within hours, thousands of visitors were swamping Eepybird. com. The videos spread with a viral rapidity the likes of which had never been seen before. Over the weekend, staffers at "Late Night with David Letterman" learned of the video from a blog in Australia. By mid-day Monday, Voltz and Grobe had invitations to perform the experiment on "Late Night" and "The Today Show."

Everything's been a blur since then. The pair scrambled to pull off twice in two days on national television what had they only accomplished once before, and with barely any preparation. But the TV appearances went well. "There were articles in *The Wall Street Journal*, *Rolling Stone* called us 'wizards,' *The New York Times* said we were 'hilarious'…we were even in *GQ*," says an account on the Eepybird site. "We were on Mythbusters twice, and we even went to Las Vegas to do a live performance at Caesar's Palace for HBO's 'The Comedy Festival.'"

Perfetti, which had been struggling to make a name for itself in the crowded U.S. candy market, jumped all over the publicity, carving out a chunk of its home page to show off the experiment. According to an article in Me-diaPost, "The Bellagio Fountain video was downloaded 20 million times and more than 10,000 copycat mint-soda videos were

Secret: Give video a homegrown feel to make it look more genuine.

posted online, which created a multiplier effect: Mentos tallied a staggering 215 million mentions of its product in TV, print, or radio stories over the past nine months, and it estimates the free publicity was worth $10 million to the company—half its annual marketing budget." Sales climbed 20 percent.

At Coca-Cola headquarters in Atlanta, though, the mood wasn't so exuberant. Coke lawyers fretted about liability problems from amateur chemists trying to duplicate the experiment. When the *Journal* called for comment, a spokeswoman said the "craziness with Mentos ...doesn't fit with the brand personality" of Coke. "We would hope people want to drink [Diet Coke] more than try experiments with it," she said.

Coke Gets on Board

But Coke's interactive marketers saw a gold mine. Sales of Diet Coke, which had been flat for some time, spiked between 5 and 10 percent, the company's interactive director told MediaPost. In August, they contacted Eepybird asking how they could help pull off more experiments. Voltz and Grobe, who were tired of buying out the local grocery's stock of soda, were happy to accept. In October, they recorded a sequel video called "The Domino Effect," involving 251 bottles, more than 1,500 candies and a network of trip wires, pulleys, and nozzles that sent choreographed foam spewing in every direction.

The Internet ate it up. Google and Yahoo featured the clip on their video home pages. Voltz and Grobe personally contacted dozens of bloggers who had helped promote the first experiment, encouraging them to link to the latest video. Eepybird was flooded with traffic, more media outlets called, and offers began coming in from casinos and corporate events departments asking for command performances.

Coke supported the experiment with unlimited supplies of beverages, ad buys on Google, and a sponsored contest with Voltz and Grobe as judges. Coke got 1.5 billion ad impressions from the stunt.

Coca-Cola was convinced. Traffic to the company's video home page doubled and, while Coke didn't disclose sales figures, Perfetti's report of a 20 percent jump in business demonstrated that the videos lifted sales. In February 2007, Voltz and Grobe put on a command performance before thousands of wildly cheering employees at Coca-Cola headquarters. By summer, Coke had relaunched its corporate website around a multicolored logo showing a geyser erupting from a soda bottle. In September, Eepybird broke the world record by triggering more than 900 geysers at a demonstration in Holland. By December, Voltz estimated that the videos had been downloaded more than 40 million times.

The success of the viral videos has made it possible for Voltz to set aside his law practice and for the two men to pursue Eepybird full-time. They're talking to Coke about "a wide range of projects," Grobe says, while tinkering away at other "cool stuff" they aren't yet disclosing.

Secret: Involve professionals in concepts and storyboarding.

What Eepybird hasn't done is go big-time. "We're two guys in the woods of Maine exploring things off on our own, and that's what we love doing," Grobe said. And they think that genuineness is part of the viral videos' appeal.

"I think that's what people like seeing: something that's made by real people for them," Grobe adds.

The pair has resisted offers from studios to film their stunts with professional crews. Voltz explains that the amateur feel of Eepybird's work is one of the secrets of its success. "We want to make production values as high as they need to be to tell a story, but no higher because that can get in the way of the story," he says. The experiments continue to be filmed with a single off-the-shelf video camera.

Home-brewed production doesn't mean skimping on preparation, though. Voltz and Grobe can spend months preparing for a new experiment. As accomplished performers, they understand that their deadpan looks and personal chemistry are essential to the package. That's why

Voltz recommends involving professionals in the concept and scripting stages while still giving the video a homegrown look and feel.

The duo also fight to keep branding subdued in their experiments. "We actually had a lot of discussion with Coke about branding," Voltz says. "Our concern wasn't for Coke but for our own viewers. If we started using typical TV commercial product shots, our audience would tune out."

Grobe adds that the experiments' success testifies to the power of viral promotion. "Having worked in theatre for 20 years, you understand how important word-of-mouth is," he says. "It can carry you right to the top."

Gold from Sawdust

The idea sprang from a pile of sawdust on a laboratory floor. Fifteen months later, it had transformed a company.

It was the fall of 2006, and George Wright had been marketing director at Blendtec for just a few months. Blendtec was a small, closely held appliance maker based in Orem, Utah that built blenders for commercial food service companies. The company's flagship products have a reputation for power and durability. The founder and chief engineer, Tom Dickson, would have it no other way.

Blendtec had a good commercial business, but Dickson wanted to get into the consumer market, where cooks were increasingly demanding commercial-grade appliances. Wright's job was to execute on that strategy. The question was how? Blendtec had a small marketing department and budget, little name recognition outside of its commercial stronghold and plenty of well-known competitors. How could it break through all the noise?

That's when George Wright noticed the sawdust.

CEO Dickson was a hands-on guy, and he routinely put the company's products through their paces. Often that involved grinding all kinds of stubborn objects in the blenders to see if they would break. Dickson had been building blenders for 15 years. He was passionate about creating the most powerful and durable product on the market. Stress-testing them with household objects was part of his routine. On that particular day, he was grinding 2-by-2 pine boards

To Wright's trained marketing eye, the sawdust was a pile of gold. He persuaded Dickson to videotape some of his tests. Next, he dropped $50 on a few household items: some ice cubes, a bag of marbles, a rake, a rotisserie chicken and a McDonald's Value Meal. Blendtec's staff video producer rigged up a simple set and the group recorded five videos, each less than two minutes long. Each video showed Dickson, dressed in a white lab coat and safety glasses, nonchalantly pulverizing items from Wright's shopping bag.

Dickson reduced the pile of marbles to powder. He then blended the chicken with a whole can of Coca-Cola to make a concoction he dubbed "CoChiken." In the video, marketer Wright can be seen sampling the concoction and declaring, "That's good CoChiken!" The team whipped up a little music, added some title slides and uploaded the five videos to YouTube, at the time a fledgling video-sharing site.

The rest is viral marketing history. Blendtec had no budget for big-market advertising, so employees were asked to spread the word about the videos to their families, friends and customers. Wright's small department submitted URLs to social news sites like Digg and alerted a few bloggers who specialized in cooking supplies. Viewers did the rest. Within a week, the videos had logged millions of downloads on YouTube. Suggestions began pouring in from viewers for other items to submit to blender oblivion.

Blendtec obliged, and in the months that followed, its CEO ground up items ranging from the ordinary (coffee beans and credit cards) to the bizarre (a Furby and Guitar Hero III game). Each spot featured the same format: a grandfatherly Dickson smiling benignly at the camera while annihilating some unfortunate tool or piece of sporting equipment. When the carnage was complete, Dickson would pour the smoldering remains onto a plate and offer a wry wisecrack. Viewers couldn't get enough.

Blendtec had a hit on its hands and it went with the flow. Video segments showing an Apple iPhone exploding into a cloud of black ash logged over 5 million downloads on YouTube and Revver alone. It also satisfied thousands of requests that Blendtec had received for an iPhone event. That barely put a dent in the inventory of suggestions, which still numbers over 100,000, Wright says.

Less than 15 months later, the Will It Blend? series was legendary. Dickson had appeared on national prime-time television and been featured in nearly every major newspaper in the country. Marketers no longer had to promote the publication of a new video; an army of enthusiasts spread the word. And sales were up fivefold. Wright had expected that the series would do well, but not this well. "I was blown away," he says. As of the end of 2007, the series had logged an incredible 70 million downloads without a second of television advertising.

The Blendtec videos are perhaps the closest thing to a perfect viral marketing campaign. They're short, funny and easy to understand. They're simple and inexpensive to produce and the stunt can be easily recreated for conferences and trade show demonstrations. "As long as there's something people want to talk about, we can throw it in a blender," Wright laughs.

More importantly, the videos are on message. Every time Dickson fires up an appliance, he reinforces the image of Blendtec as a producer of powerful, sturdy products. The company has even given tacit blessing to the hundreds of knockoff videos that enthusiasts have submitted to YouTube, although they caution admirers to keep their experiments safe. "There are people who take their mother's blender and put their sister's Barbie doll in it and upload the video to YouTube," Wright says. "Whenever they do that, they mention Blendtec."

And there's been one more surprise: the videos are profitable. Companies have paid Blendtec to produce custom versions to promote corporate mergers. A radio station commissioned the video team to grind up CD's to celebrate a new blend of music programming. Each month, the video-sharing site Revver.com sends a commission check for ad revenues that the series generates.

> ## Blendtec's Viral Video Secrets:
> ☞ Have a plan
> ☞ Don't get fancy
> ☞ Be creative with promotion
> ☞ Plan for success

All this has been a windfall for Blendtec. But its success wasn't entirely an accident. Wright offers the following secrets:

Have a plan. Although the magnitude of Will It Blend?'s popularity was surprising, the campaign's success wasn't. Wright created a marketing plan before the first video was shot, outlining a sequence of programs and strategies to promote them. The objective was never to generate millions of downloads. Rather, it was to find the right customers. "I wanted to find something that people who are in the market to purchase a blender could enjoy and help us to promote our product," Wright says.

"Whether it's 50 views or 5 million, as long as it's in front of the right people, it's a successful campaign."

Don't get fancy. The dime-store set and home-video quality of the Blendtec videos are by design. Viewers actually like the grainy authenticity of many viral videos and react suspiciously to programs that look too slick. Video quality also has to be harmonized with the limitations of Internet delivery. Files have to be small enough to be e-mailed.

Be creative with promotion. It would be obvious to market the Will It Blend? videos to cooking enthusiasts, but the company's marketers went a step further. They notified golf bloggers when Dickson ground up golf balls and football writers when the Super Bowl special was planned. Targeting these tangential markets drove plenty of traffic.

Plan for success. When Will It Blend? took off, the company was ready to exploit the program's success. That meant clearing the decks for mainstream media coverage and public appearances. It also meant ramping up the production scheduled to provide more videos faster.

Today, Will It Blend? has transformed the company. Blendtec has become a household name without spending any money on mainstream media advertising. Moreover, the quality proposition hammered home by the video series carries over to future products. "I could show you equipment in our engineering department that would make your jaw drop," says Wright. "We're now perceived to be a high quality player. That makes it much easier to launch new products."

14

Promote Thyself

"The consumer has become the brand advocate—not the marketer."
—Carol Kruse, VP, global interactive marketing, Coca-Cola,
quoted in *USA Today*, Nov. 2007

Social media presents vast new potential for promotion; so vast, in fact, that many marketers don't know where to start. Blog entries today are bedecked with dozens of icons that automatically submit content to a wide variety of social bookmarking sites. Popular linklogs like BoingBoing.net and Fark can drive hundreds of thousands of visitors to a site in a matter of hours. Some companies are experimenting with group instant messaging services like Twitter to publicize time-sensitive offers. Public relations programs increasingly incorporate blogger outreach as an essential activity.

The choices are mind-boggling. Set up a Google Alert for "social media marketing" and you're pelted with 10-15 new blog posts a day. Sign up for newsletters from services like MediaPost, eMarketer, iMediaConnection, MarketingSherpa, and the Word of Mouth Marketing Association and you'll have a dozen or more additional articles to read.

Marketers often tell me that they're overwhelmed by the volume of social media marketing information that assaults them and frustrated that they can't keep pace. I tell them I feel the same way. So do plenty of other people who spend their days immersed in this topic. No one has the perfect formula for social media marketing and you shouldn't even try to keep up with it all. Use this chapter to help you focus your energy and choose the options that pay off the best for your company or clients. I'll also suggest a few tips for keeping up with the deluge of information.

Links indicated in the text above may be found at SSMMBook.com

Blogger Promotion

The market has run so far ahead of itself that it's sometimes easy to forget that most companies are still struggling with the basic issue of what to do about bloggers. These new influencers are a potentially significant new constituency for public relations efforts, and they are the engine that drives successful viral marketing promotions. Nevertheless, the decision of whether and how to engage with them is not a simple one.

In order to promote to bloggers, you first have to engage with them. Some highly visible companies are stuck on the question of whether to even take that first step. One large consumer firm I worked with had no formal program for engaging with the blogosphere, despite the fact that there were literally dozens of dedicated blogs and fan sites devoted to its products. This company enjoyed a strongly positive public image and an adoring customer base, yet bloggers had disrupted several of its recent promotion programs by "scooping" its announcements. To make matters worse, the media were increasingly quoting these disruptors as credible independent sources of information.

Publicists fretted that if they recognized prominent bloggers through a formal program, they would lend legitimacy to a group of influencers that didn't play by the mainstream media rules. If they remained silent, however, they were effectively letting the bloggers run the show.

This scenario isn't unusual. Blogger relations can present big logistical problems. Mark Cuban, who owns the Dallas Mavericks, touched off a rancorous debate in early 2008 when he barred a newspaper blogger from the Mavs' locker room. Cuban declared that the locker room was too small to accommodate every blogger and so access would be limited to credentialed media. Although the blogger in question worked for a newspaper website, he was barred because he wasn't a reporter.

Cuban, who is an active and popular blogger, was trying to make a point. He wanted to treat all bloggers the same, even if that meant excluding them from privileges. With thousands of sports bloggers already publishing online, that policy created some difficult choices.

I believe that prominent bloggers should be treated in the same manner as mainstream media, but that not all bloggers are equal. In the same way that small weekly newspapers can't get into a Presiden-

Secret: Treat bloggers like mainstream media, but you don't have to treat every blogger equally. Use publicly available metrics to distinguish levels of access. tial press conference, casual bloggers shouldn't expect the same treatment as their prominent peers. In my opinion, it's okay to make a conscious choice to engage proactively with a limited number of influential voices. Ideally, you should establish clear criteria for these decisions and be open about them. Among the possible—and publicly available—metrics you can use are:

- Longevity;
- Output (frequency and quantity);
- Inbound links;
- Technorati, Bloglines or Blogpulse ranking;
- Number of comments; and
- Media citations

None of these metrics is perfect, but all are measurable. The best approach is to combine metrics into a single weighted average. Bloggers who don't clear the bar are out of luck. The rise of alternative publishing platforms has made this task a little trickier. A blogger may have 1,000 active followers on Twitter and as many friends on Facebook, but that influence might never show up in a blog. Many writers also maintain or contribute to multiple blogs, meaning that their aggregate influence is greater than what is evident in any single forum. To alleviate this confusion, look at the profiles that people publish on their blogs. Often they will list the IDs they use on other services.

Communities present another variable. Many people are passionate about a topic such as travel or food, but don't want to go to the trouble of maintaining a blog. They use recommendation engines such as <u>Boo</u> and <u>FoodCritics</u> to share their opinions, and some of them can acquire quite a following. Social networks make this easy by spotlighting and rewarding their most active members. These people are, in effect, blogging but they are using the shared resource of a network to get their message out instead of concentrating their comments in one place. In Chapter 3, we looked at some ways to find these influencers.

Various standards are being proposed for creating unified identities, but it's unlikely that they will have much impact in the foreseeable future. It's okay to ask online influencers to apply for the equivalent of press credentials. If they want to be taken seriously, they won't mind jumping through a hoop or two.

Whatever access criteria you choose, I recommend you define a policy for blogger engagement. Choosing to ignore these voices is not practical in the long term. Conversations will happen with or without your participation, and your absence will be perceived negatively.

> **Secret: You need to have a written policy on blogger engagement, even if you choose not to engage. The blogosphere is too big to ignore.**

While it's usually best to engage with critics directly, you don't have to do so in every case, particularly if a chorus of voices is singing the same tune. It's perfectly okay to speak directly to the public about an issue that arises online. DuPont did this successfully a few years ago when unfounded allegations were raised about links between its Teflon products and cancer. The company chose not to get into a shouting match with its critics but instead set up a website devoted to clarifying the issues of health and Teflon. The storm quickly died down once the company had stated its side of the case (the charges turned out to be groundless).

Little Pain, Mostly Gain

Most companies can only gain from blogger promotion. If your brands and products aren't well known, then influential enthusiasts can put you on the map quickly. If a community of enthusiasts already exists, they're probably eager to learn more about your new products. Nokia has conducted more than a half-dozen campaigns for its high end cell phones over the last three years. It

> **Secret: Sending new product samples to bloggers can be a cheap source of word-of-mouth marketing.**

sends new models to a hand-picked list of cell phone bloggers; no strings attached. The company has a website on which it posts the reviews these enthusiasts write—both positive and negative. Nearly 90 percent of the reviews have been favorable. The independent validation by this technically proficient community is invaluable to Nokia. Camera maker Nikon conducts similar promotion for its new cameras, sending evaluation units to prominent photo bloggers and linking to their reviews.

Working with bloggers isn't all that different from working with mainstream media, but there are some important distinctions. Prominent bloggers tend to be passionate about the topics they cover and their level of expertise often exceeds that of their professional reporters. When promoting to them, be ready for intelligent and often pointed questions. Have your product experts standing by.

Bloggers are also likely to be more resistant to PR pitches than journalists. Whereas reporters quickly learn the ropes of dealing with pitches and press releases, bloggers don't have that media grounding. They expect contact to be personalized and specific to their interests. They may react badly if they believe they're just a name on a list. Never add a blogger to your press list without first asking permission, and respond promptly to their requests for removal. Once you engage with them, treat them as you would any other media influencer. If you imply that they are second-class citizens, you will jeopardize the whole outreach effort. I describe some best practices in this area in MediaBlather, a weekly podcast I produce in partnership with veteran tech journalist David Strom.

Engaging with Influencers

Your tactics for engagement need to vary by the situation. A conversation with an openly hostile influencer demands a different approach than an engagement with someone who's never heard of your company. Use common sense and good public relations practices. Never lose your cool. Most people will welcome your outreach if you have something useful to offer.

The bad old days of "spray and pray" press releases are over. Marketing to any influencer, whether in mainstream for new media, demands a personal approach. This tactic is particularly important in the social media domain, where traditional marketing is regarded with such suspicion. Some tips:

Know the influencer. In the age of search, there's simply no excuse for not knowing something about the person you're reaching out to. A simple Google search will turn up examples of their past activity, and you can complement your knowledge by searching on services such as Zoominfo, Spock, and LinkedIn to learn more about them. Social media enthusiasts tend to be active in a lot of places, so it's usually not a challenge to find them. Read a couple of their recent posts and be ready to compliment them on something they've said. You don't need to be effusive, but show that you've done your homework. This is the quickest way to make a friend or to disarm a wary or negative person.

> Secret: Know something about the influencers you're trying to reach. Search engines make it fast and easy to look informed.

Have something of value to give. Influencers like to feel important, so have something that's just for them. This can be as simple as a link to an interesting article, an invitation to listen in on a webcast or a free trial of a new service. The offer doesn't have to be expensive, but it should be out of the ordinary.

In fact, a lavish offer can backfire. That's what happened in late 2006, when Microsoft sent some top bloggers high-end laptops preloaded with its Windows Vista operating system. The thinly veiled bribe from a company whose wealth was already a source of some resentment created such a negative reaction that Microsoft was forced to backpedal and recommend that the bloggers return the laptops or give them to charity. Negative sentiment about Microsoft's market power didn't help the matter.

Creativity will get you farther than cash. When software maker Altiris rolled out its SVS product in 2006, its PR agency sent specially labeled packages of apple juice to about 400 bloggers. Journalists ignore such gimmicks, which arrive all the time in the mail. But bloggers weren't used to the attention and the back-and-forth between them actually helped build anticipation for the product, according to publicist Cheryl Snapp Connor.

Offer help. Make it clear that you are available as a resource to help influencers better understand your products and market, as well as to serve as an entry point to the company. Make the offer meaningful by adding a cell phone number and/or instant messaging address and invite them to contact you whenever they need your help. Be sincere, though. If you provide contact information and then fail to respond to inquiries, you'll undermine the outreach effort.

> ### Secret: It's okay to give exclusives to bloggers.

Use exclusives. I have always advised against using exclusives or "leaks" to communicate news to mainstream media, but the rules are different in the community of bloggers. The reason: reporters are competitive and sometimes egotistical people who don't understand or agree with the distinctions that marketers make between media outlets. Give an exclusive to one reporter and you make a lot of enemies.

That culture just doesn't exist in the blogosphere. With the exception of a few very prominent sites, bloggers know that they aren't TechCrunch or Engadget, and they don't expect to be treated equally. In fact, rumors posted on those sites can kick off blog buzz that creates anticipation for the real announcement. Apple benefited spectacularly from this kind of speculation prior to the 2007 launch of its iPhone. More than 1,000 bloggers were buzzing about tidbits posted on Engadget and Gizmodo, creating anticipation that spread to mainstream media. Apple never acknowledged planting these rumors, but the effect was dramatic. The iPhone not only became the fastest-selling phone in history, but it spawned an ecosystem of third-party enhancement products and created a cult following.

> ### Secret: Inviting influencers into the development process is the quickest way to neutralize negativity.

Invite feedback. People like to be asked for their opinion, so take the opportunity to solicit feedback about your company, market position, product features or another topic with which they're familiar. If possible, arrange to connect bloggers with a technical resource or executive in order to re-emphasize their "insider" status. This tactic is particularly effective with negative influencers. Once you invite them into the product development process, they take ownership of the outcome. It's difficult for people to criticize something they helped create. You need to have buy-in across your organization to make this strategy work because if influencers believe their suggestions are being ignored or patronized, they'll strike back angrily.

Follow up. One of the most common mistakes that media relations people make is initiating a conversation in the name of establishing a relationship and then disappearing once the message has been delivered. This tactic makes marketers look shallow and insincere. Avoid it. Once you start a dialogue, make it a point to check in every three to four months, especially if you don't have any news to share. The fact that you occasionally call without an agenda actually reflects favorably upon you. Social networks make this easy. As explained in the vignette "What Motivates Social Networkers," creating "friend" relationships with bloggers enables you to stay in touch easily and efficiently.

Online Promotion

In Chapter 10, we touched on the importance of search in content development. Suffice it to say that discoverability should be a foundation for any promotion effort. But search engines aren't the only way to get noticed online. Social bookmarking services, RSS feeds and widgets can drive traffic, sometimes in spectacular fashion. Know how they work, but keep them in perspective.

The Web is teeming with advice on how to drive traffic through link exchanges, recommendation engines and creative approaches to content. In late 2007, blogger Tamar Weinberg listed more than 250 of the best online marketing blog entries of the year in a summary article on her techpedia blog. It would have easily taken a couple of days just to read every article she cited—and hers was only one of several similar lists that came out that December.

Secret: Linkbaiting can work, but analyze traffic to be sure visitors aren't entering and leaving on the same page. If they aren't investigating the site, you aren't gaining much.

Many of these posts offered advice on how to increase traffic by registering content on sites like Digg, Sphinn, reddit, StumbleUpon, and Ma.gnolia. Others had advice on how to write headlines or spin content to get the maximum traffic. These linkbaiting tactics are intended to generate traffic from social bookmarking services.

Social bookmarking sites can be effective short-term traffic engines. Submit an article to StumbleUpon and you may see hundreds or even a few thousand visitors within a day. Earn a few dozen Diggs and enjoy many times that amount.

Linkbaiting is quickly becoming a cottage industry, which invites the potential for abuse. Some companies actually hire offshore firms to put low-paid teams of people to work posting comments and links on as many sites as they can find. In November 2007, Dan Ackerman Greenberg posted a controversial guest commentary on TechCrunch in which he described how his company drove large volumes of traffic to his clients' videos through an assortment of dummy accounts, phony recommendations and social bookmark ballot-box stuffing. I wouldn't recommend that anyone try these tactics, but it's interesting to read the article to see just how the system can be manipulated.

It's a good practice to post your best stuff in places where other people have a chance to see it and either link to or vote on it. However, as I mentioned in the previous chapter, traffic for traffic's sake isn't very useful. The vast majority of visitors that you draw by linkbaiting will never return. In fact, they may be annoyed if they believe they were misled to your site in the first place. Analyze any traffic you get from these services to look at visitor paths, time spent on site and return visits. This will give you a sense of whether the traffic they're sending you is useful.

In the long term, you'll do better by following guidelines for developing content that I outlined in Chapters 10-13 and by practicing good promotional blocking and tackling.

Fundamentals of Online Promotion

Whether your online outpost is a website, blog, podcast, video, photo or some combination of those, a few basic promotion tactics apply.

Write for search. As we discussed in Chapter 9, using the words and phrases that your constituents use will help your search engine performance. To the extent that you can use these words in page titles, headlines and in the upper left hand corner of your website, you'll help your cause further. Tag every item of multimedia content, or else search engines can't see it.

Update often. Search engines monitor websites for activity and adjust their crawl schedules accordingly. The more often you add content to your site, the more often the search crawler comes back. This is one more reason to keep your entries short and frequent.

Online Promotion Secrets:

- ☞ Write for search
- ☞ Update often
- ☞ File a site map
- ☞ Use tags
- ☞ Promote link exchanges
- ☞ Cross-link within your own sites
- ☞ Syndicate everywhere
- ☞ Use bookmarking sites

File a site map. This often overlooked tactic can immensely improve your search performance. Most search engines don't try to find every page on your site but instead focus on those that are linked to by other pages. Sites with lots of pages that aren't connected with others (for example, back-issue archives) may be under-represented in search engines. In fact, chances are good that a quarter of the pages on your site have never been visited by a search spider at all. By registering a site map, you notify the engine of every page that you own. Most web hosting and search engine providers offer tutorials on how to do this.

Use tags. Many search engines give tags special consideration and assign better placement in search results to those sites that have categorized themselves this way. Tag-

Secret: Select tags carefully so that aggregation sites place your content in the right groups.

ging your content also makes sure that those engines will group your content with similarly tagged material from other sources. Choose tags wisely. Visit sites like Technorati and del.icio.us to see with which tags you should be associated. Standardize the use of those tags throughout your content. If you're interested in learning more about the power of tagging, pick up a copy of David Weinberger's fascinating and entertaining *Everything is Miscellaneous: The Power of the New Digital Disorder*.

The Well-Tempered Blog

Are you getting the most bang for your blog? Successful blogging is all about generating awareness, repeat visitors, search engine visibility and lots of inbound links. Take the following test to see how well your blog shapes up. Give yourself one point for each "yes" answer and 0 points for each "no." Check your score at the end.

1. Do you use a domain name that matches the search terms that are most important to you (for example, "photoprofessional")? Alternatively, does your blog live within your business domain (such as "photofinishing.com/blog")?
2. Does your blog title include a description of what the blog is about?
3. Do you post new entries three or more times per week?
4. Do you vary the length of entries, with some short and some long?
5. Do you tag your entries?
6. Do you list your tags alphabetically or in a tag cloud?
7. Are your headlines simple, descriptive and declarative?

8. Do you make it easy for visitors to subscribe to your RSS feed?

9. Do you regularly include photos?

10. Do you regularly include streaming audio or video?

11. Do you write mostly in first person?

12. Do you always attribute and link to source material?

13. Do you have a blogroll?

14. Do you include a link to your company website or your other personal websites?

15. Do you write about a variety of topics, some professional and some personal?

16. Do you frequently file reports from conferences or events you attend?

17. Do you invite comments from visitors?

18. Do you respond to comments from visitors?

19. Does the number of comments you receive exceed the number of entries you post?

20. Do you have an "About" page with descriptive information about yourself?

21. Do you have a photo of yourself somewhere on the blog?

22. Do you provide a way for readers to contact you?

23. Do you provide a search option?

24. Do you make it easy for people to bookmark your entries to Digg, del.icio.us, StumbleUpon and/or other social bookmarking sites?

25. Do you have a copyright or Creative Commons statement?

Scoring:

20—25   Bloggi master

15—19	Accomplished blogger
10—14	Purchase *The New Influencers*
5—9	Surprised you're still doing this
0—4	You are a spam bot

Promote link exchanges. Use your articles and your blogroll to link to people in your community who share your interests. Then reach out to them and ask them to link back. There's no shame in sending a "link love" e-mail to someone you think would genuinely be interested in content you've posted. As long as your demonstrate sincerity, they'll be inclined to return the favor.

> Secret: Setting up "link farms" for the sole purpose of improving search performance can get you blacklisted by the big search engines.

Cross-link within whatever sites you control. If you have 15 bloggers in the company, be sure they're linking to each other as well as to all relevant pages on the company website. If you have employees blogging on the outside, ask them for a link. The more links, the better the search engine performance. Do not, under any circumstances, set up websites for the sole purposes of creating links. These link farms are not only considered bad form, but they can get you blacklisted from the major search engines.

Syndicate everywhere. Every section of your site that is updated regularly should be accessible through RSS. No longer just a plaything for geeks, RSS is now being embedded in everything from AOL homepages to cell phones. Subscribing to RSS feeds is easier than ever. And not to beat a dead horse, but "Search engines and news aggregators really like RSS," says Sally Falkow, a Web content strategist. An RSS feed is also a starting point for delivering your content through alternative channels like a Facebook profile or a website widget. RSS feeds can also easily be embedded in widgets [see side bar below]. Effective use of RSS feeds can generate many times the traffic you would get from your own website. Make sure that any content you develop can be delivered this way.

Use social bookmarking sites. It's worth joining a few services that let you maintain your own bookmark collections, such as del.icio. us, <u>diigo</u>, <u>clipclip</u>, and <u>furl</u>. It doesn't hurt to register your own content there, and someone else just might find you. Be careful with community bookmark sites like Digg, Sphinn, and reddit, though. Those sites encourage members to vote on submitted content, and members who repeatedly register uninteresting material are branded as spammers. A surprisingly small number of people influence the decisions on these sites, and you don't want to get on their bad side.

You should also make it easy for people to vote for your content using whatever bookmark sites they favor. It's simple to add buttons to your blog or website that enable visitors to bookmark your pages with one click. Check the individual sites for instructions or use a service like <u>SocialSubmit</u>, which can submit to multiple bookmarking sites simultaneously.

What about Widgets?

Widget mania seized the marketing world in 2007, becoming the must-have tool for online marketers and experiencing predictable over-saturation in the process. Widgets are a cheap and easy way to syndicate content to constituents' blogs and websites. They're a kind of linkable eye candy. One of the earliest and most popular examples is the Amazon Associate widget, which promotes books of the site owner's choosing, with Amazon paying a small commission for sales that result.

"Think of it as a shared open window to a single site or a banner campaign where each user gets to dictate the content that appears in exchange for giving that brand the space on their site," wrote Michael Leis, Vice President of Strategic Services at Publishing Dynamics, a developer of desktop widgets, in <u>an article in iMediaConnection</u>.

Marketers love widgets because they're cheap and trackable. Enthusiasts use widgets to dress up their blogs or websites while showing affinity to a favored brand and adding some original content. Marketers can see real-time data on how people are interacting with widgets and find out whether the program has been embedded in a blog or Facebook profile. They can also be tied back to affiliate programs to reward users with commissions for referring sales. When they work, they work very well. When they don't, there's not a lot of money lost.

All commercial blogging services support widgets, which can be easily added with a few lines of HTML or Javascript code. Applications delivered on social networks like MySpace and Facebook are also sometimes called widgets. Widgets can also be delivered as desktop applications or via containers like Google Desktop.

Researcher eMarketer expects U.S. companies to spend about $40 million on widgets in 2008, nearly triple the previous year's total. The small number is reflective of the low cost of production and the fact that most companies promote widgets through their own websites or via Facebook. Jupiter Research says user awareness of widgets jumped from 5 percent to nearly 40 percent in one year. comScore counted nearly 148 million unique views of Web-based widgets in November, 2007 alone.

Widgets are generally used to deliver regularly updated information. This can be news, blog entries, videos, press releases or simple Internet services like a guest book or a chat window. You can create the content or license it from partners. Yahoo! Widgets and Widgetbox both have collections of thousands of examples. Other widget makers include Clearspring, Slide, AppsSavvy,

MuseStorm, iLike, and RockYou. ThinkDesktop specializes in desktop widgets.

On the desktop, widgets have been around a long time, with Weatherbug and Southwest Airlines' Ding! being early examples. Ding has been a gusher for Southwest, which attributed $150 million in ticket sales to the simple applet that updates users on exclusive promotions.

Creativity and fun are critical to success with widgets, and businesses of all kinds are embracing them:

- Ford used widgets to advertise Sync, a voice interface for mobile phones and digital music players. The widget offered free song and video downloads, as well as links to more information about the product.
- Dating site eHarmony has a widget with rotating questions and answers about dating. The call to action is a free personality profile.
- Paper maker Kimberly-Clark has the Scott Common Sense Community Calendar, a widget that delivers time- and money-saving tips through a desktop widget.

The popularity of widgets has quickly led to a predictable feeding frenzy. With so many now on the market, the chance of realizing significant marketing benefits is shrinking. However, given their low cost and relatively easy deployment, it looks like widgets will be with us for a long time.

The Social Media Press Release

The lowly press release is the Rodney Dangerfield of the media relations world. Although long reviled by journalists and even the PR people who produce them, press releases remain the most common way to distribute news about a company and its products.

The arrival of social media has sparked efforts to overhaul the century-old press release and make it more relevant to the online world. As of this writing, the jury is still out on whether those efforts will succeed. Nearly everyone agrees that the press release, with its impersonal language, manufactured quotes and one-sided perspective, is a relic. However, no one has come up with an alternative that seems to be worth the extra effort needed to produce it. What's more, many regulatory agencies require companies to create conventional press releases whenever there's material news to report, thereby perpetuating this outmoded form.

In early 2006, Shift Communications created the social media press release, a flexible template that accommodates text, feeds, tags, streaming media and lots of links. The concept was to recognize the many forms in which information is communicated in new media and to create a multifaceted vehicle to deliver that information.

The social media release has had mixed success. On the one hand, many PR organizations have experimented with it, including Cisco, Ford, Verizon, Gatorade and Coca-Cola. General Motors and Electrolux are among the companies that have created social media-powered online newsrooms. On the other, practitioners say the format requires substantially more work than a text press release and the results haven't justified the additional effort. However, fans continue to advance the idea.

"Done right, they enable direct conversations between newsmakers and stakeholders," says Shift's Todd Defren. "Whether there's a call for this remains to be seen, but imagine that Apple were to allow moderated comments within its newsroom. I'd anticipate a flood of interest."

In early 2008, Toronto-based Social Media Group released a template for what it called version 3 of the social media press release. The company said the new format "updates the story with any combination of available multimedia assets including photos, videos, audio clips, graphs, PDFs, textual facts and any other type of story update imaginable." The model also allows source content to be hosted on sites like YouTube and Flickr, where it can get extra search engine and community visibility. Shift also released a new version of its template. The debate is likely to continue for some time. Meanwhile, it's clear that the plain text press release, for all its warts, is likely to be with us for many years.

Syndication Success

Jody DeVere calls <u>AskPatty</u> "The Little Blog that Could." It's an apt description, because after two years of chugging away, DeVere has turned the site into a word-of-mouth marketing machine.

Jody DeVere

I wrote about AskPatty in Chapter 6 of *The New Influencers* because of the startup's innovative use of blogging to promote its agenda of empowering female drivers. DeVere started her business because she believed that women were an underappreciated source of influence in automotive decisions. AskPatty's goal is to train auto dealers to address the female audience and to become a destination and membership site for women who are interested in cars.

A lot has happened since I first met DeVere at the company's formal launch in late 2006. Today, AskPatty is actively training more than 200 auto dealers and has a backlog of 1,500 inquiries from other prospects. What started as a blog has evolved into a rich amalgamation of expert advice, community discussion and software applications. A panel of 50 female automotive experts answers questions from members via a blog and podcasts. There's a configuration and comparison engine for members to use in making car-buying decisions, and a calendar that reminds them when their vehicle is due for services. Traffic continues to grow by double digit percentages every month. All this has come without any mainstream media advertising and only a smattering of Internet advertising. ("Don't waste your money," DeVere says).

Secret: Syndicate everywhere.

The secret? Spread your content around. Jody DeVere has mastered the art of syndication, bookmarks, e-mail and plain old personal networking as a means to spread AskPatty's 2,000-plus original articles all over the Web. The valuable lesson: Posting content on your website is just the beginning. Promoting it effectively through syndication partners and your own alternative channels can deliver 10 or 20 times the exposure. You can even make the jump into mainstream media.

Go to women's sites like WomenCorp, Mommytalk, Fabulously40, CoolMomPicks, and DivineCaroline and you'll find AskPatty occupying a niche as the automotive expert. Newspapers are beginning to syndicate material, too. DeVere is generous with these deals; she usually asks for nothing more than a link. But there's a method to her madness.

For one thing, the syndication deals cost nothing. An RSS feed automatically streams any new material that's posted on AskPatty to any site in the partner network. Most social network operators like having lots of new content because it improves their search engine performance and attracts repeat visitors. Their reciprocal links also drive search engine visibility for AskPatty, which lead to more traffic. That, in turn, creates more syndication demand. It's a big self-sustaining traffic lovefest.

DeVere has also staked out a distinctive online niche. If her site was all about cars, she'd be a face in the crowd. But it's a site about cars that's aimed at women. That makes it a search engine magnet. It also makes the topics, tags and feeds that AskPatty creates distinctive by default. Jody DeVere understands the power of niche markets.

"We're basically syndicating the questions that women ask about cars, so I get a tremendous amount of search traffic from others asking those same questions," she says. "We stick to a vertical and create keyword-rich content so women find us naturally."

It helps to be a geek, of course. DeVere has tried every viral promotion tactic she can find. A new social bookmark site for women called Skirt is a recent favorite. She's also an enthusiastic StumbleUpon user. DeVere also takes pains to promote content produced by her friends and business partners. They appreciate the gesture and often return the favor.

DeVere also regularly submits interesting new content to the Squidoo, del.icio.us and Netscape bookmarking sites. There are AskPatty profiles on Facebook and MySpace, Twitter and Jaiku. AskPatty even has an island in SecondLife called Motorability, which is dedicated to raising awareness about her favorite charity, UnitedSpinal.org, and car culture. Devere hosts a regular chat called Caffeine and Cars. "We've found that the real power Internet users are in Second Life," she says.

Not surprisingly, the company is also building its own social network. CarBlabber will feature car reviews written by women for women. It will recognize the fact that women look at cars differently from men. "The guys immediately want to look under the hood, but the women take in the whole car," she says. "They ask questions like 'I have four toddlers; how can I carry all of them?'" CarBlabber will treat those questions seriously.

AskPatty's online promotion plan works because DeVere understands the dynamics of online media. She knows that bloggers and network operators like cheap and frequently updated content. She knows that conventional media are increasingly turning to bloggers as expert sources while cash-strapped newspapers are more willing than ever to accept content from commercial publishers if the quality is good and the price is right.

At this point, momentum has taken over a lot of the work. DeVere fields two or three media interviews each week and blogger mentions come daily. She admits that she sometimes has to ice her hands in the evening from all the keyboard work, but an expanding network of volunteer contributors is picking up more of the slack.

Her advice: "Pick a niche, stick to it and become very competent at that conversation."

15

Measuring Results

Online marketers face a paradox: The Internet is the most measurable medium ever invented, yet the lack of commonly accepted metrics continues to stymie marketing initiatives.

The controversy over online metrics frustrates practitioners and holds back investments. Television and radio promotion is far less measurable than online marketing, yet those media have a track record. They've been around so long that executives are comfortable with them. Little on the Internet is predictable, and the new world of social media is still a virtual free-for-all. This puts marketers in a difficult position: They're encouraged to experiment with new media, but rewarded based on predictable results. It's not surprising, then, that many social media initiatives are so tentative.

Metrics are frequently cited as the biggest barrier to marketers' adoption of online media. A McKinsey study of 410 marketing executives reported that "insufficient metrics to measure impact" was the number one factor holding back online investment. A late 2007 survey of 120 marketing pros by digital advertising consultancy Sapient found that 51 percent felt only "somewhat confident" or "not confident at all" in their ability to track campaigns in real time across multiple channels. Thirty-five percent said social media is the category they're least confident about.

Even as people argue about metrics, their variety and sophistication continues to race ahead. Just a decade ago, server hits were the accepted standard. Today, that unit of measure is almost entirely ignored. Page views, unique visitors, visitor paths, referring URLs, return visits, search engine referrals and at least a couple of dozen other metrics have gained acceptance recently. Each has value but also shortcomings.

The best metrics may also have nothing to do with website traffic. For example, an increase in blog referrals, press mentions, Diggs or performance on brand awareness studies may track back to a successful social media campaign yet deliver few visitors.

Secret: According to new research, the vast majority of active Internet users never click on ads.

Some commonly accepted metrics may also be dangerously misleading. Landmark research by media agency Starcom USA, behavioral targeting network Tacoda, and digital metrics firm comScore in early 2008 turned up some startling information. The research established the existence of what researchers called "heavy clickers," or people who click on a lot of online ads. They make up just 6 percent of the online population but account for 50 percent of clicks on display ads. Another 10 percent of the population accounts for an additional 30 percent of clicks, the research found. The conclusions were that *less than one-sixth of online users drive 80 percent of advertising clicks.*

It gets better. Researchers also found that 68 percent of all Internet users *never click on ads at all* and that heavy clickers tend to be young and have household incomes of less than $40,000. Heavy clickers are also online four times as much as other users and skew toward heavy usage of auction, gambling, and career services sites. Are these the targets of your online advertising campaign?

The Starcom/Tacoda/comScore research, if it holds up, will only complicate the metrics debate. Marketers yearn for simple performance indicators like reach-and-frequency or share of audience that can be tied back to sales performance. If clicks aren't representative of visitor activity, then what is?

As we'll see later in this chapter, more sophisticated measures of engagement are emerging, but the debate over metrics is likely to continue for some time.

Back to Basics

Any metric can be valuable if tied to a goal, so the first step in measuring success is also the least quantitative one: Figure out a strategy. The whole argument about metrics can be minimized if the marketing team, management and any outside agencies can agree on what to measure.

Katie Paine is a thought leader in on-line measurement. She began and still writes the <u>first measurement blog</u> and founded the <u>Summit on Measurement</u>, a leading event on the topic. Paine doesn't debate the merits of page views versus unique visitors. "There are no standard metrics. Measure what's important to you," she says.

> **Secret: What metrics you choose are irrelevant as long as all the stakeholders agree on the choice.**

In her latest book, *Measuring Public Relationships*, Paine offers seven basic steps of any measurement program:

1. Identify the audiences with whom you have relationships. Communications professionals rarely have a consensus on this, particularly in large firms. Even within the communications group, people have different constituencies. Before any campaign begins, you need to put the stakeholders in a room and figure out who your audience is.

2. Define objectives for each audience. This can include building awareness, generating leads, increasing sales, educating the public or addressing a crisis. Paine advocates force-ranking these goals and then assigning measurable criteria for success, such as a 25 percent boost in press mentions.

3. Define measurement criteria. The more specific you can be, the easier it is to assess performance. An example would be increasing the number of news headlines that mention your company by 25 percent or increasing your share of media quotes versus your competition's.

4. Define your benchmark. This is the baseline standard by which progress will be measured. The base metric often relates to mind share versus a competitor or a definable past performance level.

5. Select a measurement tool. Metrics of success may have nothing to do with website traffic, but could include press clips, primary research, blogger mentions, or comparative mind share. Paine emphasizes that traditional measurement tools like online surveys are still relevant, as long as they represent an apples-to-apples comparison.

6. Analyze data, draw actionable conclusions and make recommendations. Look at all the results, both good and bad, and decide what has to change. Focus on those factors that you can control. You can't do much about market conditions or your competitors.

7. Make changes and measure again. Good measurement is an ongoing process that grows in value over time. Resist the urge to look at snapshots; they're meaningless without context.

Paine boils down the issues to a few key factors. *Outputs* are the results of publicity efforts, such as video clips, media citations and blog mentions. *Outtakes* are how people think as a result of experiencing outputs. *Outcomes* are how their behavior changes. All are measurable, she argues, so once you decide what tools you'll use to measure them, the rest is just execution.

As Paine works through the various audiences that PR people must satisfy—journalists, bloggers, event audiences, local constituents and even internal employees—she repeatedly drives home the point that measurement is all about sweating a few basics. It's not about page views vs. unique visitors. It's about choosing the right metrics for your situation and then applying them in a disciplined manner.

Scuderi Group looked at a variety of internal and external factors when it created the Air Hybrid Blog in early 2006. The company's objective was to raise awareness of an innovative new internal combustion engine design that it claims can improve fuel efficiency by more than a third while cutting toxic emissions. "We decided to create more of a newsfeed without a lot of first-person personality elements," says Tim Allik of Topaz Partners, Scuderi's public relations agency. "We use the blog as a way to distribute news and information about the company to a select list."

In viewing the blog tactically, Scuderi considered outward facing metrics like placements in key publications and blogger mentions. It also displays demonstration videos from YouTube, delivers podcasts and promotes an e-mail newsletter. Viewership and open rates on all those media arc monitored. "We see this as free worldwide distribution of video and audio," Allik says. "You're pulling people in instead of sending stuff out."

> **Secret: The most useful measures of success are often intangible, involving factors like learning or testing new ideas.**

Envision Success

Jeremiah Owyang, a Forrester Research analyst, abstracted these principles at an even higher level in an early 2008 post on his blog. Noting that too many of his clients are focused on tools rather than what to build with them, he urged companies to model what success should look like. His examples of possible success metrics:

- We were able to learn something about customers we've never know before;
- We were able to tell our story to customers and have them share it with others;
- The blogging program had more customer comments than posts;
- An online community led to customers supporting each other and reducing costs;
- An experimental project paved the way for a successful future project;
- We gained experience with a new form of two-way communication;
- We connected with a handful of customers we hadn't reached before for feedback and knowledge exchange;

- We learned something from customers that we didn't know before.

Owyang proposed that if management can sign off on big goals like these, marketers are much more likely to achieve success. Social media campaigns need to allow for the novelty and rapid change of the market. Too much focus on short-term metrics can set up a campaign for failure. As noted earlier in this book, really successful campaigns often extend for a year or more, with the payoffs growing as awareness and community builds.

Secret: Social media metrics need to include activity on other sites, which you often can't measure.

Sweating the Basics

While high-level goals are ideal, the reality is that many campaigns must be tied to defined metrics and short-term ones at that.

Today's projects demand richer metrics than the online marketing programs of just a few years ago. One reason is that social media campaigns must account for what happens on *other* sites as much as your own. It used to be that unique visitors, page views and visitor time spent on a site were a pretty good indication of success. Today, you may need to consider factors like:

- Search engine rank;
- RSS subscriptions;
- Social bookmark activity;
- Comments on your site and others;
- Inbound links;
- Blog mentions;
- Discussion group posts;
- Social network membership;
- Technorati, Bloglines, or Blogpulse rankings;
- Mainstream media references;
- Referral links;
- Alexa or Compete performance rankings;

- Search engine performance;
- Positive/negative sentiment analysis;
- Video viewership;
- Mashups based on your content;
- Copycat or parody videos;
- Contest entries.

And you must be able to measure each of these factors against your competitors' performance.

There are so many possible ways to measure performance that it's impossible to designate one metric as being superior to the others. That's why it's so important to go back to Chapter 2 and define the objectives. If the goal is to build brand awareness, then comparing mentions in social and traditional media versus a competitor is useful. If it's to generate leads, then referral traffic to an informational video might work. If it's to increase sales, then track referrers to a product description/order form.

Web analytics tools grow more sophisticated all the time with high-end professional products like Omniture, WebTrends, and Core Metrics now able to track integrated campaigns spanning multiple types of content and delivery formats. Meanwhile, free tools like Google Analytics and StarCounter sport features that would have cost thousands of dollars in software license fees just a few years ago. However, no one has combined all the possible internal and external metrics.

There are some excellent blogs and websites that can give you deep dives on this topic. They include Hitwise Intelligence, Occam's Razor, Captain Blackbeaks Blog, and FutureNow. Here are a few basic tactics that every online marketer should be aware of. It's remarkable how often even these simple tips aren't followed:

Use tracking codes. Every piece of collateral that goes out, whether it be printed, e-mailed or on a website, should have a unique tracking code. This makes it easy to find out where your traffic is coming from, which is essential for campaign analysis.

Secret: Visitor paths and repeat visitors are two valuable but under-appreciated measures of success.

Use unique landing page addresses. It's surprising to see that even sophisticated Web marketers sometimes direct advertising traffic back to a simple home page URL. This makes traffic from e-mail promotion untraceable. Unique landing page URLs tied to e-mail marketing avoids this problem. And it's not just e-mail. If a visitor bookmarks a link from an e-mail message and then shares it with others, the referring URL may end up coming from a social bookmarking site. Make the address distinctive so you can track performance back to the original campaign.

Double down on winners. Your analytics analysis will almost certainly turn up a few referring URLs that outperform all others in terms of driving visitors to desired destinations. These URLs may be on your website or on somebody else's. These are your winners, and you should focus energy on driving more traffic to them. Perhaps that means buying ads on that site or setting up a link exchange. Update and share the list of winners regularly with your own bloggers and Web stewards, making sure they take every opportunity to link to them.

Pay attention to search terms. All analytics packages can show you which search terms are working for you. Consider buying these terms as part of your search marketing efforts and using them more frequently on your site to improve organic search results.

Scrutinize repeat visitors. This standard metric can be very powerful for you because it identifies your most engaged audience. Correlate that with entry pages, visitor paths and referring URLs to create a model of how your best prospects navigate your site.

Analyze visitor paths. This often-overlooked tracking feature shows what pages visitors looked at once they reached your site. While most visitors come and leave on a single page, some stay and look around. Identifying patterns in their navigation can reveal what links are working for you. In particular, look at the links that attract people to your ultimate destination page, meaning the one that delivers the download, captures the lead or makes the sale. Think of how you can spread these around more liberally.

Most importantly, choose metrics that matter to you and to your executives. This should be part of the goals defined in Katie Paine's seven steps at the beginning of this chapter. The metrics that matter to you will vary by the objective. For example, Lee Odden of WebProNews suggests that each of the following types of blogs favor different metrics:

- Blogs designed to generate advertising revenue—unique visitors, page views and subscribers;
- Blogs intended to generate leads—inquires, time spent on site, repeat visitors;
- Search engine optimization blogs—keyword rankings, links, referring traffic;
- Thought leadership blogs—media mentions, links from prominent bloggers, subscribers, inclusion in "best of" lists.

Personal Favorites

For the half-dozen websites and blogs that I personally maintain, here are the metrics I value most:

Page views—For a quick-hit view of how your site is doing, this simple metric is still the best.

Returning visitors—This is the most important number I monitor over time. A high level of returning visitors indicates "stickiness," which means that people are bookmarking you and paying attention.

Pages per visit—This number tends to move very little, but if you can keep it trending upward, it shows that you're giving people interesting content and useful navigation.

RSS subscriptions—My goal isn't to generate advertising revenue but rather to sustain visibility. I don't care whether or not someone visits my site as long as they see my content. An RSS subscriber is as good as a daily visitor, in my view.

Referring sites—It's nice to know that someone is linking to you, but it's particularly nice to know which links drive traffic. I find that it's often worth linking to these sites from my own blogroll or reaching out to the owners by e-mail to ask if they want to subscribe to my newsletter.

Search engine placement—Hitting the first results page of Google can raise the traffic floor permanently. When the website for *The New Influencers* hit the top 10 Google results on the term "influencers," traffic tripled immediately.

Search terms—It's often illuminating to see which search terms are driving traffic. They may not be the ones you expect. This can help you optimize your keyword and tag usage.

Above all, I recommend that you focus. You can go batty trying to monitor the daunting number of metrics offered in even the most basic analytics tools. It's better to understand a few indicators well than to have only a cursory knowledge of many.

> **Secret: The Net Promoter Score is a simple but powerful measure of results.**

New Metrics Emerge

As long as disagreement over metrics persists, people will try to come up with better standards. One popular and elegantly simple concept is the Net Promoter Score (NPS) proposed by Fred Reicheld in his book *The Ultimate Question*. The index is calculated by subtracting the number of unhappy customers from the number of happy customers in a given sample. NPS is a good way to identify that problems exist, although not necessarily the best way to pinpoint the exact problem.

In *Marketing to the Social Web*, Larry Weber tells how General Electric used NPS to identify that its European diagnostic imaging business was perceived poorly. A deep dive turned up problems in the company's customer support system which, when fixed, immediately improved the division's NPS.

Reicheld maintains that most companies have only marginally more happy customers than unhappy ones and that the Net Promoter Score has a direct correlation to business performance. It's relatively simple to apply this metric against a sampling of bloggers.

That view is supported by Dell Computer's experience. When the company began monitoring and responding to bloggers in 2006, the percentage of negative blog comments was nearly 50 percent, according to Dell's Richard Binhammer. The company made rapid progress, but about 18 months into the outreach project the volume of negative comments stalled at about 20 percent of total mentions. It has stayed there stubbornly ever since.

Binhammer, whose background is in politics, believes that 20 percent may be a permanent floor, at least for Dell. In the same way that 20 percent of the U.S. population votes for the same political party regardless of the candidate, businesses are likely to find that about 40 percent of their customers are either relentlessly positive or persistently negative, he says. That means that your playing field is in the middle.

Viewpoint Corp. has the User Engagement Index, an online advertising effectiveness metric that looks at such factors as "roll-overs, panel expansions, hovers, click-to-full screen, data capture and viral effects," such as pass-along messaging, according to the company. Viewpoint tracks these factors across all the ads it serves to identify the most effective messages. Many of these metrics are unique to social media channels or to Flash or Java programs. If your site uses those tools, specialized metrics may deliver unique insight on what visitors are doing with them.

Bottom line: Marketers will debate the minutiae of metrics for years. Waiting for everyone to agree on standards is pointless because different measures apply to different situations. There are plenty of useful metrics available. It's better to choose something—anything— and get started rather than waste time waiting for consensus.

Two Novel Approaches to Measuring Online Influence

With so many variables affecting the influence equation, some creative PR pros have taken a mix-and-match approach to creating their own metrics.

David Brain, the CEO of Edelman Europe, took a shot at coming up with a Social Media Index that he described in a July, 2007 blog entry. The index is a weighted mashup of metrics, including Google PageRank, Technorati rating, frequency of posts, number of comments, Facebook ranking, Twitter friends, Digg score, and other factors that assess not only a blogger's popularity but also his or her activities in other media. The results confirmed that active bloggers are also prolific in other venues and individuals tend to perform especially well compared to companies. The more than 130 comments on the blog entry testify to the interest in aggregate rankings like this.

PR blogger Brendan Cooper also attempted to create an aggregate index combining factors like Technorati authority, inbound links and Google and Blogpulse citations over different time periods. He then compared the aggregate rankings to the basic Technorati authority ranking and found that Technorati does a pretty good job of measuring overall influence. He also concluded that inbound links as measured by Yahoo were the least reliable indicator of authority.

16

Celebrating Change

"The media world has changed more in the last five years that it has in the last 50 and it will change at that rate again in the next five years."

—Wenda Harris Millard, President, Media, Martha Stewart Living Omnimedia, Feb. 12, 2008

"There has been more change in the media world in the last five years than in the previous 500."

—Peter Horan, President, Media & Advertising, IAC

A decade from now, people may look at the title of this book and think it an historical curiosity. The idea that customer conversations could ever have been assigned solely to the marketing department will seem baffling. By then, interactivity will be so embedded into the fabric of business that we will wonder how we ever did without it, much as we think about e-mail today.

It's not surprising that social media was delegated to marketing in its early days. After all, marketing owns the message and social media is mostly seen as just another communication channel. But it's a far more disruptive force than that. Online communities will fundamentally change the way in which organizations interact with their constituents. Marketing's opportunity is to lead that transformation.

The legacy of one-way communication that has defined business since the Industrial Revolution is being dismantled as methodically as the Berlin Wall. It will be replaced by a dialogue in which customers, the media, shareholders and other influencers expect to be heard and heeded. Marketing will only be one player in these conversations. In the future, every potential contact point between a company and its customers will include mechanisms for seeking out and accommodating customer feedback.

This idea is frightening to many people, particularly those who've grown up in the traditional command-and-control structure of business. Success in many organizations is predicated upon a pyramid of authority, with individual advancement depending on a person's ability to manage the expectations of just a few people. When the wisdom of crowds inserts itself into that process, dramatic change will happen.

For example, consider the impact of incorporating customer feedback about a product into performance reviews of the product management team or the ramifications of testing a hotshot engineer's new idea before a committee of customers instead of an internal review board.

How will the world change when customers can quickly organize and strike because of a company's labor practices or environmental policies? How will the dynamics of an annual meeting change when shareholders can form consensus using Twitter messages while the meeting is still in progress? No, this isn't a marketing issue at all.

My perspective on social media is somewhat different from that of my colleagues. Most authors and consultants in this field are professional marketers, people who have spent many years in the agency or corporate world and have trench warfare experience.

My background is as an information technology journalist. This is both a strength and a weakness. The weakness is that I lack sensitivity to the day-to-day challenges—including the internal politics—that marketers face. If I've glossed over any of those issues, or ignored any obvious questions, I apologize.

The strength is that my background gives me a unique perspective on the transformation that is going on around us. This is why I'm so convinced of the permanence of this new dialogue and its potential for massive change.

Changing the Rules

Veterans of the information technology market know that the industry tears itself apart and rebuilds about once every decade. It's hard for some people to believe today that Cullinet Software and Lotus Development Corp. were once orders of magnitude larger than Microsoft, or that Wang Laboratories once had a stranglehold on the word processing market. Companies like Digital Equipment and Apollo Computer went from industry leaders to has-beens in two or three years.

In almost every case, these companies posted their biggest profits less than three years before they died or were acquired. Their seemingly unassailable dominance was shattered by a change in the rules. Their mastery of one evolutionary stage had no bearing on success in another. Clayton Christensen documents this phenomenon brilliantly in his book *The Innovator's Dilemma*.

Social media changes the rules, and history teaches that we can't even comprehend the ripple effect of that fact. Businesses will learn to incorporate customer conversations into nearly everything they do. In the past, their success was based upon anticipating customer requirements and responding at just the right time. In the future, success will be a byproduct of continuous innovation and outstanding customer service wrapped around a continuous feedback loop. We live in an age when a company's best ideas are quickly duplicated by overseas competitors and sold at a fraction of the price. There is no such thing as a barrier to entry anymore. Innovation and service are the only sustainable advantages. That means businesses need to be in constant contact with their markets.

Big institutions often give lip service to change while actually changing very little. Their cultures and investors don't permit them that luxury. Media companies are learning the frightening consequences of this failure to change. Newspapers are in the early stages of an epic collapse that's driven by the fact that the environment that defines their value—information scarcity—has disappeared. Record companies are learning the hard way that the assets that used to define their value—recorded media and a network to distribute them—have no value in the age of digital downloads. Business models sculpted on the expectation of scarcity are irrelevant in an environment of abundance.

Changes in customer behavior will force every one of our institutions to re-examine its values and culture. Those that value secrecy and insularity will have a hard time adapting to the new culture of openness. Those that thrive on vigorous and honest exchange will find the new online channels to be a gold mine of ideas and innovation.

Marketing Must Own the Customer Relationship

Marketing can lead this charge, but it must first change its perspective. As the group most often tasked with managing the social media initiative, marketing must redefine its value around stewardship of the customer. The Chief Marketing Officer must, in effect, become the Chief Conversation Officer. Given that most experts estimate the average job tenure of a CMO to be about 18 months, this change may be welcome! But it will also involve internal political struggles and a lot of retraining.

Owning the customer relationship is the most enviable task any marketer can hope for, but it requires thinking differently about communication. Customers will no longer tolerate interruption or inconvenience in order to get what they want. If someone annoys them, they simply go somewhere else. Today that's easy.

Unhappy customers no longer call support lines to voice their displeasure. Today, they blog or Twitter or post a complaint on their Facebook FunWall, log a review on Yelp or send an e-mail to The Consumerist. They may not get their problem resolved, but they get the satisfaction of sharing with others a message that would have otherwise been lost.

In many ways, social media marketing is a return to basics. Conversation marketing is as old as human relationships. In his seminal essay about the software market, _The Cathedral and the Bazaar_, Eric Raymond contrasts the barely organized chaos of a street market with the unyielding formality of the church. The high priests of the cathedral enjoy power at everyone else's expense and have no reason to change. In contrast, innovation flourishes in the bazaar.

The business world is transitioning from a cathedral to a bazaar. Barriers to entry are falling and fortunes will be made and lost more quickly than ever before. Successful street marketers are those who communicate constantly with their customers, seeking "win-win" deals. Human contact defines their success.

We learn the essentials of human relationships at an early age, yet our business institutions force us to discard these practices in favor of messaging and talking points.

We understand instinctively that imperfection is an endearing trait; it makes people more human and likable. Yet as businesses, we fire people for trying new ideas that fail.

We know that advertising is unnatural. It involves delivering one-way messages without any expectation of a response. We market this way because, until recently, there has been no viable alternative. But now there is.

We measure the success of our marketing programs through data mining with formulas and spreadsheets, even though we know instinctively that passion and commitment are far more important to successful customer relationships. The problem has been that we've had few ways to measure customer passion outside of sales performance. Now we do.

Conventional marketing and mainstream media have a future, but it will be a diminished role alongside an increasingly rich set of tools that build on human relationships.

It's All About Us

One of the most provocative comments about social media that I've heard in the last two years was made by a luncheon companion at a conference. Until recently, he had relied upon professional editors at newspapers and television stations to provide him with interesting and useful information. But now those people have been replaced by his network of friend and contacts who delivered to him a continuing stream of interesting and personalized information. These were people he knew and trusted, and that made the advice all the more valuable to him. By divesting himself of mainstream media, he had lost something but had gained much more in return.

This truth is essential to adapting to the changes that are going on around us. If there's one thing that 25 years of information technology industry experience has taught me, it's that you have to discard old assumptions in order to embrace new opportunities. This goes against the grain of human nature. People tend to look at the future in the context of the past, and this makes change frightening. We focus on our losses instead of our gains.

When I speak to groups about the disruptions going on in the media world, I often hear people express regret at what they've lost. They no longer have the security of knowing that the facts they read have been rigorously checked or that trusted brands are watching out for their interests. They fear that much of this work has now been thrust on them, and they worry that they're unprepared for the responsibility.

I try to point out that there's another way to look at the situation. It's true that there will be fewer gatekeepers in the future. However, new services will emerge that perform these tasks at a much more personalized level. Information may not be filtered and interpreted for us the way it has been, but we will have our choice of vastly greater amounts of information. Events that wouldn't have merited the attention of the local newspaper or TV station will be available to us on community websites. We'll be able to witness them firsthand through video and audio recordings or read blog entries posted by the participants. Instead of having others tell us what is true, we'll be able to witness truth ourselves. What could be more credible than that?

Take Action

I started this book by discussing the difficulty that organizations have in adapting to change, and I'll end it on the same thought. The past five years has witnessed the beginning of an epic transformation in the relationship between institutions and their constituents. Change of this magnitude creates waste and uncertainty as people struggle to define a new world order. That's normal.

We are privileged to have the opportunity to play a part in creating the new ground rules. At a time of great uncertainty, people have a tendency to assume that everyone else is figuring out the answers ahead of them. That's simply not true. Over the last three years, I've had the privilege of spending time with some of the most influential thinkers in social media. Most of them will admit, after a couple of beers, that they have no idea where this is all going. Take some comfort in that.

There are only two unpardonable sins in the current environment. One is fear. Fear not only stops progress in its tracks, but wastes time and resources in the pointless exercise of chasing the past or hoping that change will just go away. That leads to the other unpardonable sin, which is inaction. Tumultuous change creates great opportunity for experimentation. When no one knows the right course of action, there is very little downside to taking chances.

That's what I recommend you do right now. Find the low-cost, low impact ideas that no one has ever tried and take a risk with them. Dedicate yourself to becoming really proficient in just one of the networks we profiled in Chapter 7. Start a blog and stick with it. Make it your goal to accumulate 500 followers on Twitter. Learn how to create a Google Maps mashup. Even if you're not a geek, I predict you'll have more fun than you expect. And now that you've read this entire book, you'll have a leg up on everyone else.

:-)

Glossary of Terms

Prepared by the editors of whatis.com,
an online encyclopedia of technology terms

AdSense—Google's online advertising program that delivers contextually relevant advertising on websites and pays on a per-click or per-impression basis. Many bloggers use AdSense to generate revenue from their blogs.

advocacy blog—A blog with a mission. The author's purpose is to advance a particular point of view and influence public opinion. Advocacy blogs are often used to raise money for a cause, either through partnership programs, contextual advertising, sponsorships or direct donations.

Alexa.com—A website popularity engine owned by Amazon.com. Alexa is best known for allowing a user to view a site's traffic patterns, inbound links and competitors.

A-list—Jargon for an influential blogger, generally used as an adjective: "A-list blogger."

bandwidth—A term for data transfer rate (DTR), the amount of data that can be carried from one point to another in a given time period (usually a second).

banner ad—A graphic image advertisement used on Web pages. When a visitor views the ad on the page, it's called an impression. If the visitor clicks on the banner and is sent to the sponsor's website, the event is known as a click through.

blog—Short for Web log. An online journal that is frequently updated and intended for general public consumption. Blogs are defined by their format: a series of entries posted to a single website page in reverse-chronological order.

blogswarm— An event in which thousands of bloggers comment on the same story or news event, usually with strong opinions. A blogswarm can become the "hot topic" of the day in both the blogosphere and mainstream media.

blogger—(1) Someone who writes for or maintains a blog. (2) A free blog hosting service owned by Google.

blogosphere—The online community of bloggers and the content they publish.

BlogPulse—Blog search engine operated by Nielsen Buzz-Metrics. BlogPulse is best known for its trend analysis and data mining tools.

category—In blogging software, a feature that allows a blogger to group posts together by topic. Categories can be labeled by short descriptions called tags or elements.

citizen journalist—An amateur journalist who usually publishes online by using a blog or community website.

Classmates.com—Founded in 1995 and widely considered to be the first successful social network, Classmates.com enables people to find classmates, share information and plan reunions and events.

click—The action of clicking on a banner or text advertisement. A click triggers an event, such as starting a video or sending the visitor to the sponsor's website.

comment—In blogging, a software feature that allows the reader to publicly respond to a blogger's post. Comments may be published automatically or moderated (filtered) by a human being or computer program.

Comment spam—A form of spam delivered as comments on a weblog.

company blog—A type of blog maintained by an organization to publish news and opinion about itself or an issue. Company blogs frequently have multiple authors, most of them employees.

Connection—On LinkedIn, a relationship between two members that allows each to see each other's personal information and connections. Similar to Facebook's "Friends."

consumer-generated media—Also called user-generated media. A broad term referring to content posted on blogs, message boards, discussion boards and review sites. The term includes articles, photographs, audio recordings and video.

Consumerist—One of the most prominent consumer advocacy sites on the Web, consumerist gathers and republishes consumer experiences and also provides news and advice of interest to consumers.

conversation—(1) In a social media context, refers to two-way communication facilitated by blogs and other personal publishing tools. (2) In marketing, the evolution of a message or sales pitch into a discussion with customers.

Creative Commons—A nonprofit organization devoted to promoting an alternative copyright framework. Based on a similar public license for software, Creative Commons seeks to expand the range of creative work available for others to legally build upon and share, as long as the reuse is not for commercial purposes.

Del.icio.us—A social bookmarking website that allows members to store, categorize, annotate and share favorite Web pages.

Digg - A form of social bookmarking service in which members can comment and vote upon bookmarks submitted by each other, with the most popular items gaining increased visibility on the site; also used to describe an endorsement of bookmarked content.

Digg.com—A self-described "social news site" in which users submit and vote on online content. The more popular the Web page, the more prominent its position on the site.

eBook—Short for electronic book. An eBook can be downloaded and read on an electronic device such as a desktop computer, pocket PC, eBook reader, Internet-capable cell phone, PDA or notebook computer.

executive blog—A blog written by a high-ranking official in a business or organization.

feed—Push technology used to syndicate Web content. Users subscribe to feeds through an aggregation program, which periodically polls all the servers in the user's feed list and downloads new content.

follower—Popularized by Twitter, a type of social network relationship in which one member unilaterally chooses to monitor another member's comments and activities without the other member's explicit permission. In most cases, the member being followed has the option to block followers.

friend—In social media terms, a relationship between two members of a social network in which both parties agree to exchange information with each other, usually on an ongoing basis.

group blog—A blog with more than one regular contributor.

hosting site—A website that houses, serves and maintains files for other websites. Blogger and WordPress are two popular blog hosting sites.

hyperlink—An icon, image or text link that, when clicked upon, brings the reader to a different part of the page, or to an entirely new Web page. Most hyperlinks appear as underlined and/or colored text on a Web page.

iPod—A popular portable digital media player and data storage device from Apple Computer.

Linkbaiting—Catchall term for practices that are intended to attract search engine traffic and links from other websites. While the term is often used in a negative context, it can apply to tactics ranging from writing catchy headlines to using contests and giveaways to attract attention.

link blog—A blog that primarily contains links to other websites. Some of the most popular blogs on the Internet are link blogs. However, this format can also be used by spammers to generate traffic to advertising sites.

LinkedIn—Popular social network for business professionals that enables members to build relationships through direct and indirect contacts for the purposes of generating business value.

long tail—A frequency distribution pattern in which most occurrences cluster near the Y-axis and a long distribution curve tapers along the X-axis. The term was first used by Wired magazine to describe the business models of online retailers, many of whom derive a large percentage of their income from sales of low-volume products.

mainstream media—Broad term used to describe major print and broadcast outlets.

microblog—A form of weblog consisting of short entries, often posted via a mobile device.

moblog—A blog that is maintained by using a mobile device such as a PDA (personal digital assistant) or cell phone. In theory, any blog can be a moblog.

Moveable Type—Business blogging software developed by Six Apart, Ltd. Best known for the trackback feature, which enables bloggers to know when other bloggers have linked to their posts.

MP3 player— A portable digital audio device that stores, organizes and plays digital audio files.

MySpace—A popular social networking website where members occupy individual "spaces" and selectively share information with friends. Originally founded as a venue for aspiring musicians and bands to share music and concert dates, MySpace is now the most popular community site on the Internet. Acquired by News Corp. in 2005.

News Feed—In Facebook, a constantly updated list of activities, messages and recommendations provided by members of a person's friend network.

Open Social—Created to resolve the problem of duplication across social networks, Open Social provides a set of common application programming interfaces that participating networks can employ to share information. In theory, this permits members to share core identity data and applications.

page view—A request to load a single HTML page. website traffic expressed in terms of page views is a widely accepted indicator of online popularity.

PageRank—A Web page's prominence in Google search results determined by Google's proprietary algorithm. The formula is a secret, but is known to include factors like page title, keywords and the number and prominence of other sites that link to a page.

permalink—Short for permanent link. A unique URL assigned to an individual blog post.

podcast—Digital audio or video programming that can be streamed over the Internet or downloaded to a portable device. Podcasts differ from streaming audio or video in that podcasts use a subscription mechanism—RSS—to deliver content to subscribers.

podosphcrc—The community of people who create and use podcasts.

PodSafe—A trademarked term referring to licensed content that may be legally used in a podcast, usually without a fee.

post—When used as a verb, the act of publishing online content. When used as a noun, a single online content item.

RSS—Abbreviation for Rich Site Summary or Really Simple Syndication. RSS is a publish-and-subscribe mcchanism that delivers information automatically to a subscriber.

server—A program that awaits and fulfills requests from client programs. A Web browser is simply a client that requests HTML files from Web servers.

show notes—Online text summaries of podcast or videocast episodes that document or provide additional information about the recorded information. Show notes often include time stamps to allow users to fast-forward to specific parts of the show.

snarky—Early twentieth century British slang for "to nag" or "to find fault with." In the blogosphere, it is frequently used as an adjective for cynical or sarcastic.

social bookmarking—A form of social network in which members store, share, annotate, describe and comment upon information found on the Internet.

Social network—Online community in which members discuss topics of common interest. Social networks are usually distinguished from discussion groups by the ability of member to publish personal profiles and to create "friends" connections with others.

Social shopping—A form of social network in which members share recommendations and opinions about products.

Spam blog—A weblog created for the sole purpose of attracting search engine traffic for the delivery of advertising messages.

tag—A keyword label that a user can assign to online content. Tags can be used to categorize, sort and search information and can also be shared to help others find related content.

tag cloud—A visual representation of a website's or blog's content as determined by the number of tags assigned to that content. Frequently used tags appear larger than other tags, making it easy for a visitor to determine what topics the author covers.

Technorati.com—A popular search engine for blogs.

time-shifted media—Audio or video content that is downloaded and stored locally for playback at the user's convenience.

topical blog—A highly focused blog whose contributors limit their posts to a narrow range of topics.

trackback—A protocol for an Internet program that lets a blogger know when another blogger has linked to his or her posts. Software that supports the protocol will display a Track-Back URL at the end of each post.

transparency—In blogosphere jargon, an honest and forthright attitude about one's beliefs, motivations and practices.

Twitter—The most prominent form of microblog, Twitter limits entries to 140 characters – each one is called a "tweet" - and enables members to easily monitor each other as "followers."

Usenet—Abbreviation for user network, or a collection of electronic bulletin boards. Messages on this distributed discussion network are organized hierarchically by subject. Each topic is known as a newsgroup. Messages posted to a newsgroup are usually distributed to other members in the group by e-mail.

viral marketing—Any marketing technique that encourages the spread of information by word of mouth. Also called buzz or guerilla marketing.

virtual world—A type of social network in which the user experience is depicted as a three-dimensional image intended to mimic real-life. Users employ proxies called "avatars" to interact with others and with their surroundings.

visitor—A person or robot program that comes to a site. A unique visitor is one who visits a site at least once in a specified time period (usually 24 hours).

vlog—Short for video blog; a blog that is composed of video content or has video as well as text posts.

Web 2.0—Originally defined by O'Reilly Media Founder and CEO Tim O'Reilly as "The web as platform," Web 2.0's definition has evolved to encompass a range of technologies encompassing collaboration, continuous development, personal publishing and software delivered as a service over the Internet.

White Box social network—Service that provides a variety of social networking features for use by organizations to construct their own networks for marketing, market research or other business purposes.

wiki—A server program that allows users to collaborate in forming the content of a website. With a wiki, any authorized user can edit the site content, including other users' contributions, by using a regular Web browser.

Wikipedia—The Internet's largest online encyclopedia, with 2.5 million articles created and maintained entirely by anonymous contributors and a team of volunteers. Wikipedia is published in more than 250 languages, although nearly 100 of those languages have fewer than 1,000 articles.

word-of-mouth marketing—A form of marketing that encourages customers to promote brands and products by sharing recommendations with each other. The Word of Mouth Marketing Association (WOMMA) is a prominent trade organization and promoter.

Wordpress—An open source blog publishing and hosting site distributed under the GNU General Public License.

XML—Abbreviation for Extensible Markup Language. XML is a flexible way to create common information formats and share both the format and the data on the World Wide Web, intranets and elsewhere.

Yelp—Prominent example of a category of location-based social networks in which members share recommendations and reviews of local businesses, services and attractions.

YouTube—A video sharing site. YouTube is often held up as an example of a success story for user-generated content. It was acquired by Google in October 2006.

Index

About the Author

Paul Gillin is a veteran technology journalist with more than twenty-five years of editorial experience. Since 2005, he has advised marketers and business executives on strategies to optimize their use of social media and online channels to reach buyers cost-effectively. He is a popular speaker who is known for his ability to simplify complex concepts using plain talk, anecdotes, and humor.

Gillin was previously founding editor-in-chief of *TechTarget*, one of the most successful new media entities to emerge on the Internet. Prior to that, he was editor-in-chief and executive editor of the technology weekly *Computerworld* for 15 years.

His critically acclaimed 2007 book, *The New Influencers*, chronicled the changes in markets being driven by the new breed of bloggers and podcasters. In addition to his consulting and speaking, Gillin writes columns for *BtoB* and *Deliver* magazines and for Ziff-Davis Enterprise. His work has appeared in scores of publications, including *The New York Times*, *Advertising Age*, and *The San Jose Mercury News*. He also writes the popular NewspaperDeathWatch.com blog, as well as his own blog: paulgillin.com.

Gillin is a Research Fellow and a member of the advisory board of the Society for New Communications Research and he co-chairs the social media cluster for the Massachusetts Technology Leadership Council. Married with two children, he lives in Framingham, MA, where he lives and dies by the fortunes of the Boston Red Sox.

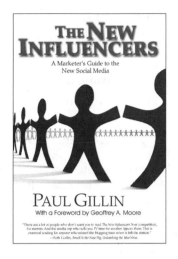

Check out Paul Gillin's first book, *The New Influencers,* part of Quill Driver Books' "Books to Build Your Career By" series.

Blogging, podcasting, and other social media are profoundly disrupting the mainstream media and marketing industries. *The New Influencers* explores these forces at work, identifying the new influencers, their goals and motivations, and offers strategies for both large and small organizations on how to influence the influencers.

"Persuasive."
—David A. Price, *The Wall Street Journal*

"This is a Five Star Book."
—Paul Greenberg, author of *CRM at the Speed of Light*

"Gillin expertly unwraps the dynamics behind this fast-evolving phenomenon."
—Ellis Booker, Editor, *BtoB* magazine

Hardcover • $25.00 ($32.95 Canada) • 272 pages

BOOKS TO BUILD YOUR CAREER BY
QUILLDRIVERBOOKS.COM

More titles from Quill Driver Books' Books to Build Your Career By series

If You Want It Done Right, You *Don't* Have to Do It Yourself!
The Power of Effective Delegation
by Donna Genett, Ph.D.

Whether you are the one delegating or you wish to help your boss become a better delegator, these six simple steps are guaranteed to lighten your workload and give you more time to focus on what's really important—on and off the job.

Hardcover • $19.95 ($27.95 Canada) • 112 pages

The Shipbuilder
Five Ancient Principles of Leadership
by Jack Myrick

Leadership is the most critical ingredient in any organization. Enter *The Shipbuilder*. This delightful business-management parable set in ancient Greece teaches the five principles of leadership.

Hardcover • $19.95 ($27.95 Canada) • 96 pages

Signature for Success
How to Analyze Handwriting and Improve Your Career, Your Relationships, and Your Life
by Arlyn J. Imberman
with June Rifkin

In this new, updated edition, Arlyn J. Imberman shares her handwriting-analysis techniques to help you the reader better understand yourself, your co-workers, and your friends and family, thus improving your relationships.

Trade paperback • $16.95 ($16.95 Canada) • 304 pages

Books to Build Your Career By
QuillDriverBooks.com

MAR — 2009